Kingsley Amis

Twayne's English Authors Series

Kinley Roby, Editor
Northeastern University

TEAS 552

KINGSLEY AMIS
Jerry Bauer

Kingsley Amis

William Laskowski

Jamestown College

Twayne Publishers
An Imprint of Simon & Schuster Macmillan
New York

Prentice Hall International
London • Mexico City • New Delhi • Singapore • Sydney • Toronto

Twayne's English Authors Series No. 552

Kingsley Amis
William Laskowski

Copyright © 1998 by Twayne Publishers

All rights reserved. No part of this book may be reproduced or transmitted in any form or by any means, electronic or mechanical, including photocopying, recording, or by any information storage and retrieval system, without permission in writing from the Publisher.

Twayne Publishers
An Imprint of Simon & Schuster Macmillan
1633 Broadway
New York, NY 10019

Library of Congress Cataloging-in-Publication Data

Laskowski, William E.
   Kingsley Amis / William Laskowski
      p. cm. — (Twayne's English authors series ; TEAS 552)
   Includes bibliographical references and index.
   ISBN 0-8057-1663-7 (alk. paper)
   1. Amis, Kingsley—Criticism and interpretation. I. Title.
II. Series.
PR6001.M6Z766 1998
828'.91409—dc21   98-12893
[B]   CIP

This paper meets the requirements of ANSI/NISO Z3948-1992 (Permanence of Paper).

10 9 8 7 6 5 4 3 2 1

Printed in the United States of America

To the memory of my parents,
William and Doris Laskowski

Contents

Preface ix
Acknowledgments xi
Chronology xiii

> *Chapter One*
> A Life in Letters 1
>
> *Chapter Two*
> Letters 25
>
> *Chapter Three*
> Genre Fiction 47
>
> *Chapter Four*
> Mainstream Novels 83
>
> *Chapter Five*
> Thinking about Amis 140

Notes and References 147
Selected Bibliography 153
Index 159

Preface

In 1981 Philip Gardner complained, in the predecessor to this book, that no full-length studies of Kingsley Amis existed.[1] That dearth has been more than filled. Between 1989 and 1995, five book-length studies of Amis appeared (three of them by Americans), each in its own way good, as well as an authorized biography and a collection of essays about him. And yet only a few years later, most of the novels on which those studies were based went out of print in the United States, with only *Lucky Jim* widely available, and Amis's last two novels were not published in the States at all. The only Amis who has a row of titles on U.S. bookstore shelves is Amis's son Martin.

The reasons for Amis's disappearance from U.S. readers' attention just as he began to acquire sustained critical notice are not readily apparent, although his tendentious reaction against what is generally called "political correctness" probably had more than a little to do with it. (At least one of his novels, *Stanley and the Women,* was reportedly difficult to publish in the United States because of its depiction of women.) He might have jokingly wondered at the connection between his critical success and popular failure; he always held that at the moment an entertaining popular art form was academically dissected—science fiction, detective fiction, and jazz are his favorite examples—it inevitably declined. Amis's own work, however, showed little influence from the analysis practiced on it, unless Eric Jacobs's probings of Amis's early years led to the autobiographical elements of his penultimate novel, *You Can't Do Both.* At any rate, his work is still widely available in Canada and the United Kingdom.

The purpose of this study is not to rectify this neglect, although I hope it does accomplish that in some small way. Rather, I want to consider Amis as a complete writer.[2] Most of the studies of Amis have—rightly, given his talents—considered him mainly as a novelist. I would like to consider him as short-story writer, poet, critic, and editor as well, in short, what Paul Fussell rightly called Amis's lifelong vocation as a man of letters.[3] The reader of any late Amis work is faced with an impressive and bewildering array of titles on the "by the same author" page. The purpose of this book is to explain what is in all of those books (as well as those not listed, such as *The Book of Bond*) and how they are connected to the writer Kingsley Amis. For all Amis's supposed political wanderings, he is a remarkably consistent figure, which his later blusterings and posings have obscured. Because of this examination of Amis as a complete writer, along with exigencies of length, I have not gone into Amis's mainstream novels as extensively as I would have liked. And because of Amis's extensive critical studies into what he called "genre fiction," I have divided my discussion of his fiction into genre and mainstream categories, a false dichotomy, perhaps, considering the thematic consistencies between the two. At any rate, Amis's arrangement of his own short stories in his *Collected Short Stories* into two such groups provides some justification for such an approach.

Acknowledgments

I would like to thank my editor, Kinley Roby, for his support and encouragement on both my volumes for Twayne, and Jennifer Farthing, editor at Twayne, for her help with this volume. A special word of thanks to Dr. Richard Smith for all his help and advice at Jamestown College. Once again I owe a large debt to Raugust Library at Jamestown College, under the direction of Phyllis Bratton, and particularly to Beth Sorenson. Of course, writers are time stealers, most often from those they love most, and nothing for me would be possible without the love and forbearance of my family: my thanks and love to Dina, Billy, and Danny.

Chronology

1922	Kingsley William Amis born 16 April in London.
1927–1934	Attends St. Hilda's and Norbury College, both secondary schools. First story, "The Sacred Rhino of Uganda," in Norbury College school magazine.
1934	Enters City of London School. Later publishes first poem, "Prelude," in school magazine.
1939	City of London School evacuated to Marlborough School in Wiltshire. Amis sergeant in Officers' Training Corps.
1941	Enters St. John's College, Oxford, on a scholarship in English. Participates in Senior Training Corps. Becomes an open student member of Communist Party. Meets Philip Larkin.
1942	Edits Labour Club's *Bulletin*. Enters army as officer in Royal Corps of Signals.
1943	Sent to Second Army Headquarters Signals unit, in which he remains for duration of war.
1944	Begins first unpublished novel, *Who Else Is Rank,* with fellow soldier E. Frank Coles. Arrives in France 30 June; becomes lieutenant and signalmaster. Begins to reject communism.
1945	Returns to Oxford in October.
1946	Meets Hilary (Hilly) Bardwell.
1947	Receives a First in English; stays on in Oxford to obtain a B.Litt. in English with a thesis on Victorian poetry and its readers. Begins second unpublished novel, *The Legacy*. First poetry collection, *Bright November*.
1948	Marries Hilly 21 January; Philip Amis born 15 August. Commissioned to do a study on Graham Greene for the University of Tucaman, Argentina.

1949	Coedits *Oxford Poetry* with James Michie. Martin Amis born 25 August. Becomes assistant lecturer in English at University College of Swansea, Wales.
1950	Thesis on Victorian poetry turned down.
1951	Writes libretto for ballad opera *To Move the Passions,* music by Bruce Montgomery; also writes libretto for Montgomery's one-act chamber opera *Amberley Hall.* Finishes *Dixon and Christine,* first draft of *Lucky Jim.*
1953	Second volume of poetry, *A Frame of Mind.* Writes coronation ode "The Century's Crown" with Montgomery. Excerpt from *Lucky Jim* read by John Wain on BBC 26 April.
1954	Sally Amis born 17 January. *Lucky Jim* published 25 January by Gollancz. "The Movement" inaugurated by J. D. Scott in a *Spectator* editorial 1 October.
1955	*That Uncertain Feeling. Lucky Jim* wins Somerset Maugham Award. Amis goes to Portugal to spend prize.
1956	*Times* editorial (26 May) and later *Daily Express* link Amis with the Angry Young Men, a pseudomovement that arose after the May premiere of John Osborne's *Look Back in Anger. A Case of Samples. New Lines,* edited by Robert Conquest, appears in June, with nine of Amis's poems. Amis's marriage almost dissolves in October.
1957	Fabian Society publishes pamphlet *Socialism and the Intellectuals. Touch and Go,* radio science fiction play, performed.
1958	Goes to Princeton University to teach creative writing. *I Like It Here.*
1959	Gives six lectures on science fiction in the Christian Gauss Seminars in Criticism at Princeton. Tours United States lecturing on "Problems of a Comic Novelist."
1960	Gauss lectures published as *New Maps of Hell. Take a Girl like You.*
1961	Leaves Swansea to become director of English Studies at Peterhouse, Cambridge. In April attends Albert Hall rally against capital punishment. Visits Robert Graves in Majorca.

1962 *My Enemy's Enemy*. Takes part in Cheltenham Literary Festival's seminar "Sex in Literature." Becomes romantically involved with its director, novelist Elizabeth Jane Howard.

1963 Leaves Peterhouse to become full-time writer; plans to live on Majorca. Spends summer holiday with Howard; returns to find Hilly and children gone to Majorca. Amis moves in with Howard. *One Fat Englishman*.

1964 Votes Labour for the final time.

1965 Divorce from Hilly finalized, marries Howard; they move, with various members of their families, to Maida Vale. *The Egyptologists* (cowritten with Robert Conquest) and *The James Bond Dossier*.

1966 Visits Prague to lecture on "The Literature of Protest in Great Britain." *The Anti-death League*, last novel for Gollancz.

1967 Visiting professor of the modern British novel at Vanderbilt University. "Why Lucky Jim Turned Right." *A Look around the Estate*.

1968 Extended family moves to Lemmons, a large house in Barnet. *I Want It Now. Colonel Sun*, James Bond novel, published under pseudonym of Robert Markham.

1969 *The Green Man*.

1971 *Girl, 20* and *What Became of Jane Austen? and Other Questions*.

1973 *The Riverside Villa Murders*.

1974 *Ending Up*.

1975 "The Crime of the Century" serialized in the *Sunday Times;* novel version published in 1987.

1976 Amis and Howard leave Lemmons for Hampstead. *The Alteration* (which wins John W. Campbell Memorial Award) and *Rudyard Kipling and His World*.

1978 *Jake's Thing*.

1980 Howard leaves Amis soon after cruise to France and Spain. *Russian Hide-and-Seek*.

1981 Awarded CBE. Hilly and third husband, Alistair Boyd (Lord Kilmarnock), move in with Amis. Edits *The*

	Golden Age of Science Fiction. First version of *Difficulties with Girls* abandoned around this time.
1982	Breaks leg; quits smoking and (temporarily) drinking.
1983	Divorce from Howard finalized.
1984	Amis and ménage move to his last home, in Primrose Hill. *Stanley and the Women.*
1985	Philip Larkin dies.
1986	*The Old Devils,* which wins Booker Prize.
1987	Stops writing poetry.
1988	*Difficulties with Girls.*
1990	Amis knighted. *The Folks That Live on the Hill.*
1991	*Memoirs* and *We Are All Guilty.*
1992	*The Russian Girl.*
1993	*Mr. Barrett's Secret and Other Stories.*
1994	*You Can't Do Both.*
1995	Eric Jacobs publishes *Kingsley Amis: A Biography. The Biographer's Moustache.* Kingsley Amis dies 22 October.
1997	*The King's English.*

Chapter One
A Life in Letters

Family

The births of writers in literary generations in English letters sometimes appear to cluster around a year; for the writers who grew to fame in the 1930s, for instance, one could select the year 1903, which saw the births of Edward Upward, George Orwell, and Evelyn Waugh—or equally apt, 1904, the birth year of Cecil Day-Lewis, Graham Greene, and Christopher Isherwood. The central birth year for the next famous literary generation, the so-called Movement writers, could be said to be 1922. In that year, Philip Larkin was born in Coventry, Donald Davie in Barnsley, and Kingsley Amis in London.

Although the Movement came to be seen as primarily a provincial literary group (Amis himself became famous while a university lecturer in Wales), Amis's life began and ended in London, which provided the setting for more than half his novels. Like other members of the Movement, he was the product of the lower middle class. His immediate ancestors, though ultimately French in descent, had become thoroughly Anglicized; Amis remarked that his father, William Amis, was "the most English human being I have ever known."[1] His grandparents, as he portrayed them in his *Memoirs,* were to him particularly unpleasant; solidly middle-class, they were extremely frugal and also tyrannical. His maternal grandfather, a lover of poetry and literature, was the only member of that generation whom Amis liked, but this grandfather was offset by his wife, a "horrible shrunken little old" woman who used to make faces at her husband as he read and who, after he died, allowed the book-loving Kingsley to select only a handful of his grandfather's volumes to keep.[2]

What Amis seems to have inherited from this generation was an aptitude for imitation and mimicry, which was passed on to Amis's father as well; a love for reading, which his mother also inherited; and, as readers of *Lucky Jim* will note, the means of burning off aggression by making surreptitious faces. What also appears to have been hereditary was Amis's later propensity toward phobias and fears of even worse mental illness. His mother's sister Dora, as Amis describes her, seems to have suffered from a form of obsessive-compulsive disorder. For his part, Amis suffered from fears of flying, the dark, open or public places, depersonalization, being left alone, and going mad; and from severe depressions, panic attacks, jactitations, hallucinations, and impotence and loss of libido. Most of these Amis was able, if not to overcome, at least to function through and, as his readers will notice, use in his fiction. That he was able to do so can be attributed in large measure to his parents.

William Amis and Rosa Annie (known as "Peggy") Lucas met, according to family tradition, in a Baptist chapel; however, neither was in any real sense religious, and Amis himself received no formal religious training because, as William put it, he did not want it "rammed down his [son's] throat" (*Memoirs*, 10). Yet William later blamed Kingsley's moral lapses on that very lack of religious upbringing; Amis dourly comments, "And I should not be truly his son if I had never felt he had something there" (14).[3] His father's most lasting influence was his stringent inculcation in his son of a work, if not precisely a Protestant, ethic. William Amis was what would today be called a middle-management executive in the export division of a mustard manufacturer, and whereas the prospect of that kind of daily work filled Kingsley with boredom and dread, as a writer he was a strict taskmaster with himself. No matter what indulgence the night before or at lunch, Amis always put in his two stints at the work desk each day.

Amis usually credited his mother with encouraging his development as a reader and a writer, although his father had a role in this as well. William, for instance, read mystery novels by now largely forgotten authors whom Amis disparaged, such as R. Austin Freeman, Francis Grierson, and John Rhode. Yet later on in life, Amis would declare that the American mystery writer John Dickson Carr, who wrote in the same genre and was friends with many of those same writers, was "the greatest detective story writer in the world" (*Memoirs*, 74), and Amis even wrote a book in that genre (but with characteristic adaptations), *The Riverside Villa Murders*. Perhaps the reason that Amis failed to recognize his father's influence on his literary preferences was the constant battle between father and son in almost all other areas of life.

Because Amis remained an only child, and the successive houses the Amises lived in were relatively small, the battleground between father and son was concentrated and magnified. Amis resented and rebelled against the type of person his father wanted him to become. They argued over all the familiar generational subjects of dispute. In music, Amis's tastes for classical music and jazz were ridiculed. In politics, Amis's resolutely leftist views invited his father's derision. They argued about Kingsley's conduct at home. He could not read to himself because it was antisocial. He had to stay at the table at dinner because to leave would break the family grouping. And above all, they argued about sex—at those times when the elder Amises were willing to acknowledge its existence. Amis was warned about the dire consequences of masturbation and could not lock any inner doors in the house to be by himself. A later row was precipitated when William found out that his son was having an affair with a married woman during the war. All these confrontations led Amis to vow that when he became a father himself, he would create in his own family "the 'permit' . . . to acknowledge the sexual world's existence."[4]

Although many of Amis's youthful interests were encouraged by his mother, she also coddled and cosseted him to the extent that for much of the rest of his life, he looked for, and came to utterly depend on, such relationships. When Kingsley grew too old to be spoon-fed, his mother would divide his food into portions that he had to eat, for fear of his being undernourished. As his biographer Eric Jacobs points out, Amis's mother's nurturing gave him self-confidence as a writer but made him later incapable of any degree of independence in his personal relations.

Jacobs sees the rest of Amis's life, that part free of paternal supervision, as "a kind of gigantic spree" at liberation from the claustrophobia of his home but also as an "endless attempt to live up to his father's expectations" (Jacobs, 63). Whatever the specific result in his conduct, Amis used the same word, *value*, when writing about his parents in retrospect. When thinking of how his father's conversation would bore him, Amis noted, "It is depressing to think how persistently dull and egotistical we can be to those we most value" (*Memoirs*, 18); his mother was "the first of the appalling long line of figures in my life whom I have come to value altogether more highly . . . now they are gone" (22). "Value" carries with it both the mercantile and ethical connotations his parents themselves had fostered. Only near the end of his moving poetic tribute to his father's memory, "In Memoriam W.R.A.," does Amis use the word one might expect to appear in a piece about one's parents: "Even your pride and your love / Have taken this time . . . to arouse my *love*."[5]

Education (and a Friend)

Amis initially attended several local grammar schools, at the first of which, he explained, a Miss Barr encouraged a love of literature, and at the second of which he published his first piece of fiction, an adventure story of the English Empire, "The Sacred Rhino of Uganda." It is worth noting that this is Amis's first foray into the realm of what would become known as popular culture, the appeal of which he would later so rigorously defend.

The most influential educational experience Amis received was at his next school, the City of London School, which his father had also attended. Here, because it was the subject in which he was most deeply interested, an English concentration was virtually invented for Amis's benefit. His devotion to literature was both broadened and deepened by the Reverend C. J. Ellingham, a religious man whose love of the atheist A. E. Housman's poetry demonstrated in the most practical way to Amis that "a poem is not a statement and the poet 'affirmeth nothing' " (*Memoirs*, 29).

Even more significant were the lessons that the City of London School taught Amis about life in England, which contributed so heavily to the moral center of his being. From this point on, because of his family's financial circumstances, Amis had to win scholarships (or "exhibitions") to pay for his tuition and board. Thus, unlike many of the writers of the previous famous literary generation, the writers of the thirties, who attended England's most prestigious public schools (even George Orwell attended Eton), Amis received much of his most formative education at a more democratically based, heterogeneous institution. It was remarkably free from racial or religious prejudice. There was little or no class snobbery, which became all the more noticeable when the school was evacuated during the early days of World War II to the environs of Marlborough school, one of the upper tier of public schools, and not one of its students made an attempt to be friendly with their guests from London. Above all, the City of London's faculty allowed Amis to develop his individuality.

Also at City of London School, Amis honed his mimetic powers; one of his more unusual acts was an imitation of Frederick Delius in the throes of tertiary syphilis. His political sympathies led him to join the League of Nations Union; however, like his attendance at Communist Party functions later at Oxford, his intentions were partly fueled by the opportunity to meet young women. He discovered an aptitude for military drilling in the Officers' Training Corps. And his literary interests led him to write a quasi-Eliotic poem (with a smattering of Oscar Wilde), "The Prelude."

Amis ended up at St. John's College, Oxford, because he won an exhibition to attend that school. He soon made friends with the writer to whom he was to be indissolubly linked for the rest of his life. Philip Larkin's account of their initial meeting goes into great detail about how Amis memorably enacted the expiration of a shooting victim; Amis recollected only that Larkin had, with instinctive generosity, offered him a cigarette—not a trivial gesture in a period of heavy rationing. Linked by a love of jazz, a sense of humor, a devotion to the mystery novels of John Dickson Carr (whose works they had been introduced to by their mutual friend Bruce Montgomery), and a deep mistrust of received literary authority, Amis and Larkin became the center of a group known as the Seven, who, in the words of Larkin's biographer Andrew Motion, "wished to distance themselves from their parents' generation, but not to abandon traditional forms and beliefs."[6]

By the time Amis had returned from military service, Larkin was at the beginning of a series of librarian's jobs that would form his livelihood, and their friendship resumed at an even more intense level; according to Motion, it was most meaningful immediately after the war, and most closely linked on the level of art. They submitted their work to each other, and they continued to collaborate, this time on parodies of poets and the parody competition in *New Statesman*. They became, in a sense, each other's ideal audience: the only novel that Amis ever admitted letting anyone else see was *Lucky Jim*, about which he asked Larkin for advice, and Larkin claimed that the poems of *The Less Deceived*, his first major collection, were written with the mental echoes of Amis's derisive laughter in his ears.

Although they both hated the posturings and dishonest enthusiasms that had to be adopted to get an English degree, there were important differences between Amis and Larkin. Whereas they both felt that jazz had lost its greatness with the demise of the 78-rpm record and the rise of bebop and stars such as Charlie Parker, Larkin was more interested in how jazz operated with his unconscious mind. Indeed, as one reads through Larkin's early correspondence, it quickly becomes apparent that Larkin is much less intimate with Amis than with other friends, even when they are discussing artistic matters. Later on, Larkin's fiancée, Ruth Bowman, thought Amis had a pernicious influence on Larkin, hardening him against women; when Larkin made an off-color joke to Bowman, she replied, " 'I'm not Kingsley, you know' " (Motion, 123).

The relationship between Amis and Larkin was also implicitly competitive. The most obvious difference between them was in their divergent literary careers; as has been often pointed out, at Oxford it was felt that Amis would end up the poet and Larkin the novelist, with *Jill* and *A Girl in Winter* to his credit. When Amis became wildly successful with his first novel, Larkin was chagrined that few people had remembered that he was the first of the Movement writers who had had anything published. As Amis's career continued to thrive, and Larkin found it harder and harder to write, he became almost ruefully jealous. Near the end of his life, Larkin admitted that Amis had actually made himself what Larkin had always dreamed of being—a novelist. Yet they continued to share certain implicit attitudes toward life. For instance, Larkin told John Betjeman that a passage in Amis's *The Green Man* showed that Amis agreed with Larkin's view of death, so memorably discussed in his late poem "Aubade." In 1952 Amis applied for a job at Queen's College in Belfast because Larkin worked there. Perhaps the difference in the arc of their careers boiled down to their relationships with their fathers. Sydney Larkin was an enormous influence on his son's thoughts, and when he died, Larkin in a sense became rudderless. Amis, in turn, always wanted to escape William Amis's influence, but later in life found the motivation his father instilled in him beneficial. Whatever their differences, Amis's warm tribute to Larkin ends: "He was my best friend and I never saw enough of him or knew him as well as I wanted to" (*Memoirs,* 64).

The Oxford in which Amis and Larkin found themselves in 1941 was at the tail end of the mythification it underwent after World War I, at least as far as literary figures were concerned. Amis realized that he would not be able to complete his degree before he had to serve in the army; nevertheless, he promised to become a schoolmaster after the war, thus ensuring himself four terms of study. He also joined the Senior Training Corps, which meant he would be an officer in the army. As far as academics went, many of the dons were already participating in the war, so finding a tutor was difficult, but Amis came to respect his first tutor, Gavin Bone, even though his specialty was Old English poetry, a subject Amis and Larkin both quickly came to detest.

In politics Amis was still a leftist and even became an open student member of the Communist Party, meeting, among others, the future novelist Iris Murdoch, although Amis later termed this the mandatory "callow marxist phase" for his generation.[7] When Amis returned to Oxford from the war, his experiences in it had soured him on communism. Many of his friends, such as Larkin and Montgomery, were now gone, but Amis made new friendships with people such as John Wain. Wain is important because he pushed Amis into going for a First (which he succeeded in getting) and into becoming a serious writer. (Their friendship later foundered on professional jealousy and Wain's alleged contention that Amis's first wife found Wain's attractions irresistible.)

But by far the most important person Amis met during his return to Oxford was Hilary—always known as Hilly—Bardwell, a woman Larkin (no mean judge in such matters) called in his last letter to Amis "the most beautiful woman I have ever seen without being in the least pretty."[8] An instinctual animal lover, she had undergone a rocky educational career, running away from Bedales, the liberal British secondary school. She was 17 years old when Amis first met her, so they underwent a somewhat prolonged courtship, getting married after Amis had received his First. It is difficult to glean the history of Amis's first marriage. He wished to make no deeply personal revelations in his *Memoirs*, explaining the lack of intimate details by admitting he did not want to hurt anyone, and it seems obvious that the person he most wanted to shield was Hilly. Hilly Bardwell was the most important figure in Amis's adult life, his domestic manager at its beginning and its end.

In order to obtain a better academic position, Amis stayed at Oxford to pursue his B.Litt. degree. Lord David Cecil was appointed Amis's supervisor, but because Amis could never find him, he changed over to F. W. Bateson (who later published Amis's more serious early academic essays, including a short version of his thesis, in Bateson's journal *Essays in Criticism*). They agreed on the topic of English poetry and its readership during the second half of the nineteenth century. Amis's main point was that Victorian poets wrote for ever-widening circles of readers, ranging from intimate friends in the closest circle to the general public in the broadest. Poets failed when they ignored their readers entirely (such as Swinburne) or pandered to them slavishly (the later Tennyson). Of course, such a prescription fit Amis's own methodology in poetry; he called Larkin his "inner audience" and "the ideal reader" (Jacobs, 142, 143). The one observation he thought worth repeating when he discussed the thesis in *Memoirs* was Dante Gabriel Rossetti's "unexpected insistence on entertainment as an essential quality of poetry" (*Memoirs*, 105). This insistence would be borne out in Amis's own poetic—and fictional—theory and practice.

Unfortunately, when Amis returned to Oxford to defend his thesis, he found that the head of the two-person examining board was none other than Lord David Cecil, and thus it came as little surprise that his thesis failed. Whether Amis was the victim of academic politics, or whether Cecil truly felt the thesis unworthy (witnesses claim Cecil's written comments peter out after a few pages), its failure had no deleterious effects on Amis's academic career. This confrontation with a guardian of British literary culture was the culmination of the main lesson Amis learned at Oxford about literature (a lesson that would be confirmed when he returned to teach at Cambridge): that for some people, usually members of the upper class, literature was to be protected as the domain of the highly educated (and usually highly bred) few; as he put it, British culture was "the property of some sort of exclusive club" (*What Became of Jane Austen*, 181). But as he had learned at the City of London School, that didn't necessarily have to be so. Yet at the same time, those who were learning to master literature *really* felt that literature at Oxford was "a pure commodity, a matter for evasion and fraud, confidence trickery to filch a degree" (*Memoirs*, 54). The realization of the hollowness of these two attitudes, and the accompanying omission of the thought of pleasure or enjoyment in experiencing literature, would charge Amis's writing on every level throughout his career and was perhaps the most lasting legacy—besides the friendships—of his educational experience.

Military

In reading through memoirs and documents pertaining to the Movement writers, one is often struck by how blasé some of their attitudes toward World War II were. Amis himself signed up for the Signals unit on the advice of his friend Norman Manning because it would necessarily involve little frontline action. Perhaps because of the time of their births, the war was something to be got through for what Larkin called "the 20's lot" (Larkin, 491). Because the thirties generation had seemingly just missed out on serving in World War I, some of them (such as Christopher Isherwood) saw war as a test and used the Spanish Civil War as a substitute. (When the real fighting came, however, it appeared that they ran.) History had shown Amis's generation that the world had not been made "safe for democracy," so there was little talk by them of World War II being a "good" war or a "crusade."

Whatever the specific reasons, Amis's war was not particularly dangerous, although he did humorously recount how British soldiers under bombardment in their tents at night had to decide which portion of their anatomy—crown or crotch—to protect with their helmets. What Amis came up against, as did so many others in England and America, was an entrenched, purblind military bureaucracy in which only the lifer NCOs seemed to possess an innate spark of common sense or decency. According to his friend and coauthor Frank Coles, in the army, Amis was too frank, too intelligent, too polite to subordinates, and too young. Moreover, his political views got him into trouble at times, as his superiors would subtly get back at him—a snap inspection, an unexpected piece of work—for views he had too freely shared in the officers' mess. He vocally supported Labour in the so-called khaki elections of 1945 that threw out Churchill and installed Clement Atlee, establishing the beginning of what would later be termed the welfare state. As Amis later remembered, "I did share in the general feeling of optimism and liberty abroad at the time."[9]

Some of Amis's other observations about army life will be discussed in the section on his short stories. On the whole, to Amis, the army was like a meticulously imagined society in a science fiction novel where the rules for living were just slightly—but rigorously—different. Although he admitted that the military life held a certain fascination for him up until around 1980, he remarked in another context that the period of life he would least like to experience again was his time in the army.

Teaching

When Amis finished up his studies at Oxford in 1949, he was already a family man, with one small son and another about to be born (the future novelist Martin Amis). He desperately needed a teaching position and applied everywhere, even for a job in Prague, Czechoslovakia. At the last minute, he was offered a position on the English faculty at the University College of Swansea, which he readily accepted. This not only provided him with a job that he would to all reports perform admirably for the next 14 years but also introduced to him an area of Great Britain that would have a profound effect on both his writing and his life. His Booker Prize–winning novel *The Old Devils* is set in Wales, and he came to appreciate the Welsh people's friendliness and warmth as he grew older. For the last 14 or so years of his life, he spent part of every summer with friends in Swansea when his London club was closed. Perhaps this return represented a wish to recapture the early years of his marital happiness: "I miss it constantly and I miss those days. . . . Often I wish I had never left" (*Memoirs,* 137).

Amis's main difficulties in Swansea revolved around politics, academic this time, but his squabbles with the bureaucracy did not seem to trouble him unduly. Even though some friends such as Philip Larkin thought that teaching was a cushy job for a writer, Amis was at pains in his published writings to point out how much work was really involved in preparing lectures. Yet Amis enjoyed teaching, for a number of reasons. He once pointed out that teaching was a two-way process of self-discovery: for the teacher, "Teaching his ideas teaches him what these ideas are" (*What Became of Jane Austen,* 189–90). Also, the very act of teaching itself was rewarding; he described, for instance, "the satisfaction, almost the excitement, of seeing your pupil take your point almost before you have formulated it yourself" (*Memoirs,* 227). Above all, under the English system of tutorials, teaching gave him a structured opportunity to talk seriously about literature, an activity that did not happen for him enough with his colleagues. As a teacher, he was described by a student in America as "anti-academic, anti-literary, almost anti-intellectual" (Jacobs, 293), qualities that might have endeared Amis to his pupils but not always to his superiors.

While at Swansea he took up the offer in 1958 of teaching for a year at Princeton University. On the whole, he enjoyed his experience; his primary responsibility was teaching creative writing, and although he was struck by his students' talent, none of them became famous writers. Besides teaching, he had to give six lectures in the Gauss Seminars in Criticism. R. P. Blackmur suggested that Amis, given his penchant for science fiction, should base his lectures on that interest. Separated from his science fiction collection by the Atlantic Ocean, Amis, after a frantic request to his friend and fellow devotee Robert Conquest, went to a bookstore in New York and scoured the shelves. Because his audience included literary illuminati such as Hannah Arendt and Mary McCarthy, who furthermore might be predisposed to disparage science fiction, he wanted to be as well prepared as possible. The resulting lectures were a success and formed the basis for Amis's book-length study *New Maps of Hell,* one of the first academic discussions of science fiction, a volume that ironically Amis later came to regret.

Some of Amis's friends thought his first tenure in the United States was not entirely serious; Larkin wrote, "He seems to have spent his time drinking and fucking, as if this should surprise me" (Larkin, 306). Amis was academically so successful at Princeton that he was offered two further years there, but even though he liked the United States, particularly upstate New York, and his new friends well enough, England loomed too large in his family's life and history (and now they were five, with the birth of daughter Sally in 1954). America always retained a high place in Amis's estimation, partly because it had given birth to, and excelled in, the forms of popular entertainment that had given him so much pleasure, such as jazz and science fiction.

On his return to England, Amis was offered—at the suggestion of his friend George Gale—a position at Peterhouse College at Cambridge in 1961; although Amis had no pressing reason to leave Swansea, he accepted the position at Cambridge. This was somewhat unusual in that Peterhouse was nominally a historians' college, and it provoked various violent reactions—"a scream of laughter or rage" as Larkin called it (Larkin, 324). Although the time constraints under which Amis had labored at Princeton had indicated to him that a full-time academic career seriously interfered with his progress as a writer, Amis made one more attempt at plunging into academia, prompted, he later supposed, by a wish to recapture some of the magic that had occurred for him and others at Oxford.

Yet certain drawbacks in his position quickly became apparent. For one, people just seemed to be ruder at Cambridge than in Wales, a fact he attributed to Cambridge's high percentage of upper-class, public-school students. F. R. Leavis, the high priest of literature at Cambridge, made it known that he considered Amis's addition to Cambridge a less than stellar appointment; Leavis remarked that it was impossible to take Peterhouse seriously because they had hired a *"pornographer"* (*Memoirs,* 217). Amis felt that the faculty and students should attempt to bridge the glaring gap between them by establishing more informal and personal relationships: a lack of these led, he felt, to the student upheavals of the later 1960s. However, much to his chagrin, when Amis tried to establish such relationships by meeting students for a drink in a pub, the rumor quickly went around that he was a homosexual.

The final straw for Amis occurred when, dining out at High Table at a college he pointedly says was not Peterhouse, his dinner companions got into a typically affected conversation about art collecting. When Amis politely remarked that he had little interest in such matters, one of his companions observed, "I think that's a dreadful thing to say" (*Memoirs,* 219). In his *Memoirs,* Amis says that he wished he could have left the country, or at least gone back to Swansea. As a matter of fact, at this particular moment in his life, Amis was contemplating moving to Majorca to live the writer's life near Robert Graves; at any rate, with his marriage to Hilly almost at an end, Amis resigned from Peterhouse, making his feelings well-known enough to prompt Larkin to observe that he thought Amis's departure too full of "public posturing" (Larkin, 348).

Amis underwent one more stint of teaching when he was offered a one-semester position at Vanderbilt University teaching modern British literature. Although he enjoyed the students and the teaching itself, in most other regards it was the second-least-favorite period in his life. Besides the scarcity of good drinking spots because of local blue laws and the general paucity of decent architecture, the virulence of the racial attitudes appalled Amis. Most apparent in the faculty he met, racism extended even to the student body, members of a younger generation Amis had hoped were beginning to unlearn the more repugnant attitudes of their elders. Jacobs presents the faculty's later defense that all this was an act assumed for the benefit of a notorious right-winger, but this exculpation seems pushing southern hospitality a little too far.

Education in Britain remained a key concern for Amis for the rest of his life, and because it formed the core of his professional experience outside of writing, he felt most qualified to pronounce on what he regarded as pernicious trends. Ever since Jim Dixon pointed out the ease with which students passed at his university in *Lucky Jim,* Amis let his opinions be known, whether in novels seemingly concerned with other subjects, such as *Jake's Thing* and *The Russian Girl,* or in *Black Papers on Education,* issued in opposition to government educational policies. Amis's most famous pronouncement about education was "More will mean worse" (*What Became of Jane Austen,* 170), by which he meant that admitting more students to higher education would entail the lowering of passing standards. Amis's unyielding vociferousness on these subjects, according to Jacobs, precluded his ever being awarded an honorary degree, while the equally tendentious but much less prolific Philip Larkin received seven.

Writing (and Loving and Politics)

As mentioned, Amis's first serious professional attempts at getting published were in poetry. Outside of school publications, the easiest (but ultimately least satisfying) outlet for young writers of the era was R. A. Caton's Fortune Press. Even though it had published other distinguished writers such as Roy Fuller and Dylan Thomas, and eventually Philip Larkin as well as Amis, its main line was in pornography, as both Larkin and Amis were well aware. Caton never gave his authors any royalties and often required a semisubsidy that placed his form of publishing only a narrow rung above that of vanity presses. But the Fortune Press did offer young authors a chance to see their work between covers, and Amis's first poetry collection, *Bright November*, came out in 1946. Only 6 of its 33 poems, however, were preserved by Amis in his *Collected Poems*. Caton himself became a terrific figure of derision for Amis, appearing often as the shiftless and despicable character L. S. (read Lazy Sod) Caton in Amis's first seven novels.

Amis's first two attempts at novel writing remain unpublished. During the war, he worked on an unfinished novel about army life, *Who Else Is Rank*, written with a friend, Frank Coles, each alternately taking a chapter. The character based on Amis has the same last name, Archer, as that of the main character in Amis's later published short stories about the army. Two chapters cover in thinly veiled fiction Amis's affair with a married woman at this time. Amis's second novel, *The Legacy*, is much more substantial and much more interesting, in that it employs some modernistic techniques and strategies that Amis was later to disparage strenuously. *The Legacy* adopts the modernist strategy of having its main character named "Kingsley Amis," but little of Amis's actual biography is involved: the plot concerns whether the fictional Amis will acquire the title inheritance by marrying a girl whom his brother champions and by going to work in the family business. The book was rejected for, among other things, "total lack of humour" (Jacobs, 127), according to a reader for Collins, but Larkin for one felt that *The Legacy* was in fact "very funny" (Larkin, 552). It is also interesting to note that by naming his main character after himself, without its really being an accurate self-portrayal, Amis was beginning to employ a practice that would lead him to much critical grief: the confusion of his fiction with his life.

Amis's other major writing before his first published novel included a critical study of Graham Greene written for an Argentinean university, which was never published, the manuscript unfortunately being lost. Amis also collaborated with his friend Bruce Montgomery in several works, including a ballad opera, *To Move the Passions*, written in consonantal rhyme and adapted from Amis's lectures on Augustan literary theory. Montgomery, however, was not industrious enough a collaborator for Amis and was also too involved with writing film music. He turned out to be the most egregious example among Amis's friends of an artist who did not live up to his talent, other than the mysteries he wrote under the pseudonym "Edmund Crispin."

The genesis for Amis's first great success, *Lucky Jim*, a success so overwhelming in relationship to his later fiction that it seems almost American in magnitude, has been widely discussed. On a visit to Larkin at the University of Leicester, Amis, on being left alone in the common room for a few moments, noticed that this particular slice of academia could prove to be untapped riches for the novelist. Other parts of the novel arose from his own and friends' experiences. Jim Dixon's last name came from the street name on which Larkin's mother lived. The odious Professor Welch was modeled quite consciously on Hilly's father, "Daddy B," and on some of his avocations, such as folk dancing—and Amis hoped his victim would notice the resemblance. Parts of Jim Dixon (his face making) came from Amis himself; some from Larkin. (Students would later wonder how the reticent librarian could possibly have been the "real" Lucky Jim.) Perhaps cruelest of all was the modeling of Jim's girlfriend, the passive-aggressive, manipulative Margaret, on Larkin's companion, Monica Jones. Larkin had to ask Amis not to make their names so similar. Jones held Amis in similar disfavor, insisting that Amis was "trying on" the faces he made so often because he was unsure of his own identity (Motion, 169).

Lucky Jim was published, much to Amis's chagrin, in January 1954, not December 1953, because Victor Gollancz thought that books by new authors published just after Christmas had a better chance of being noticed. Ten months later, a leading article appeared in the *Spectator,* anonymously at first but soon attributed to its literary editor, J. D. Scott. Entitled "In the Movement," the article almost single-handedly defined, for better or worse, an entire generation of British writers. Arguments raged right from the beginning about Scott's accuracy: had Scott identified a real, verifiable literary phenomenon, or was it all just a literary con game, played on an unsuspecting public for reasons of self-promotion? The advocates of the latter position could point to evidence such as John Wain's including Amis in a series of poems published by his university, or Wain's reading an excerpt from *Lucky Jim* on the BBC more than half a year before it was published.

Yet evidence certainly exists that within the Movement was a genuine desire to appear as a distinct literary group. For instance, Amis used the word "movement" (Jacobs, 166) in a letter to Larkin in March 1954 in reference to contemporary writers (even though he admitted the only authors they really liked were each other) while urging Larkin to write more fiction. Larkin wrote to a friend that Amis had suggested a pamphlet with his, Larkin's, Wain's, and Davie's works in it; "he is very anxious to form a 'school' " (Larkin, 226). Now that 40 years have passed since Scott's initial annunciation, it seems fairly obvious that both sides of the argument have some merit. A school of writing was emerging that had certain unmistakable features; at the same time, critics and some members within it did all they could to make sure such a "movement" existed. Certain literary generations appear obvious only after the fact, whereas others are quite obviously discrete right from their birth. The generation of British writers that was known as the thirties generation, or in Samuel Hynes's phrase, the Auden generation, quickly defined themselves. The intermediate generation of the 1940s came to be known as the New Apocalypse but failed to produce during World War II the striking series of war poets (Rupert Brooke, Siegfried Sassoon, Wilfred Owen, etc.) that World War I had. (Amis himself felt this was because most of the best poets, such as Larkin, never served in the military.) Britain in the early 1950s, caught up in the cultural hype that produced talk of a New Elizabethan Age, was hungry for the signs of a creative renaissance among its writers. A whole cluster of needs may have been created by the diminution of Britain as a world power; whatever the cause, the Movement existed, and Amis was at its center, in both his poetry and prose.

The Movement emerged in contradistinction to the romanticism of the New Apocalypse: one favorite target of Amis's critical animus in both essays and fiction is the poetry of Dylan Thomas. The Movement stressed, according to its ablest chronicler, Blake Morrison, "rationalism, realism, [and] empiricism" (Morrison, 9). Because so many of the writers—Amis, Wain, Davie, and Larkin—were employed in what were called "red-brick" universities, and their poetry was often reminiscent of eighteenth-century models, they were also dubbed "the University Wits." Because Jim Dixon also taught at such a university, he soon became conflated with his author. In a memorable diatribe, Somerset Maugham expressed with the mandarin anathema "They are scum" his distaste for the generation that the figure of Jim Dixon summarized.[10]

Walter Allen pointed out that many of the Movement writers had served in the military during the war, and that among their chief influences were George Orwell, F. R. Leavis, and the British philosophical branch of the Logical Positivists (Morrison, 53). Amis would later repudiate Leavis and his school because of its sneering at contemporary literature without attempting to place its writers. Orwell's influence on Amis, however, is more interesting and problematical. Some of Amis's cadences when generalizing have a definite Orwellian rhythm: for example, "thinking is a notorious difficult exercise, and there are always inducements to giving it up as soon as convenient."[11] As Morrison points out, Orwell's heroes, such as Gordon Comstock in *Keep the Aspidistra Flying,* had a profound influence on those of Movement fiction. Orwell and later Amis both attacked the intelligentsia while not quite denying that they belonged to it; Lindsay Anderson said of Amis that he "will rather pose as a Philistine than run the risk of being despised as an intellectual"—an accusation that also could be applied to Orwell.[12] Orwell also exhibited a catholicity of taste that parallels Amis's; Orwell the democratic socialist could appreciate Kipling, for instance, and Amis the unbeliever never lost his enthusiasm for the proselytizer G. K. Chesterton. Yet Amis also thought that the essential sociological basis for much of Orwell's literary criticism was unsound. Most important, Amis considered that in his last years, Orwell became "a supremely powerful . . . advocate of political quietism," not realizing, perhaps, that the political reforms he, Amis, advocated in 1958—broad nationalization of industry, the elimination of the House of Lords, public schools, the monarchy, and the aristocracy—were precisely the program Orwell advocated for England after World War II.[13] Ironically, of course, if Orwell actually became the "right-wing propagandist" (*Socialism and the Intellectuals,* 8) Amis calls him (a dubious claim, considering all the evidence), the career that most closely resembles his is Amis's own.

The other British literary movement of the 1950s with which Amis was quickly linked was that of the Angry Young Men. The name quickly arose in general use after the premiere of John Osborne's *Look Back in Anger* (1957), whose hero, Jimmy Porter, was almost immediately taken as the embodiment of the decade's Zeitgeist. His anger, which seems so much out of proportion to the events that ignite it, is directed at those around him because there are no "good, brave causes left," like those that so entranced the writers in the 1930s.[14] Critics, writing in newspapers such as the *Times* and the *Daily Express,* remembering Jim Dixon's similar anger, mixed up character with author and dubbed Amis another Angry Young Man. Nineteen fifty-six was a seminal year for political activists because it saw the Soviet Union's successful invasion of Hungary and the failed invasion of Egypt at Suez by the British, French, and Israelis. In fact, the former event destroyed any positive feelings Amis might have had for the communists, and the latter inspired him to march in protest against the government and to attend a Labour Party rally and promise to join the party. But as he explains in his pamphlet *Socialism and the Intellectuals,* the stupefying amount of political rhetoric at the rally put him off that last commitment. Indeed, he felt at the time that both crises would prove to be so short-lived that their ultimate political effect would be negligible. He lamented that there were no burning issues such as the Spanish Civil War or the rise of fascism or the economic ravages of the Great Depression to engage his decade and generation; the closest hot spot he saw—and this shows the paucity of causes—was Cyprus. Even though Paul Johnson claimed at the time that Suez "killed" Lucky Jim and his apoliticism,[15] Amis's pamphlet, instead of ending with a banging clarion call to action, ends with a whimpered musing: "How agreeable it must be to have a respectable motive for being politically active" (*Socialism and the Intellectuals,* 8).

Of course, Amis would become more politically active as he got older and his political course swung further right. He would find causes there—the dangers of totalitarianism, the decline of educational standards, the war in Vietnam—to engage his political interest. Ten years after *Socialism and the Intellectuals,* he explained "Why Lucky Jim Turned Right" (1967). At this point, he claimed he was a political centrist, "equally opposed to all forms of authoritarianism" *(What Became of Jane Austen,* 203). Three years later, in a postscript to this article, he had completed his journey to the right but complained that even there "many of the faces and voices and attitudes I find round me are horribly like what I was used to on the other side of the water" (211). He was not completely satisfied and indeed never would be.

His political stance now centered on an unrelentingly fierce anticommunism. His views on the Vietnam War were cogently enough held that his son Martin was sufficiently influenced to be one of the few writers of his generation in favor of it. Every week Amis met with like-minded friends, including Robert Conquest and Tibor Szamuely, at what were mock-defiantly called "Fascist" lunches. One cannot escape, however, the feeling that perhaps Monica Jones did have something of a point about Amis's trying on of faces, and that one in particular got stuck on and could not come off: as Larkin said, somewhat facetiously but nevertheless accurately in 1984, Amis had become "the E. Waugh des nous jours" (Larkin, 710). Even though Amis did not in the least share Waugh's least likable quality, his snobbishness, Amis's own pronouncements on education soon came to resemble Waugh's lament that the 1944 Butler Education Act had allowed the wrong kind of people to attend a university.

At the same time that Amis was being linked with the Angry Young Men politically, in his private life he was facing a marital crisis, as did Jimmy Porter in Osborne's play. Amis's was fueled principally by his infidelity. Amis did not hide his diary from Hilly, who quickly learned of his indiscretions. Many of his journeys to London had a double purpose in mind, as disclosed in his poem "Nothing to Fear," in which the speaker is using a friend's apartment for an assignation. In 1956, according to Jacobs, Hilly struck back with an affair of her own, which almost ended the marriage. They did manage to patch things up, and Amis complained in a letter to Larkin, "You can't have it both ways"— meaning having a family and carrying on affairs (Jacobs, 180). This phrasing is suggestive when considering the biographical implications of Amis's penultimate novel, *You Can't Do Both*.

Amis's second novel, *That Uncertain Feeling*, was his first major piece of fiction set in Wales. The same year it was published, *Lucky Jim* won the Somerset Maugham Prize, the height of irony considering Maugham's reaction to its hero. The problem was that the prize of £400 had to be spent abroad, so after consultation with friends, Amis and his family left for Portugal. Some kind of book would result; the problem was, exactly what type of book? Amis himself hated the "prose-poetry" of many travel books, and their misplaced idealistic portrayals of the inhabitants of foreign lands. At first, Amis thought of having *Lucky Jim*'s Gore-Urquart send Jim Dixon to Portugal, where he would have met Kingsley Amis (shades of *The Legacy*), but Amis settled on a more conventional approach, which resulted in the underrated *I Like It Here* (1958).

The relatively long intervals between novels in this stage of Amis's career reveal the effect teaching was having on his writing. For many readers, his next novel, *Take a Girl like You* (1960), was something of a departure in tone, subject matter, and point of view. Jacobs claims that the novel's portrayal of its heroine, Jenny Bunn, was considered by friends to be Amis's "love-letter" to Hilly (Jacobs, 263). The same year saw Amis's Gauss lectures published as *New Maps of Hell*.

Soon after Amis had begun teaching in Cambridge, he and his family visited Majorca, for the ostensible purpose of interviewing Robert Graves. The influence of Graves's poetry on Movement writers had been noted ever since Scott's "In the Movement." Even though Amis later speculated that the main reason Graves had established himself so far away from British literary circles was to evade literary competition, Amis became so impressed by Graves's lifestyle that the idea took root in his mind that one day soon, he too would come to Majorca to live the writer's life. Perhaps a subconscious factor was the cavalier manner in which Graves treated wives and mistresses. By this time, Amis's marriage was ready to collapse. Perhaps the most distasteful episode related in *Memoirs* occurred around this time, when Amis and Malcolm Muggeridge took part in a drunken, and consequently impotent, orgy with Sonia Orwell. One wonders why, if Amis did not want to hurt anybody, he felt this particular anecdote needed telling, yet one of Amis's more admirable characteristics is that he never withheld information that told—sometimes stunningly—against himself. Jacobs, in his biography, prints a photograph taken on vacation around this time, which shows a sleeping Amis, his back to the camera, on which Hilly has written in lipstick, using the title of Amis's next novel to refer to him: "1 FAT ENGLISHMAN I F___ ANYTHING."

What hastened the breakup of his marriage was Amis's growing attachment to novelist Elizabeth Jane Howard. In 1962 Amis had been invited to participate in the Cheltenham Literary Festival, at which he met Howard and began to get involved with her. Some people thought that because of Howard's upper-middle-class background, Amis's interest in her was another example of life imitating art, in that so many of Amis's plots involved hypergamy—becoming involved with someone above one's own class. But given that hatred of snobbery is the cornerstone of Amis's criticism, whether literary or political, this interpretation seems highly unlikely. By the time he left Peterhouse, he felt for some reason—perhaps he thought, if Robert Graves can do it, why can't I?—that he could remain simultaneously and openly involved with both Hilly and Jane Howard. When he returned from his vacation with Howard, Hilly and the children had left for Majorca alone, and Amis's first marriage had effectively ended.

One Fat Englishman was in part the product of Amis's sojourn in America and turned out to be the last novel produced while he was married to Hilly. It would be five years until Amis's next mainstream novel would appear. His first project, appearing in the year that he married Jane Howard, 1965, was a collaboration with his longtime friend Robert Conquest. *The Egyptologists* was originally entitled *Mummy Knows Best,* and Amis came up with new incidents and characters and much of the plot.[16] This year also saw the publication of *The James Bond Dossier,* which, according to Jacobs, was Amis's defiant valediction to academia. This study was the iconoclastic fruit of Amis's enthusiasm for reading that merely afforded pleasure, but the reading required for it, Amis claimed, soured him on reading any Bond ever again. Ian Fleming, however, took the study seriously enough to consider delaying publication of his next Bond novel, *The Man with the Golden Gun,* with which he was dissatisfied, until after Amis's work appeared, the implication being that Fleming could use Amis's literary conclusions to improve the novel.

(After Fleming's death, Fleming's publisher, Jonathan Cape, asked Amis to read the manuscript to point out its weaknesses.) A less well-known product of this same period was a small handbook entitled *The Book of Bond, or Every Man His Own 007,* published under the pseudonym of Lieutenant Colonel William ("Bill") Tanner, a character in the Bond novels. ("Bill" was Amis's nickname during the war.)

During 1966, for reasons he could never fathom, given his widely known anticommunist stance, Amis was asked to come to Prague to lecture on the topic "The Literature of Protest in Great Britain." Anyone at all familiar with Amis's writing by this time should have known that the lecture he would deliver in Prague would conclude that there was not much in Great Britain to protest about. His novel of 1966 was *The Antideath League,* the first fictional product of his research into Bond and the world of spying. It is ultimately impossible to decide precisely which genre—espionage, science fiction, mainstream—this novel fits into. It turned out to be the last novel he wrote for Gollancz, whose founder, Victor Gollancz, died that year, and to whom Amis felt personally loyal, despite his conviction the company was not doing all it could to promote his work.

Amis's next novel was the more obvious result of his Bond researches. Glidrose, the company Fleming had formed for his literary rights, decided that Amis was the ideal candidate to continue the Bond franchise after Fleming's death. Ann Fleming, Ian's widow, however, was not pleased and considered Amis a "left-wing opportunist."[17] Peter Fleming wanted Amis to use the pseudonym "George Glidrose," but eventually the name "Robert Markham" was agreed on. When the result, *Colonel Sun,* was published, Ann Fleming was to review it for the *Sunday Telegraph,* but because of the review's intemperateness, especially toward those who had contracted the novel, it remained unpublished. Her reaction to Amis shows that her knowledge of his works ended in the mid-1950s: "Amis will slip 'Lucky Jim' into Bond's clothing, we shall have a petty-bourgeois red-brick Bond, he will resent the authority of M, then the discipline of the Secret Service, and end as Philby Bond selling his country to SPECTRE." Amis himself, according to Fleming's biographer, took these complaints "in good spirit," particularly considering the monetary rewards involved (Lycett, 449).

Amis's next mainstream novel, *I Want It Now,* was published in 1968, the same year that *Colonel Sun* appeared, and arose from a question by Jane Howard about what kind of a child that a wealthy (and childless) friend of theirs would have. That same year, Amis and his by now extended family, consisting of Jane Howard, her mother, brother, her brother's friend, and frequently Amis's two sons, moved into Lemmons, a striking house in Barnet, which was unfortunately for the nondriving Amis too far from London to be easily reached by public transportation. Even though Amis's sons had initially reacted negatively toward Amis's domestic arrangement, Howard encouraged both boys to excel in their education. The entire ménage gave rise to the portrayal of Sir Ralph Vandervane's living arrangements in Amis's next mainstream novel, *Girl, 20* (1971), and imagining five people in such close proximity in later life gave Amis the germ for his short novel of death and old age, *Ending Up* (1974).

Meanwhile, Amis kept producing genre novels during this period. A comment by Larkin about a ghost attempting to get into a house provided the seed for *The Green Man* (1969). Amis's love for the detective story, particularly the 1930s variety, led to *The Riverside Villa Murders* (1973), and a suggestion by the *Sunday Times* led to the serialized (and more plot-driven) "The Crime of the Century" (1975). Finally, Amis's deep love for science fiction led to the alternate history novel *The Alteration* (1976), which won the John W. Campbell Memorial Award for that year, an award perhaps more prestigious than the Hugo or Nebula awards in that it is selected by a panel of experts in the field.

Amis's reliance on genre novels during this period, successful as most of them are, perhaps indicates that something was basically not right with his marriage. Jacobs persuasively argues that portraits of female characters in Amis's novels from *The Anti-death League* to *Stanley and the Women* reflect Amis's own emotions toward Jane Howard, and I think that by retreating, in a way, into genre fiction, Amis was able, at times, to distance himself from his emotions, although in the case of a novel like *The Green Man* not very far. (A photograph taken around this time shows Amis uncharacteristically in a beard.) On a professional level, Amis and Howard were well matched, trusting in each other's criticism of their work, and, at one point, even writing a small section of each other's novels (*One Fat Englishman* and Howard's *After Julius*). But for what mainly appears to have been temperamental reasons, their marriage soon foundered. Amis later admitted it should have ended around 1970. Howard, for her part, always objected to Amis's drinking, and she made his giving it up a condition of any reconciliation. (Whether Amis was an alcoholic or not is a question only he could have answered, and he claimed not to be. If he was, he was a high-functioning one, at least as far as his work goes.)

At any rate, many of the circumstances, including the main character's impotence, described in *Jake's Thing* (1978) were based on fact. For instance, he told Larkin in September 1979 that he hadn't had sex with a woman in more than a year and with himself in more than a month. Yet however tempting it is to take the portrayals of the women in *Stanley and the Women* as images of Howard, it would be wrong to suppose that Howard actually vented at Amis the snobbish diatribe that Stanley's wife hurls at him for being lower middle class. Jacobs claims, though, that Amis assumed that Howard felt that way about their class differences. They stayed together as long as they did because Howard did not want to abandon her husband, an action she had done twice before, and Amis had a lifelong phobia about being left alone, whether traveling or at home. At any rate, Howard finally did leave Amis in 1980.

For Amis, the main problem was how to carry on the day-to-day activities of living in light of his phobia. Friends made kind offers; Conquest suggested that Amis live with him in California, but Amis had no desire to leave England more or less permanently. At some point around this time, Amis made his first attempt at a novel called *Difficulties with Girls;* its plot concerned a young homosexual who is accused of child molestation when he spurns a woman. One is tempted to say this plotline went nowhere because it did nothing to exorcise the ghosts of his second marriage. The only novel Amis completed between *Jake's Thing* and *Stanley and the Women* was his last genre novel, *Russian Hide-and-Seek* (1980), a vision of a Soviet takeover of Great Britain.[18] The four-year gap between this novel and *Stanley and the Women,* according to Martin Amis, shows how upset Amis was during this period. Amis's increased output during the last years of his life bears out this speculation. During this relatively contented last decade, he wrote seven novels, his *Memoirs,* and a short-story collection; edited four anthologies; and produced a steady stream of nonfiction and reviewed restaurants monthly from October 1985 through August 1993.

In general, most of this work is of high quality; indeed, the first of these novels, *The Old Devils,* won the Booker Prize for 1986. *Difficulties with Girls* (1988) resolved itself into a generally successful sequel to *Take a Girl like You. The Folks That Live on the Hill* (1990) is a gentler view of old age than that presented in *Ending Up,* and *We Are All Guilty* (1991) is a slight but effective artistic rendering of some of Amis's political concerns of the period about personal responsibility. His *Memoirs* was predictably controversial, but the attitudes it expressed should not have been surprising to anyone who had read the autobiographical last sections of Amis's earlier collection *What Became of Jane Austen? and Other Questions* (1971). *The Russian Girl* (1992) is perhaps the sunniest of Amis's comedies of the wars between the sexes, and *You Can't Do Both* (1994) is Amis's last fictional exploration of the world of his youth and young manhood. Only *The Biographer's Moustache* (1995), Amis's last novel, seemingly inspired by his own experience as a biographical subject, is comparatively weak.

Amis's late productivity reflects the happiness and security of the domestic situation he arranged after the collapse of his second marriage, and on the surface this situation resembled, as he once suggested, the plot outlines of an Iris Murdoch novel. He moved in with his first wife, Hilly, and her third husband, Alistair Boyd, Lord Kilmarnock. In the house that they eventually occupied, Amis slept on the ground floor and ascended to the second floor to eat or watch television. His entire typical day, complete with work, pub, or club, is memorably described in the first chapter of Jacobs's biography, "Portrait of the Artist in Old Age," although the recountings of his subject's bowel movements are (to use a favorite phrase of Amis's) "for some readers" unnecessary information. The physical locale of this arrangement in London's Primrose Hill is reproduced in the novel *The Folks That Live on the Hill*. During this period, Amis was quite close to all his children. His daughter, Sally, often came over to fix him supper, and he and Martin, by now a novelist perhaps more famous than his father, met often, either at Sunday dinner or dining out. Amis's deprecatory attitude toward Martin's experimentalist, postmodern brand of fiction was well known: Martin felt that having to read his works twice was a sign of their worth; to Amis, it was the hallmark of their failure. In Amis's introduction to an American interlude in his *Memoirs*, he specifically names as two of America's least formidable authors Saul Bellow and Vladimir Nabokov; it is perhaps no coincidence that these are two of Martin Amis's favorites. Jacobs claims, however, that Amis felt underneath that Martin's fiction might have had a "subversive influence" on his own (Jacobs, 16). And by some accounts Amis felt much more positively about his son's work than he let on; perhaps his cranky stance was another example of his adopting what Larkin called Amis's "latterday Cheltenham-colonel mode" (Larkin, 671).

Kingsley Amis died on October 22, 1995, of complications from injuries resulting from a fall. There seems little doubt that the last years of his life were rewarding and satisfying, in no little part due to the presence of his first wife, Hilly, during this period. Amis ultimately came to "bitterly" (Jacobs, 262) regret the series of circumstances that led to their separation, and there are constant hints that Amis wished they could have continued together. Although the practice of identifying Amis's heroes with the author is a dangerous and finally unproductive game, the portrait of the philandering young hero and his wife in his penultimate novel, *You Can't Do Both,* seems to be a fair reflection of Amis and Hilly in similar circumstances, and Jacobs is surely right in seeing that the novel is "an apology, a message of love and regret. And it is addressed to Hilly" (359). And at the end of his *Memoirs,* Amis places three short poems "Instead of an Epilogue." They are dedicated to "H." All three concern evanescent forms of beauty that are somehow taken for granted in the very act of classifying their rarity, including a Camberwell butterfly (shades of Nabokov) and an overnight ice storm. The third poem takes place in 1946, the year he met Hilly. In the poem, he describes meeting Hilly, who was also beautiful and possessed a gentle inner naturalness and fragility. Its placement and tone show the ultimate place Hilly occupied in his art and in his heart.[19]

Chapter Two
Letters

Memoirs

Amis's *Memoirs* is not a standard author's autobiography. It is composed of a series of short, unconnected chapters, of which only some range over various periods of his life, such as the City of London School, Oxford, the army, and Wales. Another group concerns some of his best friends: Philip Larkin, Bruce Montgomery, Robert Conquest, George Gale, and Tibor Szamuely. Still others concern writers Amis met and admired: Anthony Powell, Robert Graves, Elizabeth Taylor, Sir John Betjeman. Others deal with figures Amis felt more ambivalent about: Yevgeny Yevtushenko, John Braine, Anthony Burgess.[1] Finally, and most controversially, some sections skewer people Amis had little regard for: Lord David Cecil, Lord Snowdon, Arnold Wesker, Leo Rosten. In the end, there seems little justification for including anecdotes about aborted "orgies" with Sonia Orwell or Francis Bacon's wanting to know if Amis liked male pornography. Paul Fussell tries to exonerate Amis by claiming that these negative portraits are justified by Amis's moral sense; that somehow writing a portrait of Leo Rosten as an unconsciously egotistical buffoon elevates Amis into the realm of Swift, Pope, and Twain. It does not. Readers learn (and believe), for example, much more about Arnold Wesker's faults as a playwright from Amis's essay "Not Talking about Jerusalem" than they do by finding out in *Memoirs* that Wesker seemed to be in total ignorance of a famous quote from *Hamlet*. In general, Amis's negative pieces seem as mean-spirited as the pieces about his friends are generous, and the pieces about himself, on the whole, are refreshingly honest.

Food and Drink

As Fussell contends, Amis was truly a modern man of letters because of the scope of his writing and range of his subjects, but few men of letters can have gotten as much mileage as Amis did writing about food and drink. He wrote a food column for almost eight years in various London publications, and his judgments about food are very much of a piece with his attitudes toward literature: it must be unaffected (not necessarily plain), well prepared, and sincerely presented. For Amis the main problem here, as elsewhere in the arts, was that food was being prepared no longer for a general audience, but for a coterie of experts and fellow practitioners.

Amis wrote even more about drink, producing for a time a weekly column on it, as well as three short volumes. One suspects that this was not only a labor of love but also a thumbing of his nose at critics who had confused Amis with some of his heroes and concluded that he was some form of sot. On the whole, his books about drink are decidedly minor works, nevertheless containing at times some of Amis's funniest writing. For instance, he calls the potent drink tequila con sangria "a splendid pick-me-up, and throw-me-down, and jump-on-me."[2] Some of the observations he makes are interesting in other contexts. For example, he notes that James Bond's deduction in *From Russia, with Love* that Red Grant was not a gentleman because he ordered red wine with fish should just have meant to Bond that Grant was "independent-minded" (*On Drink*, 68). Amis also explains his stratagem against being surprised by a subject he knows nothing about: "the generic Amis Defense Against Knowledge," which is to "treat the whole subject as an eccentric fad."[3]

As Fussell correctly notes, Amis is also concerned about the moral aspects of drinking, particularly in the social sphere. Amis grounds the reasons for drinking in this milieu: one drinks in situations involving "sudden confrontation with complete or comparative strangers in circumstances requiring a show of relaxation and amiability" (*On Drink*, 12). Thus Amis's chapter in *On Drink* (1972) "The Mean Sod's Guide" is a hilariously ironic how-to manual for those who want to shortchange their guests on their drinks. To Amis, generosity in the social sphere is a moral touchstone; in *Memoirs,* when Leo Rosten jokes about two drinks being enough for his guests, the reader knows what kind of a character he will turn out to be in Amis's moral universe.

Only so much can be said about drink, no matter how one applies oneself, and many sections of *Every Day Drinking* repeat verbatim parts of *On Drink.* And in at least three different places in Amis's works, the reader can find the same basic disquisition on the hangover and its prevention and cure. While basically much of the advice is good common sense, the more interesting parts are its literary and artistic observations.

In general, Amis's works on drink are exactly what Amis probably intended them to be: slight yet enjoyable—"amusing" in the best sense. And, according to a secondhand bookseller, they are still very popular.

Politics and Society

Because of Amis's political odyssey and the views to which it led, he was always involved in polemical writing on political and social issues. Many of his ideas have been discussed in the biographical section; here I want to mention briefly the provenance of some of those ideas.

Amis and Robert Conquest became heavily involved in a series of Black Papers (in opposition to the government's White Papers) on education. As Conquest points out, the series was not the result of any far-flung conspiracy, but merely like-minded writers getting in touch with each other to share their views. Amis claims that it was in academics that "I had first reason to dispute the progressive consensus I had grown up with."[4] Perhaps the most ingenious of these pieces is the "ILEA Confidential," written with Conquest, which purports to be a transcription of a meeting of the alien beings who really run education in the London area, which is why matters are so out of hand.

In 1957 Amis wrote a pamphlet for the Fabian Society, *Socialism and the Intellectuals,* which, if carefully read, already shows the reasons that would cause Amis to write his most notorious political manifesto 10 years later, "Why Lucky Jim Turned Right." Amis's other significant long piece of political writing is *An Arts Policy?* (1979), which derives from a talk Amis gave at a Conservative Party conference. In this pamphlet, Amis comes out against any government subsidy of the arts, except perhaps for the opera and the National Theatre, as well as for bookstores. In Amis's view, given the modern experience of artists under totalitarianism, when the state becomes really interested in the arts, "the artists had better start running."[5] Amis quotes an old proverb to justify his basic position: "If you have to please to live, you'll do your best to please" (*Arts Policy,* 5). This is Amis's credo in all aspects of mercantile society, whether it be selling the short story or bangers and mash. He also rejects the old English socialist doctrine (begun with writers like John Ruskin and William Morris) that every human being has the seeds of the artist within, and it is up to the government to liberate that artist. Amis counters, "That's only possible if making mud pies count as art" (*Arts Policy,* 3). Merrie England is indeed dead.

Amis's one editorial production concerning politics is *Harold's Years* (1977), a collection of essays ranging from all parts of the political spectrum selected from the *New Statesman* (generally liberal) and the *Spectator* (usually conservative), dealing with the two premierships of Labour's Harold Wilson and the intervening one of Tory Edward Heath. On the whole, Amis's selections are quite catholic. They include essays by friends such as Robert Conquest, George Gale, and Tibor Szamuely, but they also include a sympathetic report on the 1968 student uprisings in Paris by Mervyn Jones, a damning depiction of Soweto under apartheid by Kenneth Allsop, a scathing portrait of a pre-Watergate Richard Nixon by William Shawcross, and a balanced lament for the fall of Saigon by Richard West. From its title, *Harold's Years* might seem to be a dated collection of forgotten issues, but Amis's skill as an editor makes much of it still absorbing.

Literary Matters

Most of Amis's nonfiction concerns literature in some way. He regularly reviewed books for publications such as the *Spectator* and the *Observer*. This section deals with literary subjects that are not discussed under other headings.

Two of Amis's favorite writers were Anthony Powell and Evelyn Waugh. "I would rather read Mr. Powell than any other English novelist now writing," Amis wrote in a review of a volume of Powell's *A Dance to the Music of Time*.[6] Amis's feelings toward Waugh were more problematic. He disliked Waugh's lust for the upper classes, and certain aspects of Waugh's personality repelled him: characteristically, Amis criticizes Waugh above all for "his rudeness in public" (*Amis Collection,* 79). But Amis noted that students on both sides of the Atlantic chose *Decline and Fall* as their favorite work in a course he taught.

Several authors that one might think Amis would have an affinity for in reality repelled him. Charles Dickens, an author whose tradition Amis supposedly follows, is castigated by Amis for "the ubiquitous, obsessive repetition, the inability to leave anything, good or bad, alone" (*What Became of Jane Austen*, 33). Mark Twain, whose satirical eye Amis could be thought to share, is "that innocuous romancer" (*Amis Collection,* 18), and Geoffrey Chaucer, another master of humorous verse, Amis finds "the most repellent of our great poets" (172).

Two famous reviews of the 1950s could be held up to show Amis's aggressive philistine pose; however, what they really reveal is the moral basis for much of his criticism. He takes Jane Austen to task for *Mansfield Park* because in her portrayal of the social situation, she "continually and essentially holds up the vicious as admirable" (*What Became of Jane Austen,* 13–14), particularly in the character of Fanny Price, who is not the model of good conduct Jane Austen takes her for. Vladimir Nabokov's *Lolita* is "morally bad" (78) because Nabokov fails to distance his own voice from the narrator's. One can argue that these are misreadings, that enough hints occur in the text of *Lolita,* for instance, to signal the knowing reader that Nabokov is as disgusted as the reader is with Humbert's moral nature. But Amis's stances are well enough supported so that they must be taken into account by any admirer of either work.

Amis's longest work of literary criticism outside of his genre pieces is his 1975 study *Rudyard Kipling.* He rightly calls it an essay, because most of the hundred-odd pages are taken up with illustrations, not text, as is common in a volume of this type. The book was commissioned, and one wonders if it was because of Amis's growing notoriety as a conservative. Angus Wilson, who was also writing a book about Kipling at this time, was worried when he heard that Amis was working on one too, but the two books are really quite different in scope; Amis's work is slight, but it does not deserve the to be called "lazy," as Paul Theroux observed to Wilson when the book came out.[7]

In *Rudyard Kipling,* Amis again firmly rejects the biographical fallacy. Kipling's "Baa, Baa, Black Sheep" should not be taken as a transcription of Kipling's unhappy experiences on being boarded out in England as a child; "it is a *story:* the author is not on oath."[8] Similarly, the stories in *Stalky and Co.* should not even be regarded as "autobiographical in a secondary sense" (*Rudyard Kipling,* 34). Instead of being merely a revenge fantasy, *Stalky and Co.* introduces the figure of the Giant Killer, a type that would become so necessary to the operation of the British Empire. As usual, Amis prefers to go outward from the text into society instead of backward into the author.

Amis summarizes Kipling as "an oligarch who believed passionately in freedom" (*Rudyard Kipling,* 52). His poems laud virtues such as "law, order, duty, restraint, obedience, discipline," and Amis adds, without letting the ironic mask drop for a second, "Their message is, of course, a conservative one, without much application to our time" (55). On the whole, Amis generally agrees with George Orwell's assessment of Kipling's politics in Orwell's 1940 essay "Rudyard Kipling," here as elsewhere noting, as Orwell does, the truth of Tommy Atkin's charge in

"Tommy" that his sacrifices allow liberals at home the freedom to jeer at those who protect them.

Additionally, for Amis, Kipling is the "best writer of short stories," and in enumerating Kipling's range, Amis might be talking, except for the last item, about his own work: "the tragic, the comic, the satiric, the macabre, anecdote, fantasy, history, science fiction, children's tale" (*Rudyard Kipling*, 114). Also, Amis remarks on (in contradistinction to Waugh's bad manners) Kipling's "courtesy to strangers" (108). On the negative side, Amis notes, as many others have, Kipling's seeming "approval of violence" (111) without going into its causes (as Wilson does in his study), and Kipling's "uncritical" (53) respect for character types such as the courageous, self-effacing subaltern, without whom the empire could not exist.

But to Amis, Kipling's chief fault, which to other critics is a sign of his incipient modernity, is his needless obfuscation of simple narratives, which Amis traces to overzealous editing by Kipling. Thus "The Man Who Would Be King" is "grossly overrated"; its "elaboration" mistaken for "complexity" (*Rudyard Kipling*, 62–63). "Mrs. Bathurst" is also groundlessly obscure; Amis here declares that a "fundamental right of the reader" is "to be acquainted with what can be taken as the full facts" (107). Perhaps another reason for Kipling's "over-mystification" (74) might be his acquaintance with Henry James. Amis remarks, when noting James's bewilderment at Kipling's marriage, that "some might mutter that to mystify James over some piece of normal human behavior was no great feat" (66). For "some," read "Kingsley Amis."

All in all, *Rudyard Kipling* serves as a solid introduction to Kipling's life and works, presented from a standpoint that is not as iconoclastic as it at times makes itself out to be.

Grammar

Amis's last work, *The King's English: A Guide to Modern Usage* (1997), is the culmination of a lifelong interest by Amis, often expressed in the interests of many of his heroes, in correct speaking and writing. Internal dating shows that portions of the book were worked on in 1994, and some of its concerns spill over into Amis's last novel, *The Biographer's Moustache* (1995). Unfortunately, *The King's English* shows signs of its posthumous publication. Also, because many of Amis's recommendations refer to British English, the book is of limited interest to American readers, especially those who take umbrage with criticism; Amis, although declaring his respect and admiration for America, finds "Americanisms" such as the ubiquitous "glottal stop" insidiously deleterious.[9] But the book remains interesting not only because of Amis's linguistic concerns but because of what he reveals about other subjects during the course of his pronouncements.

As can be expected, Amis is a linguistic conservative; as he says early on, "Resistance to all linguistic change is obviously a healthy instinct" (*King's English*, 2). Yet he is not a knee-jerk prescriptivist; like H. W. Fowler, whose *Modern English Usage* (1926) Amis acknowledges as his model, he has no problem with the split infinitive or ending a sentence with a preposition (although he does recommend not splitting infinitives, because people who do care about such faults are often in positions of power). Nor does he find the uproar over the misapplication of a word such as *cohort* all that justified. Still, he does call the misuse of *disinterested* "a case of ignorant bullshit" (*King's English*, 56)—a most un-Fowler-like statement. On the whole, Amis's goal is to steer a course between the "berks," as he calls them, on the one hand, those who invariably misuse the language through either ignorance or laziness, and the "wankers," those whose hypercorrectness is the sign of an inflated sense of class or social superiority. His examples, characteristically catholic, range from Shakespeare to *Coronation Street*. As he says about Fowler himself, the best approach to language is "unfanatical" and balances "knowledge and common sense" (76).

Another figure who looms behind *The King's English* is George Orwell, whose seminal essay "Politics and the English Language" (1947) Amis refers to several times. He does find some of Orwell's recommendations unfounded, such as his ridiculing of the often useful "not un-" construction. But on the whole, Amis finds the rules that Orwell declares at the end of his essay sound, particularly the last one, which Amis paraphrases as "don't write anything that seems to you barbarous" (*King's English*, 207). Like Orwell, Amis realizes that the main purpose of writing and speaking is communication, and all questions of correctness must be subservient to that goal.

Along the way, Amis is able to reflect on linguistic matters that have come up in his own writing. For instance, he discusses the use of swearing and profanity, pointing out that when he and Larkin used it in their works and correspondence, it was more a matter of rebellion than anything else. Amis deplores the replacement of "sex" as a term by "gender" because it is based on a false premise—sex is present not merely in the physical differences but in every aspect of a relationship: "[T]he larger part of sexual behavior is not physical but no less sexual for not being so" (*King's English,* 84). E. M. Forster is castigated for not offering democracy the "four cheers" it rightly deserves (231).

On the whole, Amis is his usual combative and polemical self in this book, which appears, as he says, in a period of "renascent prescriptivism" (*King's English,* 30) in linguistic matters. Because of his humor and curiosity, he is much more enjoyable to read than other prescriptivists such as John Simon or William Safire. But there is a valedictory air about the whole proceeding, perhaps caused by Amis's own sense of impending mortality, or else because he shared in the sentiment that he quotes (as an example of the use of the word *around*) from the hymn "Abide with Me": "Change and decay in all around I see" (Orwell also quoted this line more than once). Several entries end with the phrase "as if anyone cared" (96). At any rate, Amis fought the good linguistic fight, and his book deserves three cheers at least from all who are concerned with the way language is used.

Short Stories: Criticism and Editing

For Amis, the short story is in a sense a shorter version of a novel, a "telescoped novel" in his phrase, usually revolving around one central idea. Thus his own short stories are "chips from a novelist's workbench."[10] And because of the short story's construction around an idea, it is particularly related to genre fiction: science fiction, the detective story, the humorous story, and the ghost or terror story. He notes that few authors can excel in both novel and story: Graham Greene, he declares, is a notable exception; however, given Amis's own tastes and prejudices, he does not mention Henry James.

Thus, the short story in its mode of "the impression, the untrimmed slice of life, the landscape with figures but without characters" (*Collected Short Stories,* 10) does not interest Amis. He is all for the plot-driven story as tale. This predilection emerges in his selections for *The Amis Story Anthology: A Personal Choice of Short Stories* (1992). Half its selections, as he admits in his introduction, are genre stories. Two of the science fiction stories, Anthony Boucher's tale of a robot saint "The Quest for St. Aquin" and H. Beam Piper's alternate-world story "He Walked around Horses," appeared in Amis's earlier collection *The Golden Age of Science Fiction* (1981). The other science fiction tale, Brian Aldiss's "Outside," a story of solipsism and identity, is thematically related to Amis's own story "Something Strange." In the case of several authors (M. R.

James, G. K. Chesterton, and P. G. Wodehouse), Amis had more than one candidate for inclusion, and interestingly enough, they are all genre authors. Amis ultimately chose Chesterton's first Father Brown story, "The Blue Cross," M. R. James's ghost story "Oh, Whistle, and I'll Come to You, My Lad," and Wodehouse's "Jeeves and the Song of Songs." Amis's final genre selection is Dick Francis's tale of racecourse fraud and deception, "Twenty-One Good Men and True."

The "mainstream" stories Amis selected usually revolve around some insight characters obtain into their own lives or the lives around them: James Joyce's "A Painful Case," Angus Wilson's "Fresh-Air Fiend," and Elizabeth Taylor's "Summer Schools." Two of the stories concern the British Empire and the effect of colonization on the colonizers: Rudyard Kipling's tale of interracial love "Beyond the Pale," and Somerset Maugham's story of empire and cowardice "The Door of Opportunity." Amis also selected Ambrose Bierce's often-anthologized tale of the Civil War, "An Occurrence at Owl Creek Bridge," and Irwin Shaw's story of anti-Semitism during the last days of World War II, "Act of Faith." Surprisingly, considering Amis's general abhorrence of Vladimir Nabokov's style (see his review of *Lolita*), Amis included Nabokov's "First Love." What is most interesting about Amis's overall selection is the way it parallels in subject matter and mode his own short stories.

Stories

In his own *Collected Short Stories* (1980; rev. ed. 1987), Amis deliberately separated its contents into mainstream and genre fiction. The first 6 stories are mainstream and take up about half the book's pages, and the remaining 12 are science fiction, humorous, detective, and horror stories, with several parodies and pastiches thrown in. In general, the mainstream stories recapitulate concerns Amis deals with in his longer fiction, especially human life as "the continual taking of moral decisions" (*What Became of Jane Austen*, 91), whereas the genre stories are usually complicated with an infusion of sexuality that their models originally lacked.

Amis's first three stories deal with the British army at the tail end of World War II in a Signals unit very like the one in which Amis served. A central character, Frank Archer, appeared in Amis's unpublished collaborative novel, *Who Else Is Rank,* and functioned as Amis's alter ego in that work. As Amis points out in his introduction, these stories are not fragments from any novel, and a quick glance at their structures bears this out. They are all tales of a moral education that occurs in an army unit that has never traveled on foot or fired a shot in anger. Nevertheless, the conflicts that emerge can be just as deadly as those in a combat unit. Elsewhere Amis criticizes Evelyn Waugh's war novels for not showing that army existence possesses "confusion and arbitrariness just as much as order and custom" (*Amis Collection,* 74). Beyond a recognition of these realities, what Tom Thurston learns in "My Enemy's Enemy" and Frank Archer in "Court of Enquiry" and "I Spy Strangers" is that the army, in particular its commanding officers, can be vindictive as well as arbitrary, and often for no good reason at all. Even more depressing, this type of conduct is not confined to the army.

In "My Enemy's Enemy," Tom Thurston has the chance to warn a young soldier, Dalessio, that the Adjutant has it in for him and will use the pretense of a snap inspection to send Dalessio to the Pacific theater, where violent combat is still raging. The Adjutant is an all too common example of officers who in civilian life never had the kind of power they were given in the army, and in the words of a later story, "they use it to inflict injustices on other chaps whom they happen to dislike for personal reasons" (*Collected Short Stories,* 67). Significantly, most of the settings for these stories still betray traces of their former German uses; in this case, it is an SS training school, and many of the characters are specifically linked to fascist counterparts. Later, in "I Spy Strangers," Sergeant Doll will advocate returning the Nazis to power to counterbalance the Russians. A thematic undercurrent in these stories is that the war against the mindless abuse of power is never over.

Although the Adjutant betrays a general prejudice for soldiers who use their intellects, Dalessio's main offense seems to have been mocking the Adjutant's middlebrow taste in music, in this case, Addinsall's *Warsaw Concerto*. Thurston remains silent, and it is the otherwise nondescript Captain Bentham who warns Dalessio. Bentham, unlike his Utilitarian namesake, is more concerned with the individual than the mass, because the captain is truly dedicated to the real principles of the army. At the end of the story, he rips into Thurston's moral complacency: "I think you're really quite sold on the Adj's crowd. . . . I think you're a bastard, just like the rest of 'em" (*Collected Short Stories,* 33). Thurston remains silent.

The lessons Frank Archer learns in the next two stories are similar, and the results are also equivocal. In these stories, Major Raleigh is the retributive villain who sends any offending types to the East, even though, the narrator ironically points out, by doing so he is filling that theater with "drunks, incompetents, homosexuals, Communists, ration-vendors and madmen" (51). In "Court of Enquiry," Raleigh punishes Archer for losing an otherwise worthless charging engine. Archer's chief crime to Raleigh appears to be that he is overfamiliar with his men. During the enquiry, Archer shamelessly lies to Raleigh, obsequiously thanking him for his (nonexistent) support and guidance. Archer later tells the narrator that he did so to show Raleigh that he had gone overboard in his persecution, and the story ends with the narrator's ironic comment, "The Army would lick anyone into shape. You could even say that it made a man of you" (42). What kind of man is another matter.

"I Spy Strangers" takes place in the context of Britain's Khaki Election, in which Churchill was thrown out and Atlee's Labour government voted in. The Signals unit is holding a mock parliament, and in one of Amis's characteristic fictional openings, the extensive use of dialogue makes readers work hard at figuring out what exactly is taking place: not for several pages will they realize that this is a mock debate. Naturally, Raleigh is maddened by the latitude of the freedom of speech afforded and feels that some of the suggestions, including nationalization, "could never happen in the real world" (*Collected Short Stories*, 48); the irony, of course, is precisely that they did happen. The Opposition foreign spokesman, Sergeant Doll, is a few degrees to the left of being a fascist; nevertheless, it is he who protects the liberal Hargreaves from being sent to Burma and taunts Raleigh with the information that Archer will be demobilized early to return to Oxford. For Archer, the horrible epiphany at the heart of the story is that this type of existence, with its "unique scope for vindictiveness," is not limited to the army: "You mean that this is what life is like" (63, 81). When Raleigh learns the results of the real election, he despairs that a way of life is somehow disappearing, and given Amis's political stance during this period (1962), the last sentence of the story, Raleigh's reflection that "England would muddle through somehow" (86), could be seen as ironic. Yet because even the seemingly totalitarian Doll can cooperate against mindless tyranny, perhaps the ending can be seen as ultimately hopeful.

"Moral Fibre," although using John Lewis, the main character of Amis's novel *That Uncertain Feeling* (1955), has no other relationship with that novel. Lewis and his family are asked by a social worker friend, Mair Webster, to employ a former prostitute and petty thief, Betty Arnulfsen, as a housekeeper as part of her rehabilitation. Betty eventually relapses and in fact offers herself to Lewis, who refuses her (a similar situation occurred to Amis in Wales), but this self-control is not the moral fiber referred to in the title. Rather, Mair Webster declares that the trouble with Betty and girls of her ilk is a lack of moral fiber. To John, however, in "relapsing," Betty has proved what her internal fiber consists of: "Betty burgled that place to get her own back. . . . As a method of not being the kind of person Mair wanted her to be" (*Collected Short Stories,* 105 – 6). In a review written around this time, Amis wrote that social workers should employ "the utmost kindness and patience" (*What Became of Jane Austen,* 86), qualities that Webster conspicuously lacks. The solution to the problem of the Betties of this world remains unsolved at the end of this story.

"All the Blood within Me" deals with another favorite theme of Amis's: the character who spends much of his life (and who is almost always male) seriously misjudging the people closest to him. Alec Mackenzie attends the funeral of a woman with whom he has carried on a platonic relationship for years, not realizing how she has controlled and manipulated the lives of others around her. At the end of the story, Mac muses on "how envy and pride could appreciably distort his judgement of other people" (*Collected Short Stories,* 129). The story is also interesting for its portrayal of an Anglican clergyman who no longer believes in religion; this one gives a funeral sermon on the futility of a belief in an afterlife.

"Dear Illusion" deals with the falsity of artistic—in this case poetic—reputations in the last half of the twentieth century. Edward Potter, generally esteemed to be "England's greatest living bard" (*Collected Short Stories,* 150), reveals that he has written all his poems as a temporary relief from mental depression; he himself has no idea whether they're any good or not. Potter's list of poetic favorites shows he has little real taste for poetry, according to Amis's lights; the list includes such figures as John Betjeman, Roy Fuller, and W. H. Auden (to Amis, all good), and Allen Ginsberg, Philip Roth, Sylvia Plath, and Ezra Pound (all bad). Potter's own poem "Unborn," which Amis reproduces, is fairly awful. When Potter's doctor chemically cures his depression and Potter writes in one day a book of poems utterly unlike his previous work, it is an immediate success, except to those critics who have always disliked Potter's work. The book is entitled *Off,* and Potter explains that he has deleted the four-letter Anglo-Saxon imperative that should have been the title's first word; it is his final message to his critics, and he commits suicide, because, as he explains, "if the poems are no good my life's been wasted" (142). The story is interesting because it introduces Amis's concern, perhaps arising out of personal experience, with modern psychotherapeutic drugs, but if one does not share Amis's taste in modern poetry, the story's humor can seem somewhat forced. It would take abysmal taste to see "Unborn" as the product of a major talent, yet that is Amis's main point.

"Something Strange" is Amis's only "straight" science fiction story. In it a group of four characters think they are marooned in a small space station on the edge of the galaxy but are actually the subjects of an experiment on Earth to eliminate fear. The ultimate irony of this plot is that its main thematic concerns—the relationship between reality and illusion, the problem of solipsism, and the malleability of personal identity—are all subjects that would later be connected with science fiction's New Wave, a movement whose influence Amis despised. This theme recurs in "Mason's Life," the last story of the volume, in which perhaps both main characters are in each other's dream. Amis's next four science fiction stories are all basically humorous: "The 2003 Claret," "The Friends of Plonk," "Too Much Trouble," and "Investing in Futures." These stories deal with a group of time travelers whose main concern about the future seems to be what kind of drinks it will provide, and these stories, unlike "Something Strange," have their origin in Amis's regard for sociological science fiction. In general, the less politically tendentious the story, the more successful it is. "Hemingway in Space," as the title suggests, is a parody of Ernest Hemingway's short stories, in this particular instance "The Short Happy Life of Francis Macomber," only in this case the Macomber figure gets to live and order his now docile wife to make supper.

"Who or What Was It?" is a strange takeoff on the plot of Amis's novel *The Green Man*. Originally designed to be read over the radio, the story describes the journey of the "real" Kingsley Amis and Elizabeth Jane Howard to a hotel-restaurant very much like that of *The Green Man*, which is run by a man named, like the protagonist of the novel, Maurice Allington. Here the "real" Amis rescues Allington's daughter from a supernatural Green Man, just as Allington did in the novel. When "Amis" returns to the hotel, he discovers that while he was gone, somebody or something has visited "Jane" in his guise and in fact made love to her. "Amis" and "Jane" conclude that it must have been God who has done this, and "Amis" is both relieved and disappointed when a pregnancy test proves negative. The plot, so barely stated, is obviously outrageous, but many people took Amis seriously, even his old friend Bruce Montgomery. Amis goes on about this for a page and a half in his introduction, mourning the credulity of the modern age, but one suspects that he was secretly pleased by such a reaction. Above all, the story is a satire on the postmodernist habit of inserting the "author" into the plot of the story, and readers should thus not take very seriously Amis's assertion here that he is "more like" Maurice Allington than most of his other heroes (*Collected Short Stories*, 233).

"The Darkwater Hall Mystery" is the first of the series of pastiches that wind up this collection. It is a Sherlock Holmes story without Sherlock Holmes, and Amis does a fairly good job at reproducing Watson's voice. The humor in the story lies in Watson's mistaking two characters' rehearsing of a play for spousal abuse, and the plotline is deflated at the end by having the most obvious suspect be the real villain, which almost never happens in a real Holmes story. The modern twist that Amis adds at the end is that Watson has had an affair with a Spanish maid. "The House of the Headland" starts off as a pastiche of a turn-of-the-century spy story, with its characters eating, à la Fleming, caviar, grouse, and greenhouse peaches. The plot concerns Count Axel, a Swedish nobleman who appears to be preparing an insurrection on Crete. The echoes of M. R. James's "Count Magnus" in Axel's name, and the description of the house and its hooded inhabitants, seem to indicate that we are now reading a ghost story. But Axel is really using the title house to hide his collection of severely deformed women. Again, Amis's addition of the sexual element adds in this case a truly disturbing element to the parody. The final pastiche, "To See the Sun," is a vampire story, and once again Amis faithfully reproduces the style and epistolary-journal mode of narration of Bram Stoker's *Dracula,* while the painting of a vampire's "funeral" that comes alive for the narrator owes its origins to M. R. James's work, most notably "The Mezzotint." Here Amis blends the sexual element more smoothly with the requirements of the plot, perhaps because sexuality already forms so large a part of the modern vampire. In the days of Anne Rice and numerous imitators, however, "To See the Sun" seems almost tame and restrained in its attempts for narrative authenticity of voice.

"Affairs of Death," the last story in Amis's first collection, points to a new direction his short fiction would take in several of the stories in his second volume: the "real" explanation behind certain literary or historical events. "Affairs of Death" portrays Macbeth as a somewhat heroic figure who has journeyed to see the pope to put on record the true account of his accession to the throne. The title story of Amis's second volume, *Mr. Barrett's Secret and Other Stories* (1993), reveals through another Victorian narrative pastiche Amis's theory, first propounded in a review of Donald Thomas's biography of Robert Browning (1982), that Elizabeth Barrett Browning's father was opposed to her marriage to Browning not out of the tyranny of a Victorian paterfamilias but for fear of their producing a black child because both families had a strong background in the West Indies. In an afterword, Amis points out that Barrett's true motive was probably "fear of betraying his jealousy at seeing the two unequivocally together, with their offspring."[11] Similarly, "Captain Nolan's Chance," a radio play, shows that the "reason why" behind the charge of the Light Brigade was to impress upon Russian leaders the superiority of British cavalry. Amis notes that the historical Captain Nolan was a strenuous supporter of the efficacy of light cavalry in two books on the subject; to this Amis adds a fictional conspiracy concerning "the Great Game," in which Russia would invade India if the British troops could be shown to be cowards, an imputation that the charge would refute. Although a Russian officer calls the charge "magnificent," Amis later declares that Nolan partook of "the sort of luck that comes the way of murderous maniacs" (*Mr. Barrett's Secret,* 171, 176). Amis is still decidedly ambivalent about the "glory" of war.

Two stories in this volume are works of genre fiction. "Boris and the Colonel" is a generally unsuccessful tale that combines spy fiction, literary criticism, and what sounds very much like a romance story. In it, a Russian mole sends a message via forged stanzas to Gray's "Elegy Written in a Country Churchyard" to a member of the Burgess-Maclean spy circle in Moscow so that the spy will return and the mole can kill him. The story is as implausible as the romance that occurs in it. "1941/A" is a short alternate-history tale of the "Hitler victorious" subgenre, a supposed excerpt from a history book telling how Germany and Japan won World War II. The punch line of the story, its last lines, is a variation on the end of one of Amis's favorite stories, Piper's "He Walked around the Horses." We learn that this history has been written by the "Joseph Goebbels Professor of Modern History in the University of Oxford," an oxymoron if there ever was one (*Mr. Barrett's Secret,* 185).

Amis's final two mainstream stories are of extremely varying quality. "Toil and Trouble" concerns a literary agent who is kidnapped and briefly tortured, supposedly because he told an author his book was unpublishable. The title refers to the agent's use of a quotation from *Macbeth* to discover that the "kidnappers" are actually out-of-work actors. The story is perhaps a wish fulfillment. "A Twitch on the Thread," however, just may be Amis's best story. Its title refers to the twitch that God uses to summon a lost soul back to himself. (Evelyn Waugh uses the term in this sense as the title of part 2 of *Brideshead Revisited*.) In Amis's story, the lost souls are two twin brothers, separated at birth and raised in England and America. Both became hopeless alcoholics until they received what they took to be a message from Jesus Christ, grew sober, and became Anglican ministers. For the American clergyman, the conversion is a sign of God's omnipotence. For the English protagonist, however, the revelation becomes an epiphany to him that individuality and personal responsibility are shams; as an alter ego tells him in a dream sequence, "Any ideas of free choice that may be nourished by a human unit, formerly known as an individual, are illusory and false" (*Mr. Barrett's Secret,* 105). There are two reasons for his realization. One is that his faith is based on the premise that it came from grace, "that God had planted in him the impulse to pray" (92). Thus, he reasons, if separated twins conceive of the same impulse at the same time, then the impulse is not divine but hereditary. The other reason arises out of his wife's circumstances. She has suffered for years from clinical depression, and during the course of the story, she is cured by the administration of the correct psychotropic drugs. Ultimately, this cure is ironic because its method confirms the hero's increasing doubts about the reality of free will. This brave new world is too much for the hero, who goes on a bender as the story ends. What makes the story so powerful is that Amis offers no easy answers. Elsewhere he has stated that he believes that faith is a "gift" (*Amis Collection,* 226), and an entire book written around this time, *We Are All Guilty* (1991), is based on Amis's belief in personal responsibility. But here Amis hides his tendentiousness and truly explores the possibilities present in the question. It is also Amis's most generous portrayal of a clergyman.

On the whole, Amis's stories are more than "chips" from his workbench. For one, they offer him the opportunity to test and express different fictional voices, particularly in genre fiction, something he could not do in novels. The short-story form also allowed him to combine certain genres and mix in additions of his own, as in "The House on the Headland." And in the best of his stories ("I Spy Strangers," "A Twitch on the Thread"), he was able to present and work through moral questions and problems with the same intensity that he reached in his longer fiction.

Poetry: Criticism and Editing

Near the end of his career, Amis was in the ironic position of being a novelist who read very little fiction, and a poetry writer who wrote little poetry while constantly reading it in order to anthologize it. Amis originally thought that he would become primarily a poet, and his love of poetry never left him. What he wanted to accomplish in his own poetry, he searched for in that of others. Above all, he prized lucidity and comprehensibility, as he stated in his introduction to his own selection of poems in D. J. Enright's *Poets of the 1950's* (1955). Amis noted elsewhere that a prime goal of the Victorian poet was "to be as lucid as the occasion permitted" (*Amis Collection,* 158), and he declared, in one of his tirades against Dylan Thomas, that "a poem cannot just be and not mean" (209). The only translucent or opaque poet of whom Amis approved was W. H. Auden; for Amis, as for many critics, the Auden of the 1930s was "almost the only Auden" (199), and the "obscurity" of this period's work "put me off and still does, though not enough since then to prevent me from thinking his best poems as good as any in English in the last hundred years."[12]

Underlying this basic premise of the communicability of meaning is Amis's predilection for ordinary themes as well as ordinary language. For Amis, as well as other poets in the Movement, the reaching after the grandiose statement and mastery of epic themes were the basic faults of modernism and the New Apocalypse. In his 1955 statement, Amis generalized that "nobody wants any poems on the grander themes for a few years,"[13] and a year later, he declared that the resulting "minor literature" would be no bad thing (*Amis Collection,* 22). Thus poems about ordinary subjects commended themselves to him. Over and over, particularly in his poetry column and the resultant anthology, *The Pleasure of Poetry* (1990), he shows how deeply memorable poems can be written about often forgotten or unnoticed ordinary things, in poems by such varied writers as John Drinkwater, Robert Graves, Elizabeth Jennings, and Kenneth Ashley.

Amis also particularly valued the sense that a poet can impart in his or her work that the poet is speaking directly to the reader and no one else. Amis notes this feeling in Gray's "Elegy Written in a Country Churchyard," and it is also Amis's primary reason for liking another of his favorite poets, Edward Thomas, who writes "in such a direct way . . . the reader is in no doubt that he actually feels it."[14] Allied to this immediacy is what might be called a temperance of language. Amis's highest compliment in this vein is "unsensational," which he applies to the works of Edward Thomas, R. S. Thomas, Edmund Blunden, and Tom Moore.

But above all Amis seems to have been temperamentally predisposed to poems about what can simply be called the sorrows of loss. As Paul Fussell astutely notes, the poems collected in Amis's other selection of poetry favorites, *The Amis Anthology* (1988), "convey a pervading sense of loss and emptiness, a deep consciousness of the pathos of mutability and evanescence."[15] This theme was long a congenital favorite with Amis. In 1971 he approvingly found in an anthology of young British poets "a non-self-indulgent melancholy, a resignation and regret for what has been lost or is passing, a (to me) sympathetic . . . rueful shrug at life" (*Amis Collection,* 166). He commended in 1975 Rudyard Kipling's "tragic power, his understanding of pain, waste, loss and horror and the unargued stoicism that outlasts them" (68). In an introduction to a 1973 selection of Tennyson's verse, Amis found that Tennyson's "whole poetic nature was made to express loss and the feelings that lie close to it: despondency, ennui, nostalgia, loneliness, despair and the desire for reconciliation and resignation" (187). And for Amis, his favorite poet, A. E. Housman, wrote about "the old primary themes of loss, pain, and deprivation as realised and reflected in the English landscape" (197); he is "marvellously gloomy," a telling oxymoron (*Pleasure of Poetry,* 101). In his anthologies, Amis includes works such as Edwin Muir's "The Breaking" because of "its quiet acceptance of the way all things pass and are always renewed" (39), and he includes in three of his anthologies Hilaire Belloc's "Ha'nacker Mill," a "lament, for the passing of old rural England" (88).

Amis, however, is certainly not connected in the public mind with elegiac monodies; for the most part, his most popular anthologies have been stoutly tendentious. In a review, he approvingly called Charles Causley's *Poetry Please* a "Treasury of Untrendy Verse" (*Amis Collection,* 165), and the same title could be accorded in its way to each of Amis's poetry anthologies. Oxford University Press asked him to write the successor to W. H. Auden's *The Oxford Book of Light Verse* (1938); Amis's collection, which came out 40 years later, contains a rigorous defense of its selections in his introduction. Some differences can be attributed to taste; as he notes, he independently chose entirely different extracts from Byron's *Don Juan* than Auden did. Amis declares "light verse is unimaginable in the absence of high verse"; it needs something to play off of.[16] On the whole, the anthology is highly successful (and by far the easiest of Amis's anthologies to obtain), despite some tendentious inclusions, such as "On Communists" and three takeoffs on "The Vicar of Bray," one of them by Amis's friend Robert Conquest, under the pseudonym of Ted Pauwker. The anthology also includes a dialect poem by Amis, "The Helbetrawss," not included in his *Collected Poems*.

Amis's simultaneous "untrendy" anthology was *The Faber Popular Reciter* (1978), in which he performed the valuable function of gathering into one volume poems that were once "too well known to be worth reprinting" but were now in danger of being forgotten.[17] Such poems served an important public function because they were "what unites the individual with some large group of his neighbours," a connection that became impossible after "the disintegrative shock of the Great War" (16, 18). *The Faber Popular Reciter* is valuable because it locates in one place so much of English verse that is hardly ever anthologized anymore, but nevertheless forms a backbone for the rest of the poetry that arose both because of it and opposed to it.

Amis's two personal anthologies are more a labor of love. He calls his post as poetry editor of the *Daily Mirror* the "most rewarding job I ever had" (*Amis Collection,* 171), because in it he was trying to make poetry once again a satisfying mass art, a task he continued in his personal anthologies. He was perhaps more openhanded in his selections; while including a patriotic work by Henry Newbolt, he also chose an anti–Vietnam War poem by James Fenton. Amis chose what he calls "one of the first and greatest of all Leftie poems" (*Amis Anthology,* 318), Rochester's "A Satire against Mankind," as well as Gray's "Elegy," "a great Rightie poem" because of its message that the poor are "better off" than is actually the case (320). Surprisingly, Amis includes a great many religious poems. And in several instances, Amis includes poems that do not particularly appeal to him (Shakespeare's sonnets, certain works of Keats, Shelley, and Ted Hughes) but that might connect with others. None of these, however, are included in the more personal *Amis Anthology*.

All in all, Amis's lifetime love of poetry led him to a courageous, if inevitably doomed, defense of poetry as it was conceived of in earlier times. In his anthologies, he attempted to infuse a wider sense of community into the relationship between poet and audience, the subject of his failed thesis. It is based on the simple notion that "what appeals to me in this way is likely to appeal to others in the same way" (*Amis Anthology,* xvii). Amis is not entirely consistent in his larger poetic judgments: at one time, for instance, Whitman "approached greatness"

(*Amis Collection*, 18); later on, his work is "thin and eccentric" (*Pleasure of Poetry*, 114). But Amis was flexible enough to change his mind on certain points; his growing appreciation of Keats is one example. He never relented in his war against obscurity, reviling Gerard Manley Hopkins for "his obsessive affectation of singularity" (*Amis Anthology*, 330). Amis borrowed F. W. Bateson's term of opprobrium for ambiguous verse; it was "sublimer than thinking" (*What Became of Jane Austen*, 57). Such a stance inevitably brings charges of a lack of capacity to appreciate the sublime, to which Amis at times admitted.

Amis also called poets to account for the effects of their works, calling Yeats's "Easter 1916" "vicious nonsense" (*Amis Anthology*, 337). He tendentiously defended works such as Chesterton's "Lepanto" and Newbolt's "Vitai Lampada." He also predictably defended poets such as his friends Philip Larkin and John Betjeman, but here Amis's defense was grounded in a sensibility that could praise eighteenth-century poetry for "examining not the species but the individual, of numbering the streaks of the tulip if not some humbler growth" (*Amis Collection*, 155), a sensibility that could admire a poem that ended with the lines "And I alone of all mankind / Were left in loneliness behind" (*Amis Anthology*, 94). In the introduction to *New Lines*, a key Movement anthology, Robert Conquest notes that George Orwell, because of his "principle of real . . . honesty," is "one of the major influences on modern poetry."[18] Amis, in the empirical reliance on his emotions and his reason in his poetic judgments, and in his belief that this was the basis for a true communality of taste, was Orwellian in the best sense of the word.

Poetry

Amis's first collection, *Bright November* (1947), prompted him later to rejoice that its rarity made it little known. He preserved only six of its poems in his *Collected Poems,* and few contain a hint of the later distinctive voice and tone that Amis would bring to his poetry. As has been pointed out, many were heavily influenced by the early works of Auden, an influence that is borne out, for instance, in the speaker's twice addressing his words to a "stranger." Not many of the poems stay in the mind. The chief subjects are war and love, with at least eight addressed to "Elisabeth," and one to Hilary. Amis's later voice does begin to emerge in "O Captain, My Captain!" by adopting a more demotic and less hieratic vocabulary. "Beowulf," one of the poems he retained, expresses his unfavorable opinion of its literary worth. But on the whole, one can see one of the reasons Amis expressed such hostility for the collection's publisher, R. A. Caton, in his novels up to 1966. He did Amis no favors by making it possible for these poems to be published.

A Frame of Mind (1953) is much more characteristic. Although the major influence is now Robert Graves, elements of Amis's poetic beliefs that are also central to Movement principles begin to emerge, chiefly in "Against Romanticism." The speaker blames the near-mania of certain poets to replace reality with dream-constructs on the desire "to please an ingrown taste for anarchy."[19] His world, though "pallid," will at least be "temperate" (*Frame of Mind,* 19). The theme is further pursued in "Ode to the East-North-East-by-East Wind," an obvious riposte against Shelley, who is referred to in the speaker's categorization of "poetic egotists" who adulate nature because the "world . . . will not mirror their desire" (22). A more personal theme appears in "Something Nasty in the Bookshop" (later retitled "A Bookshop Idyll"), one of Amis's most famous poems. The speaker notes that men and women appear to have different poetic subjects, with women's being far more self-revelatory, leading to the notorious conclusion "Women are really much nicer than men" (29).

In the later collections, *A Case of Samples* (1956) and *A Look around the Estate* (1967), many of Amis's best poems concern the demarcation between reality and the defenses that the mind constructs against it. Even art can be mendacious because of its generalizing mania, as in "Here Is Where" and "Larger Truth." Poems such as "The Garden," "Notes on Wyatt," "They Only Move," "A Pill for the Impressionable," and "Romance" concern how the mind constructs romantic delusions to cover fear of solitude and death. As in Amis's novels from *Take a Girl like You* to *The Old Devils,* death is a recurring and indefatigable motif. "The Silent Room" is really the coffin, and "A Pill for the Impressionable" is the nostrum that we really care about others' suffering, when only our own mortality really moves us. And, as in his novels, the thought of death is often inspired by prospects of sex, as in "Nothing to Fear," a kind of "To His Coy Mistress" in reverse, in which the prospect of an illicit assignation arouses not relish, but dread. Even in a poem such as "Point of Logic," which seems to be merely another firmly antiromantic poem—love is reduced to "labouring bodies" (*Collected Poems,* 83)—an allusion to Othello's metaphor about death, "Put out the light" (5.2.7), once again connects sex with death. For all the Movement's professed rationality, poems such as these, as Blake Morrison suggests, show that the Movement is not as far from romantic undercurrents as might be supposed.

Sex itself, and its place in the human condition, is another subject to which Amis returns. "Nocturne" asks if sex is merely an animal act, or another form of representation and communication. Amis's most famous (or infamous) series of poems, "The Evans Country," concerns a Welsh skirt chaser, Dai Evans, not all that different from many of Amis's less appealing novelistic heroes. Like Maurice Allington in *The Green Man* and Robin Davies in *You Can't Do Both*, Dai makes love immediately subsequent to—one is tempted to say because of—someone else's death. At the end of the cycle, Dai is comfortably ensconced in front of the telly, satisfied, but nonetheless realizing that he will never know "all it must mean to really love a woman" (*Collected Poems*, 115). As at the beginning of the series, the speaker asks readers to compare their own situations to Dai's. "What about you?" (116). This is the question that faces readers at the end of every Amis novel as well. Are we really all that superior? If so, we had better have some good reasons why.

Amis's poetry is weakest when it becomes tendentious. Poems such as "Shitty," "Ode to Me," "Festival Notebook," and "Crisis Song," all amount to, in grittier language, the familiar lament from "Abide with Me": "Change and decay all round I see." Amis's best works in this vein include "Their Oxford," in which the speaker questions his own certitude in lamenting the passing glory of Oxford, because he doubts if he had any Oxford to call his own. Also effective are Amis's poems about his religious beliefs, or lack of them. "O'Grady Says" sounds like the child's game "Simon says" until one realizes that O'Grady is God. "The Huge Artifice" talks about the human condition revealing "an inhumanity beyond despair" (*Collected Poems*, 88). "A New Approach Needed" is Amis's most unrelenting attack on Christianity, accusing Christ of not having studied human beings enough; many have endured "worse / And more durable wrongs" (89) than he did. Even if one cannot agree with Amis's conclusions, one can sympathize with the feelings of compassion that prompted them. It is here, and not in his attacks on Leo Rosten's hospitality, that Amis can be properly compared to Mark Twain.

Amis's best poetry includes "In Memoriam W.R.A.," his poem about his father; "The Evans Country"; "South," about the American South and its physical beauty and moral squalor; "Bobby Bailey," a poem of boyhood reminiscence; and "A Reunion," about an army reunion. They all employ a vigorous and often striking use of demotic speech to reinforce a sometimes moral message, but just as often a rueful lesson that only time can teach. It is in these hard-won observations, not in the brayings from his political pulpit, that Amis's best poetic accomplishment lies.

Chapter Three
Genre Fiction

"Genre fiction" is Amis's favorite term to distinguish certain types of popular fiction from "mainstream" fiction: science fiction, detective stories, espionage fiction, the horror or ghost story, the thriller, and the Western—all of which, save the last, Amis wrote. His ultimate belief in the worth of genre fiction is grounded in the primacy that he gives to the audience in his theories about all art forms, from the novel to cooking. The audience knows what it wants, and it should be able to receive it in a direct and understandable form. Thus, although Amis has few kind words to say about rock music, he admits that it is pleasurable for its devotees because it is, on the whole, still easily comprehensible; the critics haven't gotten to it yet. Rock is as directly approachable as the work of John Betjeman; nobody had to explain it to the masses, as was the case with modernism in all its forms and its secular interpreters. On the whole, Amis argues, the percentage of truly bad works in popular art is about the same as that in high art, and the best popular art is better than the worst high art. Genre fiction, to use the Rossetti dictum that Amis admired so much, must be "amusing," and in its struggle to remain that way, it fulfills a function that mainstream fiction often no longer attempts.

Science Fiction: Criticism and Editing

Amis's *New Maps of Hell* (1960) became famous as the first notable academic study of science fiction, or, more properly, the first notable study of the genre by an academic; John Clute calls the book "certainly the most influential critical work on sf up to that time."[1] The book became notable, Amis later suggested, because it arrived at the point in culture history when science fiction began to increase its appeal because of "an unknowing consensus" in the "Zeitgeist" of the period.[2] The study quickly became the most widely reviewed of his works up until that time; however, today it is generally relegated to the space of a footnote in the history of science fiction criticism. *New Maps of Hell* has been superseded as a historical study by works such as Brian Aldiss's *Trillion*

Year Spree or as a study of the inner form of the genre by works such as those of Darko Suvin. Partly this is because of the limited scope of the book, constrained by Amis's reliance on the materials he could get his hands on in New York at the time; partly because the study, like many of Amis's other "academic" works, is almost purposefully British in the way it refuses to adopt an academic tone, stance, organization, or methodology; and mainly because in it Amis narrowed the importance of science fiction to one particular kind of science fiction. This is regrettable, because taken as a whole, the book deserves rereading for its characteristic wit, levelheaded judgments, and insights that have not yet been refuted.

As in most studies of this type, Amis attempts to come up with a definition of science fiction: "[S]cience fiction presents with verisimilitude the human effects of spectacular changes in our environment."[3] Verisimilitude is important for Amis because without it we are left with fantasy, not science fiction. Environment in the ecological sense is not precisely the term Amis really means here, although he does discuss the disaster fables that were becoming so popular at the time, such as John Wyndham's *No Blade of Grass*, but such stories do not really interest Amis because they merely show humans either splendidly adapting or horribly maladapting to the situation. What Amis is much more interested in is what he variously calls the "satirical" or "admonitory utopia," which is constructed by taking a present-day trend or tendency and projecting it into the future (*New Maps of Hell*, 31, 48). Or, in a phrase from the introductory sonnet to *New Maps of Hell*, science fiction allows us "to meet face to face / Our vice and folly shaped into a thing," and this happens most effectively in the "comic infernos" with which much of science fiction presents us (13, 120).

This perspective thus skews the way in which Amis recounts the history of science fiction. *Gulliver's Travels* is significant because it shows "a series of satirical utopias. . . . This point, where invention and social criticism meet, is the point of departure for a great deal of contemporary science fiction" (*New Maps of Hell*, 31).[4] With this perspective driving him, Amis finds modern science fiction's ultimate justification to be "a means of dramatising social inquiry, as providing a fictional mode in which cultural tendencies can be isolated and judged" (63). Only then will he look below or beneath the narrative, finding in some of these satirical utopias an allegory of "a fear of the loss of individuality and free will" (71). Thus when he finished looking through a New York bookstore's bag of contemporary science fiction that formed the reading basis for *New Maps of Hell,* he pronounced Frederik Pohl science fiction's "most consistently able writer" (119) because of the numerous "comic infernos" presented in his writing. Pohl's novel *The Space Merchants,* which satirizes modern advertising techniques, is "the best science-fiction novel so far" (Amis limits the contributions of Pohl's collaborator C. M. Kornbluth to the action sections).

Such satirical utopias leave in the minds of readers what Amis terms "the inverted catharsis" of science fiction, "some slight discomfort," or a "residual uneasiness" (124). Most critics up until this time had extolled science fiction for its "sense of wonder," a nebulous term that Amis also uses. Yet Amis is one of the first critics to argue that the purpose of science fiction is ultimately to make its readers think, and as always for Amis, we cannot have too much reason. Nevertheless, Amis's view of the entirety of science fiction at this vantage is unduly narrow, and it is no excuse to argue, as he later does, that "the immediate state of science fiction at the end of the 1950s made it easy to see it as I saw it" (*Golden Age,* 18). Amis's refusal to allegorize, to dig beneath the surface, to become what he calls a "trend-hound," blinds him to the connection between American society in the 1950s, the Eisenhower years of complacency, prosperity, and a concomitant spiritual restlessness and unease, which emerged in fables such as those of Pohl. Unfortunately, as is the case with *The James Bond Dossier,* Amis never explored the genre's origins deeply enough.

Amis uses this sociological effect of science fiction to defend it against charges of complacency. He admits that the genre does, however, give free rein to what might now be called anthrocentric triumphalism; in Amis's terms, "a boundless self-confidence, a feeling that if humanity to itself do rest but true, no situation will be too tough and no problem too difficult" (*New Maps of Hell,* 79). This portrayal of humanity was in large part due to the editorship of John W. Campbell Jr. at *Astounding* (later called *Analog*) magazine and his promotion of writers such as Isaac Asimov, Robert Heinlein, and A. E. Van Vogt during the early 1940s. Amis finds the late-1950s Campbell "a deviant figure of marked ferocity" (98) because of his advocacy of ESP and other psychic powers. As Amis says, science fiction has traditionally been "strongly activist in its attitudes," proclaiming that "chains can be broken if people try hard enough" (77). The prototypical science fiction plot of this subgenre shows the individual, often portrayed as "the deviate, the maverick" (96), sometimes marked by supernormal mental powers, in rebellion, almost always successful, against a "polity which prohibits change" (90). But because the individual is often merely trying to restore the status quo ante, such science fiction, although "radical in attitude and temper," is also "strongly conservative in alignment" (110). Whereas Amis in general approves of science fiction's approval of triumphant activism, he does say that such optimism sometimes appears "almost excessive" (79) and, with the maddening vagueness he can at times adopt, "there are a lot of other things that also should be" (80). What these "other things" are will be apparent in the endings of *The Alteration* and *Russian Hide-and-Seek*.

In 1960 Amis had certain recommendations for the future of the genre. He hoped that narratives that were sufficient for solid short stories would not be inflated to novel length; however, any sensitive reader of the later works of Heinlein, Asimov, and Arthur C. Clarke will admit that the tendency has only flourished to an even greater extent. Amis felt that as science fiction grew more popular, its community would stop incessantly worrying about the genre's future; a quick glance at the recent forewords to yearly collections such as Gardner Dozois's *The Year's Best Science Fiction* will show that this definitely has not yet occurred. Amis also advocated a better use of humor in science fiction (one of the reasons he praised the works of Robert Sheckley), a more far-reaching and mature handling of sexual matters, and a better regard for matters of style. All of these suggestions are significant in light of his own later science fiction novels, as well as the movement of the genre as a whole.

In the early 1960s, Amis and Robert Conquest edited five collections of science fiction entitled *Spectrum*. Their prime purpose was to introduce science fiction to a wider audience in Great Britain, particularly works that had not yet appeared there. They were generally successful in this task. *Spectrum* was able to present in their entirety many of the stories Amis had discussed in *New Maps of Hell:* Pohl's "The Midas Plague," William Tenn's takeoff on Van Vogt, "Null-P," Robert Sheckley's "Pilgrimage to Earth," Katherine MacLean's "Unhuman Sacrifice," Mark Clifton's "Sense from Thought Divide," Henry Kuttner's "Vintage Season," Anthony Boucher's "The Barrier," Theodore Sturgeon's "Killdozer," C. M. Kornbluth's "The Marching Morons," and Paul Ash's "The Big Sword." The introductions to these volumes were generally noncontentious, reasoned affairs, quoting authorities from Raymond Williams to Amis's favorite, Rossetti, on art's function to be "amusing." The introduction to *Spectrum IV* goes even further and reprints a discussion between Amis, Brian Aldiss, and C. S. Lewis, "Unreal Estates." In *The Encyclopedia of Science Fiction,* Peter Nichols claims that *Spectrum V* "is selected almost entirely from [*Astounding Science Fiction*], a reflection, perhaps, of [Amis's] increasing conservatism about HARD SF (and in his politics)" (Nichols, 28). Although this claim is true as to politics, it is misleading because Amis never argued for the primacy of the "hard," technocentric form of science fiction, only that the science retain a veneer of verisimilitude to distinguish it from fantasy. Of the stories in the entire *Spectrum* series, 20 were originally published in *Astounding/ Analog*, and 17 in the "softer" magazines such as *Galaxy* and *The Magazine of Fantasy and Science Fiction*. *Spectrum* presents an extremely wide variety of stories, ranging from the technological puzzle solving in Tom Godwin's "Mother of Invention" to the entropic lassitude of J. G. Ballard's "The Voices of Time," and from the brash triumphalism of Van Vogt's "Resurrection" to the indictment of innate human cruelty in Howard Fast's "The Large Ant." At this period in his career, Amis was still very catholic in his tastes, but the "reformation" that took place elsewhere in 1960s science fiction would ossify his position.

In 1981 Amis edited his final SF collection, *The Golden Age of Science Fiction,* and in its introduction, he presents the case he had been amassing against contemporary science fiction since the late 1960s. For Amis, science fiction had been infected by the same disease that had infected other forms of literature, music, and the other arts—modernism. This particular form of modernism became known as the New Wave, which Amis summarizes as "shock tactics, tricks with typography, one-line chapters, strained metaphors, obscurities, obscenities, drugs, Oriental religions and left-wing politics" (*Golden Age,* 22). Who is to blame for such a catastrophe? One culprit Amis indicts is himself. To him, *New Maps of Hell* lent a spurious academic cachet to the study of science fiction and left the door open for the academics to interpose themselves between science fiction writers and their audiences.

Amis gives several other reasons for the decline of science fiction as he knew it. One is that familiarity breeds, if not contempt, at least a diminution of that elusive "sense of wonder"; as science explored more, "*Terra incognita* was turning into real estate" (22). Also, science fiction is, for Amis, primarily an idea-driven genre, and like that other concept-dependent genre, detective fiction, the number of possible ideas was finite and becoming completely exhausted. Also, the convenient abbreviation "SF" was now being taken in some quarters to mean "speculative fiction," which allowed for fantasy, a genre Amis had never been entirely comfortable with (claiming once that budding psychiatrists should peruse the subscription lists of fantasy magazines to find prospective clients). Also, with characteristic candor, Amis admitted that he was getting old: in one's forties, "one's capacity to take in new stuff, stuff markedly different from the stuff one is used to, diminishes" (19). The stories that Amis selected for his last SF anthology include several from the *Spectrum* anthologies, such as Ballard's "The Voices of Time" and F. L. Wallace's "Student Body." Amis also included stories that he discussed in *New Maps of Hell* but were not collected in a *Spectrum* volume: Anthony Boucher's "The Quest for St. Aquin," Philip Latham's "The Xi Effect," Pohl's "The Tunnel under the World," Clarke's "The Nine Billion Names of God," and Jerome Bixby's "It's a *Good* Life." Two of them, Boucher's "The Quest for St. Aquin" and H. Beam Piper's "He Walked around the Horses," Amis later chose for his anthology of favorite stories. All in all, like the *Spectrum* series, *The Golden Age of Science Fiction* is a remarkably wide-ranging collection in terms of modes, subjects, and themes, almost completely belying the astringency of the introduction. The collection even ends with a dying fall, Poul Anderson's "Sister Planet," in which a member of an expeditionary force on Venus has to kill his team members, as well as the creatures whose intelligence he has discovered, so that Earth will not colonize the planet, wiping out its inhabitants. If this story were written by, say, Ursula K. LeGuin, it could be taken as a comment on the U.S. role in Vietnam, thematically fitting right in with New Wave considerations. Amis's tastes were often wider than his opinions.

Amis's diagnosis of the condition of science fiction is intimately bound up with his liking for the science fiction of the 1950s. Most classifications of science fiction's golden age put it somewhat earlier, from 1938 to 1946, because as John Clute has suggested, that was the golden age of *Astounding*. Amis's golden age, from 1949 to 1962, is actually the golden age of *Galaxy* and *The Magazine of Fantasy and Science Fiction*. During that period, he says, writers "poured out ideas with reckless extravagance.... And they used them up" (*Golden Age,* 34). A contrary opinion, written in 1979, was put forth by Frederik Pohl, who in addition to being a writer was also a science fiction editor and agent. "Markets create writers," Pohl declared, claiming that the proliferation of science fiction magazines during the 1950s allowed talents such as Robert Sheckley and Algis Budrys—both anthologized by Amis—to appear and grow.[5] By the end of the decade, three-dozen SF magazines had dwindled to a handful with the collapse of the American News Company. Science fiction was forced to find new ways and methods of reaching an audience.

The rise and fall of the New Wave is too problematic to go into in great detail here, except to say that its influence was not as baleful as Amis suggests, although a story such as Pamela Zoline's "Heat-Death of the Universe" is as stultifying, as inimical to a sense of wonder, as Amis makes it out to be. The New Wave did promote two areas in which Amis had pressed for improvement: sexuality and style. It was just that in the one, some of the ideas were no longer to Amis's liking, and in the other, the style sometimes came between the material and its readers. And, as Amis does note, the New Wave was not as universal a movement as it was sometimes later made out to be. The career of Larry Niven, a writer in whose works the idea always reigns supreme, began and flourished during the New Wave's halcyon days. Also, in the 1950s, Amis claimed, aficionados of science fiction, like lovers of jazz, tended to be "firmly over to the left in politics" (*New Maps of Hell,* 17), a trend that continued unabated into the 1980s. If ideas still continued to be heroes in contemporary plots, then they were often ideas Amis could no longer stomach. Ultimately, the most important reason for Amis's disdain, that calcification in his capacity for appreciation that he claimed set in after age 40, prevented him from seeing that writers such as Ursula K. LeGuin and Samuel R. Delany were presenting just the type of science fiction Amis so strenuously championed, "a fictional mode in which cultural tendencies can be isolated and judged" while still allowing readers to "frolic like badly brought-up children among the mobile jellyfishes and unstable atomic piles" (133).

Science Fiction: *The Alteration*

The idea for *The Alteration* arose when Amis heard an unusual voice on the radio; upon investigation, it turned out to be the voice of a castrato. In such a figure, the most basic questions about sex and art are emblematized: What would it be like to give up the ability to physically love for the sake of art? In addition, what kind of a society would have to be in place to create such a figure? To treat such a possibility, Amis chose the science fiction convention of the alternate world, a subgenre that does not have much claim to strictly being science fiction, as one of the characters in the novel says, "if on no firmer grounds than that writers of the one sometimes ventured into the other."[6] In the novel's alternate time line, Henry VII's son Arthur does not die and lives to have a son, Stephen III, with Catherine of Aragon; thus the Reformation never happens in England and is quickly extinguished in Europe. Martin

Luther becomes Pope Germanian I; Sir Thomas More (not the Baron Corvo) becomes Hadrian VII. Thus the Europe of 1976 is ruled by the Catholic Church, which, typically in novels that posit this particular change, such as Keith Roberts's *Pavane* (1968), has prohibited all investigations into science, and whose dogmas and beliefs have remained virtually unchanged since the Middle Ages. This change in the time line is the first sense of the novel's title: it is an altered world; the second sense is the alteration that the church wishes to perform on the gifted young singer Hubert Anvil, an operation that might turn him into the greatest singer who has ever lived. In this comic inferno, to use Amis's language from *New Maps of Hell*, the Catholic Church is the "polity which prohibits change," and Hubert is the "deviant, the maverick" who opposes the authority; here, artistic talent, not ESP, is the power that marks the individual, and the novel is definitely an "an allegory of intolerant conformism" (98), like many of those admonitory utopias Amis so admired in the 1950s.

Readers quickly realize that in Amis's vision of an alternate world, certain characters who also inhabit our time line still exist. Perhaps this strains the bounds of credulity, but it affords Amis the chance to apply one of the techniques he noted in the comic infernos of the 1950s: "[T]he constant introduction of novelties [which are] witty, in the sense that they will strike by their singularity at first sight, but are on reflection found to be just" (*New Maps of Hell*, 120). Thus we learn, from the description of the cathedral in Coverley, the alternate England's capital, that Christopher Wren is still an architect, Turner, Holman Hunt, and William Morris still artists. But then we hear about David Hockney's work as being too traditional, and one famous artist's name has been transformed into Epstone. The alternate world shows us features of our own from a skewed, but telling, perspective. Himmler and Beria here are fittingly officers of the Holy Office, the church's inquisitorial arm, and A. J. Ayer is professor of Dogmatic Theology at Oxford.

The global perspective has also changed. A cold war still exists in 1976, although here it is between the church and Islam. "Pacific concomitance" is what we call "peaceful coexistence," and the "detensione" that exists between the two warring realms is our world's "détente." As one of the characters describes the present situation, "no wars throughout Europe but the one, a war with long breaks of peace, a war against a power that can never be crushed and can be held in only by standing in arms from year to year: the best possible form to draw off any will to rebel or quarrel" (*Alteration*, 97). This is strikingly close to the situation that George Orwell posits for his eternal tyrannies in *Nineteen Eighty-Four* (1949). Indeed, in many aspects, the church of *The Alteration* resembles the Inner Party of Orwell's novel. Brother Flackerty, for instance, has what looks like a version of Winston Smith's "memory hole" in his desk to destroy incriminating documents. In a world dominated by the Catholic Church, it would seem that the only hope for freedom is New England, the country to which Hubert tries to flee. But in a customarily deflating moment at the end of the book, we learn that this Eden also contains its own serpent, what New Englanders call "separateness," which is, of course, a translation of the Afrikaans term "apartheid." (Amis subtly emphasizes the connection by having it explained by a Dutch descendant of New England's founders.) Even though Indians flee to New England to escape the rigors of the church in Louisiana and Mexico, they occupy in New England a similar position to blacks in the antebellum South, except without the institution of slavery.

Similarly, the literary situation is similar to ours, yet wittily different. Edgar Allan Poe was a famous and successful New England general. Shakespeare was a playwright, but he was excommunicated and sent to New England (with hints that he was deported for his tolerant, in this world, portrayal of a Jew in *The Merchant of Venice*). Percy Shelley burnt down the papal summer residence, the Castel Gandolfo, in 1853. In the most significant departure for this time line, science fiction, SF, is called TR, "Time Romance," and the alternate-world subgenre is called CW, "Counterfeit World." Reading is illegal, although not totally eradicated. (In *New Maps of Hell,* Amis notes a work in which the totalitarian government's "major act . . . is the banning of science fiction" [103].) Hubert and his friends get their hands on, of course, Keith Roberts's *Galliard (Pavane),* and even more significantly, Philip K. Dick's *The Man in the High Castle.* In our world, Dick's novel is one of the most famous examples of the alternate-world subgenre, as well as of that subgenre's most common alteration, that of Hitler victorious (which Amis uses in his own story "1941/A"). In Dick's work, the characters read a novel called *The Grasshopper Lies Heavy,* which portrays a world similar to, but not identical with, our world, in which the Allies win. In a dizzying whipsaw of perspectives, in *The Alteration,* it is Dick's novel that describes a world similar to, but not identical with, our own, in which the Reformation does happen. The allusions become even more meaningful when we learn who this world's man in the high castle is.

By scattering these small but significant changes throughout *The Alteration,* Amis fulfills one of the prescriptions for science fiction that he set out at the end of *New Maps of Hell,* that future science fiction must be humorous, which *The Alteration* is throughout its texture. It also fulfills another of Amis's suggestions: it handles questions of sex and sexuality as serious and fundamental. The matter, of course, is implicit in the central question of the novel: Will Hubert be altered? As in *Nineteen Eighty-Four,* the tyrannical government tries to suppress and rechannel the sexuality of its people, and rebellion against the church often takes the form of sexual rebellion, as with Winston Smith and Julia in Orwell's novel. The chaplain in Hubert's family, Matthew Lyall, rebels because of the affair he has with Hubert's mother. They both quickly grow to love each other, and punishment is equally swift; Lyall is savagely emasculated in almost a parody of what will happen to Hubert. And van der Haag, the New England ambassador, in an echo of Goldstein's analysis of the relationship between repressed sexual energy and hate in *Nineteen Eighty-Four,* explains the "ruthlessness" of the Catholic clergy as arising from "the celibacy of their priesthood" (*Alteration,* 177).

Amis goes against the typically triumphant ending of the comic infernos of the 1950s in which the rebels succeed; here, Lyall ends up dead, and Hubert is altered. In this respect, the book also resembles Orwell's *Nineteen Eighty-Four,* but with some significant departures. Lyall is slain not by any deliberate machinations of the powers-that-be after he is questioned by officials of the Holy Office but because Thynne's servant, a spy for the Holy Office, overhears him complaining about Lyall's intransigence but leaves before learning that Thynne nevertheless feels Lyall will come around. This is a distant echo of the circumstances that led to the murder of Thomas Beckett. Hubert's case is even more problematic. Hubert is not seized at the last minute before he escapes from England; rather, his own body seems to betray him when one of his testicles becomes situated so that it shuts down the blood supply to the other. The cure has the same outcome as the proposed alteration. One of the doctors says that this condition arises "it seems by chance, or as if by chance" (*Alteration,* 181). Of course, for anyone more religiously minded, chance does not exist. Amis places a broad but deliberate hint that in this particular time line, Someone Else is pulling the strings. As one of the castrati accurately exclaims after hearing Hubert sing, in the book's second-to-last line, "Deo gratia" (205).

The novel ends with a flurry of actions in the greater world. The present pope, John XXIV, is an unreconstructed Yorkshireman (supposedly modeled after the novelist John Braine), who is almost certainly the only fictional pope to tell one of his subordinates, "Fuck your facilities!"

(*Alteration*, 195). The scene takes place in the pope's new summer residence, the Castel Alto; of course, this means that the pope is this novel's man in the high castle. We learn that the church has been experimenting with biological warfare that will not work because, unlike the plague, people die before they can pass it on, as well as surreptitiously placing a birth control agent, "Crick's Conductor" (presumably a reference to Francis Crick, the codiscoverer of DNA), in the water supply of the general populace; however, the agent causes too many birth defects. The pope cannot repeal Innocent XVII's bull against "artificial regulation" (birth control) because the Sacred College would accuse the pope of heresy. So, adopting another Malthusian solution, he sanctions a war against Islam, in which, we later learn, the Moslems are stopped and quickly repelled in Belgium, presumably after the populace has been sufficiently winnowed. One final in-joke appears with the pope's mention of what is obviously Anthony Burgess's novel *The Wanting Seed,* in which the overpopulation is dealt with by sending women to war. The pope adds, "Interesting lad, Burgess. It's a mortal pity he had to go and . . ." (199). Reviews were not the only place where Amis could get in a quick jab.

On the whole, *The Alteration* deserves all the accolades it received, including the John W. Campbell Memorial Award (an irony worthy of Amis himself, considering his opinion of Campbell). The novel deals with many of Amis's typical concerns, such as the fluid and ever-changing relationships arising out of love, sex, art, freedom, and responsibility. It is interesting to compare the novel with Roberts's *Pavane,* which Amis almost certainly read. *Pavane* is much more "poetic," has broad elements of fantasy within its depiction of the "old" religion, and is also much more concerned with the technology that would arise in a twentieth-century medieval society. Most important, the inevitable rebellion with which such novels end is here wildly successful; it turns out that the church has forbidden scientific investigation because human beings were not mature enough to deal with its consequences. When the church releases the knowledge, technology explodes. In this time line, there were no World War I slaughters, no Nazi concentration camps. In the end, *Pavane* is ultimately in the tradition of those utopias such as William Morris's *News from Nowhere* in which modern technology is happily and fortunately eschewed. They are similar to the escapist utopias of 1950s writers such as Clifford D. Simak who worry, Amis says, about "the moral and spiritual dangers of a technological civilisation" (*New Maps of Hell,* 73). In *Pavane,* you can have your technology and use it safely, too. Amis's view, although on the surface sunnier and less lugubrious, is more deeply pessimistic, on the broader level in which the tyrannical institution will seemingly last forever (not for nothing did Orwell make connections in *Nineteen Eighty-Four* between the Inner Party and the Catholic Church), and perhaps on the more intimate level as well. In three years, Amis would write *Jake's Thing,* which ends with an even fiercer renunciation of love. Amis declared that in science fiction, "the familiar categories of human behavior persist in an unfamiliar environment" (*New Maps of Hell,* 177); the familiar categories that Amis elucidates in *The Alteration* are not comfortable or reassuring, and fittingly, the reader is left with that "inverse catharsis" Amis held is the hallmark of good science fiction—and many of Amis's other works, for that matter.

Science Fiction: *Russian Hide-and-Seek*

Russian Hide-and-Seek is an example of the science fiction subgenre of future history. Some critics mistakenly perceive this subgenre to be solely predictive; this was Margaret Thatcher's mistake when she told Amis to "get another crystal ball" when she learned of the novel's plot. Future histories isolate certain historical or societal trends and take them to their conclusions; they are science fiction's most widely adopted thought experiments and often lead to a depiction of the kind of comic inferno that Amis finds the hallmark of good science fiction. Yet *Russian Hide-and-Seek* is not comic, nor particularly tragic, but curiously affectless, and its inferno is devoid of fuel or heat.

The novel is set sometime in the mid-2030s. England has been under Russian rule for around 50 years. The plot centers on a group of young Russian revolutionaries who hope to return England to the English. The problem is, the English don't particularly want England anymore. Amis claimed elsewhere that the main theme of the novel is that religious belief, once stamped out, "is dead and gone forever" (*Amis Collection,* 228). I would argue that in an equal sense, the novel is an answer to Anthony Burgess's *1985* (1979), which in itself was a response to George Orwell's *Nineteen Eighty-Four.* When Amis reviewed Burgess's book, he found that Burgess had made the same mistake Thatcher had: it was beside the point whether the events of the novel resembled the events of the year or not. *Russian Hide-and-Seek* attempts to describe what life would be like in a society that believes in absolutely nothing, on both sides of the fence.

The society on the whole resembles that described in many late-nineteenth-century Russian novels. Technology has made no great advances in this twenty-first-century civilization. The Russians, because of their power, act in the forms of the upper class, and the English take the role of the peasantry. Indeed, because there are no beliefs, everyone is constantly described as acting in a play. Their props—their clothing, food, houses—are generally shabby and threadbare, which they do not even realize because no one alive has any standard of comparison. Their parties generally devolve into drunken revelry. The title refers to a game that drunken Russian officers play to prove their manhood, a version of Russian roulette. Like characters in Tolstoy who speak French to mark their class, these Russians speak English phrases, but the idiomatic expressions crudely jar with the casual brutality of their acts.

The plot revolves on a young Russian officer, Alexander Petrovsky. At first, he seems like a gentle enough soul when he cries after telling his sister about frightening a sheep while out riding. But a few days later, he has completely forgotten about it. Alexander has no moral depth, indeed no depths of any kind. He is the supreme role player, constantly inventing a face to present to the world: "[C]ertainly he often asked himself what 'Alexander' would have felt, thought, and done at some local turn of events."[7] And of course the underlying question is, what kind of a character can be formed when nothing in society exists with which to form character? The answer is that such a character will find its shape in opposition, but it will be a senseless, ludicrous shape. When Alexander inevitably joins the revolution of Group 31 and is asked to arrest his father, an important official, it is Alexander who insists on shooting him.

The English they hope to liberate are no longer interested in being free. Russian histories claim the "Pacification" (an Orwellian doublespeak term; see his essay "Politics and the English Language") of England took three days, but in reality, the fierceness of the English resistance almost forced the Russians to withdraw. But now the English have nothing left to believe in to prop up their freedom. The revolution is to take place after a festival designed by Russian experts to reintroduce English culture to the English. But everything fails miserably. In drama, the audience totally misunderstands *Romeo and Juliet; Look Back in Anger,* however, is a great success because it is considered a comedy. Religion is the area in which Alexander tries to help, but during the affecting sermon delivered by an old but still believing clergyman, most of the audience leaves. The problem here is that the rot started before the Russians took over. The churches are all now converted to other uses. "And yet there had been something about what had been here, and in innumerable other such places, that men had been ready to die for—long ago" (*Russian Hide-and-Seek*, 73)—a very faint and ironic trace of the sentiments in Philip Larkin's poem "Church Going."

And here the resemblances between *Russian Hide-and-Seek* and *Nineteen Eighty-Four* begin to mount up. Abandoned churches play an important part in Orwell's novel, too. A picture of St. Clement's Dane decorates the wall (and hides a listening device) in the illicit flat of Winston Smith and Julia; they also meet in an abandoned church. Theodore's questioning of Alexander when he joins the revolution on whether he would kill his men echoes O'Brien's questioning of Winston and Julia on whether they would throw acid in the face of children. Sonia Korochenko's reply to Alexander about the revolution, asked after a bout of lovemaking, echoes several scenes between Winston and Julia. No one in either Airstrip One or Russified England realizes that everything is shabby and debased because they no longer have any standards with which to compare them. History has become replaced by a series of what might be called "mismemories" of past history; the prole in the pub tells Winston about all the capitalists in their high hats, and Alexander thinks about "the immigrants cowering at the backs of their shops while the racist mobs looted and burned and the police stood by or joined in the rapine, of the groups of workers hastily assembling and training for the supreme struggle" (*Russian Hide-and-Seek*, 134). Both sets of memories are false, and both are tendentious. Both O'Brien and Vanag, the head of Russian security, wear dark blue uniforms, and like Winston's rebellion, Alexander's is actually instigated by the state; three of the five who started Group 31 were agents provocateurs, as O'Brien is. And although the Russians' technology is not far advanced, the security service can, like the Inner Party, record "any conversation anywhere" (239).

But Amis places certain important qualifications within these similarities. Even though historical truth may be hidden, it is not, to use Orwell's word, "vaporized"; Russians who want to find out that, for instance, the Normandy invasion actually took place, can, with some effort. Theodore and Alexander, in the end, simply desired an adventure and were not really driven by any overmastering belief. Thus Theodore, when he sees his fiancée in prison, requires no Room 101 to renounce her; it is not that he is past caring but that he has never really begun to care. Vanag is not driven by any indomitable will to power; it is merely that he and his men live by "traditions"; everyone else has "nothing" to live by (*Russian Hide-and-Seek*, 234).

So why in the end is *Russian Hide-and-Seek* so unsatisfying? The first reason is hinted at by what the English call the Russians throughout the novel: "Shits." Most of the characters are just that; even Sergei Petrovsky, the liberal who wants to return self-government to the English peacefully, is repellent when faced with death by Alexander. And Alexander is the biggest one of all, too irredeemably one to make the reader care much one way or another. Alexander is suitably shaken when Sonia offers him her daughter, but he soon goes back for some sex play in which the daughter provides the literal momentum. When an officer is finally killed playing the title game, Alexander tries to weasel his way out of blame by claiming truthfully that he had no part in it, but the major rightly blames him for not letting him know the game was going on. Alexander refuses to rescue an actress he had meant to seduce when the production of *Romeo and Juliet* goes up in flames. The look of contempt Sarah gives him for not acting mortifies him not so much because he is a coward but because he didn't live up to the role he dreams for himself. He sticks to his decision to shoot his father because "not to would be admitting to himself, and to others, that he was a trifler, a poseur, a *booby*" (*Russian Hide-and-Seek*, 184). Even when he seems to be making a moral apprehension, he's pitiful. He realizes that what separates him from an Englishman of the past is a "mental," a "moral" barrier (224), but he still goes out to kill his own troops. When his own soldier shoots him, the only resulting emotion is relief.

The main problem is thus thematic. In describing an age of no belief, Amis conscientiously sticks to his theme. The whole thrust of the book is contained in the scene in which Dr. Wright analyzes the meaning of Bunyan's "To Be a Pilgrim," which is sung during the church service. It is a work anthologized elsewhere several times by Amis. Wright can no longer understand the religious implications of the hymn, but he can appreciate its symbolic overtones: "[I]f it was at all typical of what his parents' generation had sung in church some of the early Russian [punitive] measures had at any rate not been reasonless" (*Russian Hide-and-Seek*, 171–72). All well and good, but how can one then describe with any energy, any life, a society in which everyone's main motivation seems to be to escape boredom? And that is all this hymn fills the "congregation" with: boredom. Elsewhere Amis has said that *Nineteen Eighty-Four* is "that great work of private hysteria" (*New Maps of Hell*, 99), and however accurate that assessment may be, it is precisely that hysteria, that fear of the loss of individuality, the infamous vision of "a boot stamping on a human face—forever," which makes Orwell's novel a great work, gives it its drive, its nimbus of doom and apocalypse.[8] It is what makes the novel a true "comic inferno" in Amis's terms, where the clocks unluckily strike thirteen, and the bugs in the walls turn out to be not insects but listening devices. What was wittily apt in *The Alteration* falls flat in *Russian Hide-and-Seek*. The sexual concerns of the earlier novel are far better integrated into the plot than those of the latter. The rigorous thematic consistency of *Russian Hide-and-Seek* is ironically its gravest fault. It is a comic inferno of the first circle of hell, the causeless, and the whimper with which this world ends is almost too faint to be heard or heeded.

Mysteries: Criticism

In his criticism, Amis always tries to speculate on the origins of the appeal of his favorite genres. In the case of the mystery or detective story, it is clear that its primary appeal lies in the high place the genre accords to reason and rationality. The detective, in Amis's view, shows above all the power of the human mind to find the rational cause behind events. One cannot help but be reminded of his call for a more rational age in general: "[O]ne is better off with too much reason than with none at all" (*What Became of Jane Austen*, 92). Thus any explanation of the appeal of the detective story that does not take this into account must be spurious. Amis finds Julian Symons's sociological theory about the appeal of detective fiction spurious, adducing proof of its fallaciousness by noting that Symons himself fell for the genre when he was 11 years old, when he could not have had status to protect. Amis elsewhere notes that the mania for certain genres of literature begins in adolescence, but he can come up with no further inner reason. Yet although he generally rejects sociological or psychological interpretations, he does offer one of his own in connection with detective stories. Because the great detectives provoke a need for their approbation and a fear of their scorn, they are, in a way, father figures.

For Amis, the three great detective story writers were Arthur Conan Doyle, G. K. Chesterton, and John Dickson Carr. As far as American detectives are concerned, Amis rejects the critically acclaimed works of Dashiell Hammett and Raymond Chandler and argues—unsuccessfully—that Mickey Spillane was better than either of them. Amis tries to maintain the distinction between the detective story and the thriller, and he claims that the classic detective story died around 1950. He also connects the decline of the mystery story with his theory about the decline of the arts in general: artists are writing for critics and not for audiences, and like science fiction, the detective story has run out of ideas and is inspiring works of commentary, like Symons's *Bloody Murder*—for Amis, always a deadly symptom of inner rot.

By far the author who earns Amis's highest critical praise is John Dickson Carr, the American mystery story writer who spent his most successful years of writing in England (and also wrote under the pen name of Carter Dickson). Amis and Philip Larkin became acquainted with Carr's works on the advice of their friend Bruce Montgomery, who published detective novels under the pen name Edmund Crispin. (The initials of Crispin's chief detective, Gervase Fen, reproduce those of Carr's detective Gideon Fell.) When Montgomery introduced Amis to Carr in 1955, and Carr told Amis that he liked *Lucky Jim,* Amis said it made him "feel like a fledgling composer patted on the head by Beethoven."[9] In his essays, Amis was equally enthusiastic, and whatever lapse of recollection he may have hinted at in his introduction to *The Crime of the Century,* he had a deep and abiding knowledge of, and appreciation for, Carr's works. "Words like 'gripping' and 'absorbing' should have been allowed to remain in the womb of language until the advent of Carr/Dickson" (*Amis Collection,* 125).

Carr's novels almost always deal with some sort of "impossible" crime, usually involving a locked room, in which the question of "how" is equally important as "why." The atmosphere is thus often closely allied with the supernatural, which is usually, but not always completely, dispelled by the end of the story. According to Amis, Carr's formula partook of "the following of a ritual or a recurring dream" (*Amis Collection*, 123). Carr's best work has a "highly-wrought, perfectly finished complexity" (116) that goes beyond formulaic construction. Although most critics would agree with Amis's locating of Carr's talents in the area of plotting, Amis goes further and declares that Carr's novels show a grasp of "nuances of local life" and provide "some sympathetic insight into the social history of that vanished era" (123–24). Some readers would claim that Carr, like other workers in this genre, sacrifices character to plot, as well as locating his novels in some never-never England of the 1930s whose existence was as "real" as that of Doyle's or Chesterton's London. Also, Carr does not mind toying with genre conventions, almost to the point of being postmodern, going so far as to lift the curtains on the machinery of the narrative. In the famous "Locked-Room Lecture" of

Carr's *The Hollow Man* (1935; U.S. title *The Three Coffins*), Dr. Fell comes right out and says they should talk about detective stories "because . . . we're in a detective story, and we don't fool the reader by pretending that we're not."[10]

For Amis, Carr's underlying appeal lies in the way that his detectives can explain how the seemingly irrational, indeed apparently supernatural, can be explained, without totally lifting the veil of mystery from the events. Carr's biographer, Douglas C. Greene, explains that ultimately Carr was "equivocal" about "whether the universe is ordered and rational" (Greene, 220). Thus at the heart of Carr's world still lies the mystery; he is unsure whether these detailed and elaborate explanations can ever explain the underlying mysteries of life. "That may explain," says Greene, "the fact that in his books Carr so often shied away from the question of 'why' in favor of 'who' and 'how' " (220). Blake Morrison talks about how the Movement writers in general failed "to disassociate themselves from that preoccupation with the dark, the anarchic, the irrational, the chaotic, which they took to be characteristic of the Romantic sensibility," which elsewhere they decried (Morrison, 184). In this preoccupation, coupled with his love for the rational, lies Amis's fondness for the works of Carr, and for mystery writing in general, which would emerge in Amis's best mystery novel.

Mysteries: *The Riverside Villa Murders*

The Riverside Villa Murders is set at the height of the golden age of the detective story—1936. The novel takes place in a small London suburb, and its semirural milieu reproduces what W. H. Auden calls in his essay "The Guilty Vicarage" the Great Good Place: "[T]he more Eden-like it is, the greater the contradiction of murder."[11] For Amis, the novel reproduces the Great Good Place of his youth. Many critics have commented on the resemblances between Amis and his young hero, Peter Furneux. They are exact coevals, born in 1922; they share a seemingly French-derived surname; they both commute to grammar school in London (Peter goes to "Blackfriars," an echo of Frank Richards's Greyfriars); they are both the only child of devoted but restrictive parents; they both read *The War of the Worlds* at the same time in their lives; they both live in similar London suburbs. Thus the conflict between Peter and his father reflects the arguments between Amis and his father over music and personal freedom; like Amis, Peter cannot lock the bathroom door for fear that he may be indulging in self-abuse within. Peter's statement about his place in the family dynamics has been said to be a comment by Amis about his own position: "Being an only child did not mean that you were by yourself too much; on the contrary, you got the whole of your parents reserved for you instead of divided up into three, say."[12] Peter's life throughout the novel shows us that childhood, or early adolescence, is not really free, no matter what society says. As Peter begins to learn how to obtain his freedom, the novel takes on some of the characteristics of the bildungsroman, and Peter's final realizations about the murderer and his father's secret complete his education.

The differences between Amis's novel and those of the golden age are crucial. Peter's striking good looks make him attractive to homosexual as well as heterosexual predators, and he and his best friend indulge in mutual masturbation when they get together to listen to jazz records. The degree of sexual frankness in the novel—Peter is initiated into heterosexual sex during its course—sets it well apart from other novels of the golden age. What makes the novel resemble the classic detective novels of the 1920s and 1930s is the unusual method of the murder, the figure of the great detective, and all the knowing references within the plot. There is a Carrian concern with the mechanics of murder: even though the murder takes place out of doors and not in a locked room, one of the chief elements of the mystery is not only who the murderer is but how it was done. Amis here does a nice job of combining the method itself with the thematic concerns of the plot. The detective in this case is not wholly amateur or wholly professional, to use Auden's terms: he is the acting chief constable Colonel Manton, who, like many great detective figures, is a true eccentric; as Amis elsewhere says, because the main character detects, his or her inner character cannot be shown, so he or she is depicted by personal foibles or avocations. In Manton's case, some of the foibles are innocent: he loves jazz and is a devotee of detective fiction; the books on his shelves are by writers such as Carr, John Rhode, Anthony Berkeley, Dorothy Sayers, and G. K. Chesterton—all members of the Detection Club and favorites of either Amis, father or son. But one element of Manton's eccentricity is not one that would have been described by the writers on his shelves: he is a homosexual, a fact that almost every character in the novel comments on, speculating that his concern for Peter is based on ulterior motives. Yet Manton is a truly polite and kind character, concerned for his guests' well-being—always a touchstone for Amis of a good character. And when Peter offers his friendship to Manton, Manton refuses it.

If one did not know Amis was so firmly opposed to experimental fiction, one would be tempted to call *The Riverside Villa Murders* a postmodern detective story. For instance, when Peter first goes to talk to Manton, he is given Carr's *The Hollow Man* to read; Peter goes right to the locked-room lecture: "It was good even though you knew very little more about the story than that it was utterly different from the real story of what had happened to Mr. Inman" (*Riverside Villa Murders,* 81), the victim in Amis's novel. But is it really different or irrelevant? In fact, the murder of Mr. Inman, like so many of Carr's, revolves around the fact that a crime seems to have been committed by someone at close quarters, when in reality the murderer was far away. Throughout the novel, Manton makes acerbic comments that make the reader aware that at least one character knows he is within a novel, and a very particular kind of novel. When Manton tells Detective-Constable Barrett, his assistant, to do something routine, such as canvass a neighborhood, he always adds that Barrett will learn nothing—which is true, considering the kind of novel they are in. Taking Barrett to his car, Manton explains, " 'It has all my magnifying-glasses and false beards and reference books about bicycle tyres and tattoo marks in it,' . . . making that bit sound as if he had it in for somebody or something by no means easy to identify"—that somebody being the reader (35). When Barrett makes a perceptive comment, Manton tells him, "You seem to forget that I'm the one who's supposed to work everything out in that style" (100). When the insensitive and dull policeman Cox makes a speculation, Manton comments, "There are no cases on record of people like Cox being right. It's an established rule" (179). Even though Colonel Manton is a most unusual golden age detective, he knows his role, generally stays within it, and advises other characters to do the same. The novel at times veers toward, if it does not quite indulge in, the metafictional.

A golden age detective story often has as its narrative center a young person (such as Carr's Ted Rampole) who becomes involved with the crime in some way, often falling in love with a suspect, but always remaining a separate center of consciousness, usually making precisely the wrong speculations about the crime, so that the great detective can spring his surprise at the end. By making this center of consciousness so young, and frankly introducing the elements of sexuality that would not be discussed in the classic detective story, Amis has brought the classic story into the last half of the twentieth century with his own characteristic concerns. "How nice the nice things in life were" (*Riverside Villa Murders,* 45), Peter muses early in the novel. By the end of the novel, he will have learned the extent to which the nastiness of life can be mixed up with the nice elements, to use Jim Dixon's dichotomy. When the classic detective story ends, Eden is restored, ready for the cycle to begin again, but not in Amis's version; one cannot conceive of a series of novels involving Peter and Colonel Manton. Eden is lost, but the whole world lies before Peter, who now has the knowledge to cope with it.

Mysteries: *The Crime of the Century*

Amis was contracted to write *The Crime of the Century* by the *Sunday Times* of London two years after *The Riverside Villa Murders* was published. Because that novel was conceived largely along the lines of the classic English detective story, his new novel, to be published serially, would be "one with large thriller or action elements and large forces involved."[13] Its plot deals with a serial killer whose crimes are leading up to something much larger—a deed that will earn the appellation of the novel's title. Once again previous literary models are mentioned in the text—in this case, *The ABC Murders* by Agatha Christie. Once again, the literary rules governing the genre are discussed by a character: "This bloody playing by the rules. Early mention of the criminal.... All clues shared with the reader.... No vital coincidences.... No secret passages, poisons unknown to science, twin brothers.... The really boring one is never being allowed to show what's in the criminal's mind even when it's nothing to do with the crime" (*Crime of the Century*, 4). Once again there is the almost metafictional aspect of the plot: one of the characters comments that whoever is doing these crimes "is doing a thriller" (38). After the crime is solved, one of the characters explains to another, "You couldn't be our man, because it would have meant a bloke who writes detective stories had started setting up a detective story in real life, and that kind of thing only happens in detective stories." The other replies, "Policemen aren't supposed to think like that" (146). Indeed not—unless they are in a thriller themselves.

The problems with *The Crime of the Century* are numerous. For one, there is almost no interest in character. The novel is full of types—the Rock Star, the Lawyer with a Secret, the Detective Novelist, the Ambitious Politician, the Trendy Sociologist (this is an Amis novel, after all)—but none of them has the least spark of life. Much of this can be attributed to the method of publication. Amis had to strip the narrative back to the bare minimum, "cutting the whole issue down to the bone," in his words (*Crime of the Century*, ix). Also, because the novel ended with a contest in which readers proposed their own endings, the plot was open-ended: almost any of the suspects could arguably have committed the crime. Thus when one comes to the book version of the novel and reads Amis's ending along with the contest winner's, one sees that there is little to recommend either as a satisfactory solution. (What marks Amis's as his is that one character is trying to hide a homosexual second life, and the novel ends with a call to drinks.) As the contest winner's version puts it, "at least there were enough red herrings and blind alleys in the present case for me to produce a different solution every year until [the villain] is released" (162). In a mystery by Carr, one gets the feeling of a jigsaw puzzle, that only one pattern will make sense of the chaos. In *The Crime of the Century*, one is looking through a kaleidoscope, one more turn of which will reveal a new pattern, an interpretation, just as valid as any other. *The Crime of the Century*, unfortunately, cannot even be classified as an interesting failure.

Ghost Stories: Criticism

The horror story, or more precisely, in Amis's case, the ghost story, was the genre about which Amis wrote the least, but what he does say is significant for his practice. Once again, he places the beginnings of the genre's appeal in one's childhood, but its real origin is "the biggest mystery of all" (*Amis Collection*, 133). Amis declares, "We enjoy being terrified, not horrified" (*What Became of Jane Austen*, 130), a naive view perhaps in the present salad days of writers such as Clive Barker, Anne Rice, and Stephen King, who try to out–Grand Guignol each other in the explicitness of their gore. For Amis, the pleasure of the horror story comes in the expectation, not the actuality of the terrifying being.

For Amis, the master of the ghost story is M. R. James, whose "Oh Whistle, and I'll Come to You, My Lad" Amis included in his selection of favorite short stories from all genres. He elsewhere hints that James's *Ghost Stories* are masterpieces and particularly notes with approval James's formula for ghosts and other beings: "[T]hey are malignant as well as frightening, physically solid and formidable (no nonsense about mere spiritual hauntings), and, very often, subject to certain rules and limitations" (*What Became of Jane Austen*, 128–29). In this description of James's ghosts, Amis echoes the words of a fictional detective whom he admires, John Dickson Carr's Dr. Gideon Fell, who summarizes his rules for ghost stories in the Carr mystery *The Hollow Man:* "The ghost should be malignant. . . . It should never be transparent, but solid. It should never hold the stage for long, but appear in brief vivid flashes. . . . It should never appear in too much light. It should have an old, an academic or ecclesiastical background; a flavor of cloisters or Latin manuscripts" (Carr, 109). Amis would adapt all of these strictures for the novel-length ghost story that he would write.

Ghost Stories: *The Green Man*

One of the constant dangers of reading Amis's fiction is mistaking the central character for the author, and Eric Jacobs, Amis's biographer, makes this mistake about *The Green Man,* following Amis's lead in his short story "Who or What Was It?" when Jacobs declares that Amis is "more like" Maurice Allington, that novel's hero, than any of his other protagonists. True, Amis does share a number of physical and psychological ailments with Allington: they are both heavy drinkers, both hypochondriacs, and both suffer from jactitations (involuntary muscle spasms just before the onset of sleep, when the sufferer suddenly feels as if he were falling), as well as hypnagogic hallucinations. There are also stylistic signs that Allington is related to Amis, such as Allington's reference, when confronted with frustrations in his job, to "an anti-hotelier HQ," a locution (like "bastards' HQ") favored by Amis as well as several of his other heroes.[14] Allington's long, hilarious paragraph about "Instructions to a Pimple" (*Green Man,* 114) could have come from, say, an Amis newspaper column. And some might argue that Allington's attitudes toward women are of a piece with Amis's.

Of course, Amis places large signs that Allington is not to be confused with Amis. Besides the obvious difference in their occupations—Allington runs the Green Man hotel and restaurant—one striking dissimilarity is Allington's pronounced dislike and mistrust of fiction and novels. Amis, however, places these differences in the narrative not, as Jacobs suggests, to hide his resemblances to Allington, but because Amis is simply *not* Maurice Allington. Amis exaggerates the affinities between himself and Allington, almost all of them weaknesses in perception, so that he can construct a seemingly unreliable narrator, a feature of several ghost stories since *The Turn of the Screw* by that other James who wrote ghostly tales, Henry (who is alluded to early on in *The Green Man* in the figure of a patron who cannot get to the point). Soon enough, though, the reader learns to trust Allington, as much as any

Amis hero can be trusted; Allington's unreliability becomes much more important to the plot because other characters cannot trust his observations. No one will believe him.

Perhaps Allington's greatest unreliability as a character—and his greatest resemblance to other Amis protagonists—is in his personal relationships. He is one more example, perhaps the best outside of Roger Micheldene and Bernard Bastable, of the Amis hero as shit. Allington is almost thoroughly selfish. As his wife, Joyce, tells him, he has the double talent of being able to ignore people and yet to observe them closely when it suits him. He pays little attention to his wife, neglects his father, and fails to get through to his daughter. His father calls him "a bad lad" (*Green Man,* 25) and tries to tell him what a miserable life Joyce is leading. (The narrative hints that the father is deliberately frightened to death by the ghost, who does not want Allington becoming any more self-aware.) Allington's son, Nick, arraigns him with an indictment that could apply, to a greater or lesser extent, to many Amis protagonists: "You're just too lazy and arrogant and equal to everything (you think) to take the trouble to notice people like your son, and your wife, and deem them bloody well worthy of being let into the great secret of how you feel and what you think about everything, in fact what you're like" (151).

What begins to redeem Allington is the extent to which he is aware of his faults: "[I] wish I knew how to give my daughter a life" (*Green Man,* 19); he says about his father, "Here was somebody else whose life I did not understand" (23). For all his avoidance of any true human contact, he still realizes that he needs people, for his ultimate problem is his sense of self: "[B]eing alone mean that I was stuck with myself. . . . Two's company, but one's a crowd" (46). Hell is not other people—it's yourself. Thus the underlying psychological frisson in the story is initiated by Allington's search for a means of escape; as Diana, his friend's wife, asks him early on, "Why do you look as if something's after you all the time?" (27). Any external horror has to be, says Allington, "less terrible than a portable, infinitely adaptable demon living and acting in the mind" (165).

Of course, because this is a ghost story, demons must be concretized. Amis adapts M. R. James's strategy in some of his most memorable stories ("The Treasure of Abbot Thomas," "Count Magnus," "Casting the Runes") of dividing, as it were, his ghost into two: a villain and his familiar. In this case, the villain is a ghost, that of Dr. Roger Underhill, an eighteenth-century cleric who formerly inhabited the Green Man and caused by means of a supernatural agency the death of his wife (who also haunts the hotel). His familiar is the title figure, an arboreal demon conjured up out of a patch of woods near the hotel. The creature's distant origins seem to have been Central American, but its appearance fits nicely into the local druidic myths of the Green Man (of which Allington seems to be unaware), a potent fertility symbol whose stone face decorates gardens even today.[15] The creature's sole purpose is to kill young women whom Underhill sends to it in a parody of druidic rites. Thus Amis is able to have both a "ghostly" ghost, the spectral Underhill, as well as, in Amis's own words about James's ghosts, a "malignant . . . physically solid and formidable" creature that is "yet subject to certain rules and limitations" (exorcism, for instance, works on both Underhill and his familiar, which can be controlled by a small figurine). The green man fulfills Fell's doctrines as well: solid, it never speaks, and does "appear in brief vivid flashes."

Allington comes to realize that Underhill has chosen him as the subject of his haunting not only because of his unreliability as a witness but because they share "something of an affinity" (*Green Man,* 235). This underlying affinity really resides in sexual matters. Allington is unusually callous about such affairs, even for an Amis hero. He makes love to Joyce immediately after his father dies, with little accompanying sense of love. Allington not only seduces Diana Maybury on the afternoon afterward but is subsequently intent throughout the course of the novel on getting her and Joyce in bed with him together. When perusing Underhill's diaries, Allington learns that Underhill indulged at times in just such a relationship with two young girls from the village whom he has blackmailed (one of whose physical endowments closely match one that Joyce and Diana share). Yet Allington does not make the connection between himself and Underhill until Underhill tries to kill, with the agency of the green man, Allington's daughter, Amy. This, he learns to his disgust, was Underhill's purpose in using him.

One other way in which Allington resembles other Amis protagonists is in his fear of death. Like Patrick Standish in *Take a Girl like You,* Allington becomes almost obsessed at times with the subject: "And I honestly can't see why everybody who isn't a child, everybody who's theoretically old enough to have understood what death means, doesn't spend all his time thinking about it" (*Green Man,* 100). Allington's *timor mortis,* as well as his need for a solution to the problem of Underhill and his familiar, leads to the novel's most notorious—and unexpected—scene: Allington's interview with God, a being who, for Amis, is inextricably linked with the problem of death, as *The Anti-death League* shows.

This scene is introduced by an effect that is the opposite of that of M. R. James's story "The Mezzotint," in which a picture gradually comes alive; here, time stops, and the world turns into a picture. The deity, never named as such in the narrative, has a rather unprepossessing appearance, that of a young man with a "not very trustworthy face," who signals his true identity by giving off "a whiff of the worst odor in the world," the charnel scent of death (*Green Man,* 188, 190). He has approached Allington because Maurice is "a good security risk" because of his poor reputation; Underhill, on the other hand, is "a minor threat to security"—security in this case being humanity's continued lack of any serious belief in an afterlife (*Green Man,* 191). When Allington brings up Amis's most enduring complaint about religion, the suffering of the innocent, the young man tells him "it's purely and simply the run of the play. No malice in the world" (192). In recognition of Allington's assistance in getting rid of Underhill, the young man reveals that there is an afterlife, but Allington probably won't like it very much; "you'll never be free of me" (196). (Later in the novel, Amis introduces another of his line of unbelieving Anglican clergymen, the hilariously named Rev. Tom Rodney Sonnenschein, who nevertheless can efficaciously exorcise both Underhill and the green man.)

By the end of the novel, Allington has to an extent redeemed himself. He is truly heroic in rescuing Amy, and he ultimately refuses Underhill's last and most provocative temptation, that of peace of mind, but with a characteristic qualification; Allington realizes his duty is to protect others from Underhill's further machinations. It also appears that Allington is ready to embark on a new and perhaps more meaningful life with his daughter. One customary deflation remains for Allington, however; Joyce leaves him to go off with Diana. It is a characteristic moment of revelation for an otherwise blinded Amis protagonist at the end of a novel. But Allington's more hard-fought realization concerns his greatest fear, and death no longer holds such terrors for him: "Death was my only means of getting away for good from this body and all its pseudosymptoms of disease and fear, from the consistent awareness of this body, from this person" (*Green Man,* 242). It is significant that the last word of the novel is "round" (242), referring to the evening circuit that Allington as a hotelier must make; it also alludes to the circles that Allington must transit and withstand for the rest of his life. The circles of hell are here, not in the afterlife.

In the traditional antiquarian ghost story perfected by M. R. James, the cause for the haunting, as well as the guilt of the central character, usually resides in the curiosity of the protagonist, who disturbs antiquities better left untouched. Amis modernizes this scenario by placing the guilt more firmly in the central faults of the protagonist: selfishness, sexual greed, lack of *caritas*. He combines this with characteristic concerns about death, eschatology, and the place of religion in modern society. In other words, while *The Green Man* is recognizably a work of genre fiction, it is also unmistakably a Kingsley Amis novel. It is another piece of evidence that shows that Amis has his greatest successes, here as well as in *The Alteration, The Riverside Villa Murders,* and *The Anti-death League,* when he combines genre considerations and requirements with his own novelistic interests. When he follows a formula *(The Crime of the Century, Russian Hide-and-Seek,* and to a lesser degree *Colonel Sun),* the results are less satisfactory.

Spy Stories: On Bond

Undoubtedly the most widely known of Amis's works of criticism is *The James Bond Dossier* (1965). It may well be, as Eric Jacobs suggests, Amis's farewell to an academic career; it is certainly contentious enough in its premises to rankle many academics. For one, Amis sets out to defend Ian Fleming, an enormously popular author, precisely because of his very popularity. Amis declares in the preface that after his academic career, "I can't help being slightly drawn to any form of writing that . . . reaches no part of its audience through compulsion."[16] He also defends Fleming from the subsidiary charges of being sexist (although not using that term), snobbish, immoral, and sadistic. In doing so, Amis follows the lead of George Orwell, who similarly analyzed and defended popular literature from its critics.

For Amis, Bond's chief appeal is that he is a sort of Everyman with whom his readers (the premise is that they are exclusively male) can identify. After decades of films in which Bond, by accomplishing ever more elaborate stunts, comes closer to being Superman than Everyman, such an assertion may seem unjustified, and to a certain extent, neither do the texts fully justify it, but Amis makes a strong case. For Amis, the appeal of the spy story's fantasy lies in the reader's identification with a hero who appears to be ordinary, but inside is extraordinary; this appeal becomes particularly powerful in conformist times, such as the 1950s and early 1960s. (Here the analysis dovetails with Amis's view of sociological science fiction during the same era.) Looking at television secret agents such as *The Avengers'* John Steed, Amis declares that secret agents "*must not* be different" (*James Bond Dossier,* 13), or else they would not survive in the real world. Perhaps the eccentricities of Steed can be attributed to the rise of the genre itself, which was made possible, according to Amis, by the demise of the classical "great detective" (12), who was always differentiated by outré habits. (Amis also sees the spy genre as quickly approaching decadence, as the detective story did, on the evidence of the emergence of shabby and squalid figures such as Len Deighton's Harry Palmer.) Bond, however, is basically like other human beings; his accomplishments are based on skills that are not really unique talents; they are "acquired, not innate" (16). (Amis here evades the fact that Bond is physically superior to most men, and no amount of exercise would make the reader Bond's equal in combat or sports.)

Intellectually, Bond is, for Amis, a palimpsest on which readers can project themselves; his "mind is a completely utilitarian organ" (*James Bond Dossier,* 31).[17] One characteristic sets Bond apart: his psychological makeup. Amis calls him "a depressive and a solitary" (29), traits that lead to Amis's crucial literary analysis of Bond as Byronic hero, who, after the murder of his wife in *On Her Majesty's Secret Service,* attains the final identifying mark of such a hero, "a secret sorrow over a woman" (35). For Amis, this is Fleming's real triumph, combining such a "wildly romantic, almost narcissistic, and . . . hopelessly out-of-date persona inside the shellac of a secret agent, [and] making it plausible, mentally actable, and, to all appearance, contemporary" (31). Amis, however, does not go into how such a character becomes identifiable for the reader; we may want to be Bond, but do we want to be Byron?

Although Bond himself may be an Everyman in the ordinary sense, the plots in which he is involved are not. In a phrase that Amis repeats in his essay on his own Bond novel, Amis says that "Fleming technologized the fairy-tale for us" (*What Became of Jane Austen,* 68), and Amis spends an appendix in *The James Bond Dossier* on Bond's links with science fiction. Yet the implausibility of Fleming's plots is leavened by what Amis calls "the Fleming effect" (*James Bond Dossier,* 88), that is, Fleming's relentless and overpowering use of brand names on everything. Such constant references to commercial things link the fantastic plots to the quotidian reality that surrounds us (a lesson that Stephen King has assiduously followed in his even more fantastic fiction).

Whereas Bond is Everyman, the Bond villain is extraordinary: in Amis's phrase, "somebody really big" (*James Bond Dossier,* 54) (a perhaps not unconscious play on the name of the villain in *Live and Let Die*), who has a mania for power. Amis compares Dr. No in this respect to O'Brien in Orwell's *Nineteen Eighty-Four*. The point of these characters' tirades to their victims is not so much that they are insane in their perceptions of the world but that their listeners are children compared to them, which leads to Amis's most interesting insight about Fleming's villains (which he does not follow through enough): they are father figures. Amis tries to defend Fleming against the charge that most of his novels end in the same manner, with Bond being lectured to, and often tortured by, the villain and then being left on his own to escape. Amis terms this repetitive device a narrative convention that affords the villain a logical point in the plot to explain the niceties of his schemes, and also "makes us feel admiration and sympathy for the hero and fear and hatred for the villain" (20). Moreover, it is the point at which the recalcitrant child is dragged into his father's study to have the ways of the world explained to him. In this respect, Bond's boss, M, is also a father figure, and, interestingly enough, the character whom Amis most despises, calling him brainless and unsexed. To a certain extent, this portrayal of the boss as headmaster is a convention—"boy's-paper bullshit" (62)—but Amis also points out that in one instance, M's eyes show a glint of red, the sure giveaway of a Bond villain, and M also smokes thin black cheroots, another villain's habit.

Another part of Bond's appeal, especially for an English audience, is Fleming's patriotism. For Fleming, the loss of the British Empire and the general diminution of Great Britain to a second-class world power during the 1950s never really happened. At times, this patriotism is negatively expressed in various politically incorrect assessments of foreigners, which Amis argues are not really "sinister" (*James Bond Dossier*, 71). Certain "delusions of grandeur" (74) are indulged in when Bond villains target Britain as the subject of their plots. Yet Amis makes no mention that Fleming's more subtle delusions of grandeur concern the secret service itself; in Bond there are no Cambridge spies, no betrayals by Burgess, Maclean, Philby, and Blunt.

Amis's defense of Bond against various charges is on the whole successful. As to the charge of immorality (amorality would perhaps be more accurate), Amis shows that characters such as Sapper's Bulldog Drummond and Mickey Spillane's Mike Hammer are truly immoral and sadistic; at least Bond at times reflects on what he has to do. Yet Bond must be at times unthinkingly violent; thus, "a secret agent has no choice but to be a hypocrite" (*James Bond Dossier*, 25). Amis, however, does show a chink in Fleming's portrayals on this point when he points out that many of Bond's friends, including the otherwise estimable Darko Kerim, while providing a "warmth" (64) that Bond himself lacks, are really villains in their actions themselves: Kerim with women, Marc-Ange Draco as head of the Union Corse. Their villainy is seemingly excused because they are "on the right side" (67).

Amis's discussion of Fleming's treatment of women is not as successful. In discussing their ludicrously suggestive names, he remarks, "I just relax and enjoy it, a policy the bearers of the names would surely endorse" (*James Bond Dossier,* 38). Amis surely knows the origins of the phrase "relax and enjoy it," and if he thinks it's wrong when Darko Kerim does it, then Amis shouldn't be so glib when discussing characters, some of whom (Honeychile Rider and Pussy Galore, for instance) have undergone the act the phrase refers to and not enjoyed it. (Perhaps even more ludicrous is Bond's role as eventual sexual healer of these women.) Yes, these characters have become a Fleming convention, many of them portrayed as "a defenseless child of nature, a wanderer in a hostile world, an orphan, a waif" (48). Yet this convention encapsulates an even larger fantasy, that of love without any commitments. Amis's inferences that critics of Bond's sexual success are somehow sexually jealous of him, or sexually deficient in some way, are the low points of Amis's argument in a book that otherwise combines literary scholarship and a deep knowledge of the works, and indeed the entire genre, in a work that is readable in the best sense.

Amis got a little more mileage out of his research by publishing in the same year *The Book of Bond* under the pseudonym of Lieutenant Colonel William "Bill" Tannner, M's chief of staff in the Fleming novels. The book is both slight and slightly amusing, with the premise that it is a book of instructions for any male who would like to be James Bond, or in the chapter on girls, any female who would like to be his girl. Each paragraph is handily annotated with references to the particular text(s) from which it comes. The candidate's prospects are realistically assessed when Tanner recommends that instead of doing the prescribed exercises, the candidate should lock himself in the bathroom and make appropriate noises while seated on the stool. The design of the book is clever: the chapter on alcohol is prefaced by a picture of Alka-Seltzer, the chapter on girls by a packet of birth control pills, and the chapter on culture by a black, blank page. The chapter on drink presages much of the tone and manner of Amis's books on drinking. The section on M lists all the adverbs that describe his tone of voice, and the one on girls all the adjectives that describe the heroines' breasts. But the last chapter is especially flat, and on the whole, although the book shows flashes of wit, it remains curiously embalmed in its age, a relic more redolent of Steed than Bond.

Spy Stories: *Colonel Sun*

At the end of his life, Ian Fleming knew that his inventiveness involving his chief literary creation was slipping (Amis thinks that, like modern writers of science fiction and detective fiction, Fleming was running out of ideas). He delayed publication of the last Bond novel, *The Man with the Golden Gun,* until he could read Amis's conclusions in *The James Bond Dossier.* The criticism did not help. After Amis had analyzed the posthumous novel for Fleming's estate (Amis's conclusion that Scaramanga's homosexual attraction to Bond had been excised by Fleming was not well received), Amis seemed to at least some of Fleming's heirs the ideal candidate to continue the series. Ann Fleming objected, however; this is what Amis refers to when he says that "fear was expressed in some quarters that I might produce a sort of Lucky Jim Bond" (*What Became of Jane Austen,* 70). She need not have feared, as it turns out. Amis admitted that he undertook the commission for the money and to find out "how cross with me the intellectual left will get" (66). Because of Amis's support for the American role in Vietnam, they assumed he would adopt Fleming's so-called ideology, as Graham Greene charged in the *New Statesman.* To an extent they were right, but interestingly enough, Amis himself in the novel does not completely buy into Fleming's worldview.

Colonel Sun is Amis's rewriting of the Bond myth based on the conclusions he came to in *The James Bond Dossier*. He keeps many of Bond's characteristics: Bond plays golf, he enjoys plain foods, he gets a major charge out of smoking, and he is violently afraid of becoming middle-class. Amis also adopts many of Fleming's literary devices, particularly those that enforce verisimilitude. He gives several characters detailed back stories. He makes Flemingesque pontifical generalizations about widely ranging topics. And he tries to employ the "Fleming effect" by using brand names: Ferragamo slippers, Longines and Rolex watches, Stolichnaya vodka. But on the whole, this technique is not as incessantly employed as in Fleming. Amis adopts some of Fleming's stylistic tics: the overuse of the word "delicious," for example. And he even attempts to adopt Fleming's awkwardly cloying female point of view; the heroine, for example, thinks of Bond, "That mouth was made to give her brutal kisses, not to become distorted in a grimace of agony; those hands existed to caress her body, not to be stamped on by the torturer's boot."[18] Yet Amis will not touch the scenes that Fleming does so well: when Bond takes a swim to refresh himself, he does not go beneath the water, thus averting the possibility that Amis will have to describe the milieu that Fleming depicted best.

More important, Amis tries to change and subtly improve Fleming's creation. On almost every level, the novel is a more "realistic" narrative. Most important of all, Bond does not rely at all on the gadgetry that seems to have saved him so often in the past. No "fairy tale technologized" here. The best weapons of Bond and his allies are a Thompson submachine gun and a British rifle made in 1916. Other characters are more realistic, or at least more moral. The heroine has an almost normal name, Ariadne Alexandrou, and Bond's best friend, Litsas, is no thug, but a patriotic Greek.

This Bond is not as solitary as Fleming depicts him; at least here his evening companions are named. A subtle moral change occurs in Bond as well. Bond's motives are entirely honorable: to rescue M and avenge the death of his servants. After each act of violence, Bond has moments of regret. No savage boots to the backside here, such as Bond gives Krebs in *Moonraker* (1955), even before he realizes Krebs is a villain. Now Bond rationalizes, "It was necessary, he told himself. It was duty" (*Colonel Sun,* 122). Amis even manages to include an in-joke about his own literary analysis of Bond's character; when Ariadne merely mentions Lord Byron, Bond complains, "I don't really enjoy being compared with Byron. As a poet he was affected and pretentious, he ran to fat early and had to go on the most savage diets, his taste in women was appalling, and as a fighter for liberty he never got started" (68).

Above all, the plot is more realistic. No superweapons are employed by the villain; just a trench mortar and assorted small arms. The villain's scheme, a Chinese communist plot to destroy a Middle East conference of Russians and Arabs and to blame it on the British, is almost plausible (but that he should kidnap the head of the British secret service and his best agent to accomplish this is not). The heroine mentions the real-life spies Oleg Penkovski and Greville Wynn. Even more unusual is the depiction of the Russians, which seems about 25 years proleptic. When the Russian bureau chief in Athens gives Bond a "firm and dry" handclasp (81), we know Amis is using Fleming's shorthand to indicate that Gordienko is a possible ally. Bond assures Ariadne that "the Kremlin knows perfectly well that the main threat isn't the West anymore, but the East" (110). This view, however, does not lead Amis to John le Carré's conclusion that each side is as bad as the other; Bond muses, "There were still two sides: a doubtfully, conditionally right and an unconditionally, unchangeably wrong" (64).

Amis employs the conventional Fleming ending, with Bond being captured, tortured, and escaping, but he makes the sequence more than a mere narrative convention by giving the villain a plausible motive for torturing Bond: Sun is a pathological and intellectual sadist. He can lecture Bond on his mania with even better motivation than Hugo Drax or Auric Goldfinger. But in the end, Sun is just as maniacally melodramatic as other Bond villains. Yet in a surprising about-face, he admits (here the hand of Amis is more apparent than Fleming's) that he did not feel as he thought he would when he tortured Bond: "I felt guilty and sick and ashamed. I behaved in an evil and childish way. It's ridiculous and meaningless, but I want to apologize" (234). It is as if the school bully suddenly repented.

Other Amis characteristics dot the narrative. The setting of the Greek islands is the same as in *I Want It Now* and "The House on the Headland," a short story that recapitulates some of the plot of *Colonel Sun*. At one point, Bond's perception of the plot requires him to recognize a classical allusion, as happens in *Crime of the Century*. On the whole, however, the novel is not a successful blend of Amis and Fleming, nor a convincing impersonation, nor even a successful improvement; many spy writers, from le Carré to Brian Freemantle, can invent plausible plots. Above all, Amis simply cannot reproduce the narrative momentum and suspense that Fleming could, even in a plot such as *Moonraker*'s, in which Bond also uses no gadgets. Amis's major climax is perhaps as effective as Fleming's (it is certainly more disturbing), but the minor climaxes—the fight at the Acropolis, the gun battle in Athens, the destruction of the Russian ship—simply do not cohere as well as Fleming's—the card game with Drax, the collapse of the cliff, the automobile chase at night. Amis of course realized this, and at the end of *The James Bond Dossier,* he flatly stated that Fleming "leaves no heirs" (113). That is still true.

Spy Stories: *The Anti-death League*

When it first appeared in 1966, *The Anti-death League* was chiefly marketed as the fictional result of Amis's Bond researches, with the sexual overtones of the plot heavily emphasized. In reality, the spy story is only one of the elements from which Amis constructed this novel. Not only does it contain aspects of other genres such as the mystery and science fiction, but many of its key concerns—army life, madness, drinking, and the relationship of God, humanity, and death—are those of Amis's mainstream fiction as well. Even L. S. Caton makes his last appearance here, only to be memorably wiped out by getting shot "full in the face" (an indication, says Amis, that this novel is to be taken seriously).[19] Because of this admixture of so many of Amis's fictional interests, *The Anti-death League* is in many ways Amis's most characteristic novel, and one of his most successful.

In a sense, the novel is also a reaction against the flashiness and unreality that Fleming's pervasive influence cast over the espionage genre at this time, from Matt Helm to *The Man from U.N.C.L.E.* The closest any character approaches to being a real spy is Jagger, the fat, disheveled government operative whose unruly hair and thirst for beer belie his physical and mental effectiveness. (He deduces who wrote a key document because its punctuation was correct, but its spelling was not—a point one imagines would be beyond Bond's comprehension.) The spy catcher, Brian Leonard, is a naive snob who would not have noticed the suspiciousness of Kim Philby or Guy Burgess any more than he does that of the real spy in the novel, who turns out to be almost figuratively under his nose. Leonard, however, is generally likable, as are most of the other characters in the novel, except for the ludicrously wrong psychologist Dr. Best, and the two rationalist officers, Venables and Ross-Donaldson.

The novel is set in the environs of any army base in England, which gives Amis the opportunity once again to depict realistically the army's essential nature, with all the attendant boredom, futility, and unwarranted obedience to authority. The soldiers there are supposedly guarding a new British superweapon, code-named Operation Apollo; the mythological allusion gives a clue to the exact nature of the weapon, which Amis withholds almost until the end of the novel. The reason for its existence, the threatened invasion of the Indian subcontinent by the communist Chinese, is Amis's modern takeoff on all those earlier spy novels about "The Great Game" in which Czarist Russia threatened India, the most memorable example of which is Kipling's *Kim*. And the horrible nature of the death that this superweapon will cause gives rise to a crisis of conscience in one of the main characters, the aptly named James Churchill, whose name contains allusions to both Fleming's spy and England's wartime leader.

This obsession with death and its role in the scheme of human existence troubles several of the other main characters too, as well as giving rise to several incidents in the plot. The novel begins and ends with deaths in the animal kingdom—a cat stalking a bird's nest at the beginning, a pet dog getting run over at the end—and the motif runs throughout the entire novel. A dispatch rider is killed delivering a message that could just as easily have been sent electronically, a young soldier dies of disease, the young heroine develops breast cancer: all these events lead Churchill to hypothesize that the characters are entering a "lethal node," on the analogy of newer military terminology in which "nodes" replace "fronts." These death nodes are, in Churchill's words, "a bit of life it's death to enter" (*Anti-death League,* 201); for him, they represent, in the absence of God, the operation of a mechanism beyond fate or chance in governing life.

And it is precisely this absence of God in setting the rules of the universe that bedevils the main characters. If God did make up these limits, then he must be, according to the novel's lights, a sadist. This conclusion emerges in the comments by Churchill and other characters (chiefly the alcoholic homosexual Max Hunter and the atheistic padre William Ayscue) about the events of the plot. When the dispatch rider dies, Churchill observes, "The Lord giveth by Christ and the Lord taketh away" (*Anti-death League,* 38); after the death of the young soldier, he bitterly remarks, "Just this one thing is enough to show that we live in a bad world" (88); and Ayscue later tells him that a belief in a merciful deity "is a disgrace to human decency and intelligence" (276). This despair at the way the world is set up culminates in one of Amis's most powerful poems, "To a Baby Born without Limbs," examples of which were prevalent at this time in Britain because of the ingestion of the tranquilizer Thalidomide by pregnant women. This poem, which inaugurates the short-lived Anti-death League at the base, states that such awful occurrences are God's way of showing the human race who is boss. When Churchill says after learning of his lover's breast cancer that "Hating it is what I'm on now more" (235), it is hard not to think of Amis's own reply to Yevtushenko's question about believing in God: "[I]t's more that I hate him."

Some critics have remarked that Amis's generally sunny depiction of love in this novel is the result of his beginning a relationship with Elizabeth Jane Howard; be that as it may, it is interesting to compare, for instance, Churchill's and Catharine's gentle and magical woodland idyll with the later, more brutal one of Maurice Allington and one of his mistresses in *The Green Man*. In general, Amis here provides a sympathetic portrayal of women, particularly in his depiction of Catharine's previous marriages; however, the portrait of the indelibly promiscuous Lady Hazell, which was immediately seized on by the novel's American paperback publisher (its back cover offering the lurid thrills of "a nymphomaniac lady of the British aristocracy who runs her home as any Army bordello"), seems more willfully outré on Amis's part. More successful is his continuing battle against certain charlatans in the mental-health industry with his depiction of the ironically named Dr. Best, whose knee-jerk diagnosis of every ailment as repressed homosexuality becomes ludicrous when applied to Max Hunter, whose generally sympathetic depiction leaves no doubt that he is anything but repressed. Best repulsively calls the rape of a 10-year-old girl "an *unpleasant experience*" (*Anti-death League*, 19), and longtime readers of Amis will note that Best's favorable allusion to T. S. Eliot's concept of the objective correlative is not a sign of favor on the author's part. It comes as little surprise when Best tries to force himself on Lady Hazell, whose promiscuity proves to have its limits. In general, it is only through rational analysis that the catatonia that afflicts Catharine and later Churchill can be cured.

The novel becomes most successful at its conclusion. Willie Ayscue has ironically started out as an atheist who nevertheless preaches about a "100% loving" God because without that, hope would not exist (*Antideath League*, 145). Ayscue is also a music lover, and his discovery and later performance of a hitherto unknown work at the end of the novel lead to his conclusion that music is "the true embodiment of the unaided and self-constituted human spirit, the final proof of the nonexistence of God" (312). Yet in the brief sermon following the performance, he argues that the music reveals "God's glory" (314), which has inspired the composer, which in turn leads Ayscue to feel that perhaps someone might be listening to his prayers concerning Catharine's full recovery. This might indeed become the first step to comprehending why God constructed the world as it is, "an explanation so cogent that human beings would unhesitatingly forgive all the wrongs he has done them" (315). But the same music drives Ayscue's beloved pet dog, Nancy, into the street in front on an oncoming lorry. Despite the glimpse of hope vouchsafed all the characters at the end of the novel, ranging from Ayscue's nascent faith to Churchill's renewed faith in humanity, all are doomed to succumb to the ultimate irony—death. This delicately balanced perspective, however characteristic, is perhaps the most successfully attained of all Amis's novels.

Chapter Four
Mainstream Novels

Lucky Jim

Lucky Jim was the right book for the right time. Even if it led to the mistaken pigeonholing of Amis later as one of the "Angry Young Men" (though in hindsight the label seemed apt as he appeared to become an Angry Old Man), Jim is essentially a rebel against the society in which he is forced to live. At one point, he is subsumed with "indignation, grief, resentment, peevishness, spite, and sterile anger"—all these caused by a woman to whom he is attracted.[1] This rebellion gives rise to not only the book's importance as a product of its time and place, but much of its humor. What Jim rebels against—romantic entanglement, phony culture—would give rise to the stereotypical view of Amis that dogged him throughout his later career, and Amis's method of narration, here seen for the first time, would lead to the equally erroneous equation of character with author. Both of these areas need to be examined more closely.

Many critics have pointed out that Amis's main narrative device is the heavy use of free indirect discourse, in which a narration from a third-person limited point of view adapts and adopts the language and vocabulary of the character from whose viewpoint readers encounter the action. Thus almost all of *Lucky Jim* comes to us filtered through the very words that Jim might use to describe the events; everything is mediated through his consciousness, but without the intervening and identifying effect of a first-person narration. Thus when the narrator describes a decoration in Jim's bedroom at Professor Welch's house, a small figurine is called "the representation . . . of a well-known Oriental religious figure" (*Lucky Jim*, 60–61). This refusal to use a simple proper noun—Buddha—is not caused by the ignorance of the putative narrator, but because Jim cannot bring himself to use the word in describing the self-consciously "arty" decorations of his culture-hungry host. Similarly, in the novel's most notorious instance, when the narrator employs the words "filthy Mozart" (63) to identify the composer of the tune

Welch is singing in the shower, "filthy" is Jim's judgment, not Amis's, and probably is further influenced by the attitude with which Jim regards the singer. Amis might have used this narrative device so that he could become closer to his characters, but the more damaging critical effect is that his characters become identified with him.

Jim's rebellion against academic society is pervasive and forms the backbone of the entire plot—even the romantic element seems intertwined with it. At an indefinite time after the war, he finds himself teaching medieval history at a provincial university because the subject was the easiest one when he was at college and because better-paying jobs elsewhere were occupied by Oxbridge graduates who ensured that new positions were filled by men of similar backgrounds. Jim dates the beginning of the downward slide of his reputation to his accidental kicking of a stone that hit a faculty member who had gone to Cambridge. Michie, the student who relentlessly pursues Jim in order to take his "special subject," is another exemplar of this class, in both the categorical and economic senses of the word: he knows how to speak correctly and how to dress perfectly.

Beyond Jim's simmering class resentment lies the outright hatred he feels toward his superior, the pharisaical Professor Welch, one of Amis's comic triumphs. In his dealings with Jim, Welch proves himself to be a thorough hypocrite: he hardly works at all, makes Jim proofread articles and check his research for a speech, and continually blackmails Jim into doing things because of his probationary status, even though it is fairly certain that Welch knows Jim will not be asked to return. Welch does not have enough academic acumen to assess Jim's article, claiming that its only validation will be its publication—anywhere. He is stingy with drinks—an even more mortal social sin in Amis's view. Above all, Welch is constantly in pursuit of a spurious and snobbish culture, in light of which his fondness for Mozart can indeed appear "filthy." Welch's invitations to Jim to attend "arty" (one of Jim's chief words of opprobrium through the novel) weekends are meant, he thinks, "to test my reactions to culture" (*Lucky Jim*, 24). And it is this culture against which Jim reacts so furiously that must be further investigated, because if it is the normal high culture in the Arnoldian sense, then Bertrand Welch is correct in labeling Jim a philistine—an accusation that would often be also hurled against Jim's creator.

The climax of the novel is Jim's drunken and derisive lecture on Merrie England, a subject near and dear to Welch's heart. Indeed, it forms the entire base of his particular approach to culture. Welch's idea of culture centers on the Arts and Crafts movement promoted by William Morris and others of his circle. As Welch himself explains it, in characteristic language, he is interested in "the English social and cultural scene, with a backward-looking bias in a sense, popular crafts and so on, traditional pastimes and that" (*Lucky Jim*, 176). In the fragments of the Merrie England speech that are reproduced, Jim speaks of other Morris shibboleths as "the instinctive culture of the integrated village-type community" (205) and "identification of work with craft" (223). The whole point of Jim's umbrage against this stance is that even he, who supposedly cannot recall the difference between Augustine and Aquinas, knows that this period should never be replicated or used as a model because "it was about the most un-Merrie period in our history" (227). Jim's reaction against this pose might also be a symptom of a more general revulsion against the "New Elizabethan Age" that was being heralded as Elizabeth II acceded to the throne and the Festival of England celebrated.

Similarly, Jim's main romantic entanglements arise from the hypocrisy at the heart of his relationship with Margaret, whose wardrobe is significantly always described as "arty." In delineating Jim's precise mental states as he moves from guilt to freedom, Amis is characteristically careful to note Jim's moral condition, as well as his honesty in facing up to his own selfishness and shortcomings. He got involved with Margaret from honorable motives: "[P]oliteness, friendly interest, ordinary concern, a good-natured willingness to be imposed upon, a desire for unequivocal friendship" (*Lucky Jim,* 10). Jim is looking for a kind of friendship with a colleague—outside of housemates such as Beesley and Atkinson, Jim leads a lonely existence. When he learns from Catchpole of Margaret's false suicide attempt, Jim is able to emerge from under what has seemed an "intolerable" load and to pursue Christine, a beautiful woman who after all proves to be not really "out of [Jim's] class" (162, 124). Yet what the novel calls "the awful business of getting on with women" leads to assertions that become harbingers of the kind of statements that would get Amis in so much trouble later on, such as "the feminine manoeuvre of using an innocent bystander as a whipping-boy" (11, 114). Again, it seems fairly clear these complaints are Jim's, not Amis's, but their global nature invites the confusion.

In the end, perhaps the most lasting legacy of *Lucky Jim* is its style, unadorned, plain, clearly antimandarin, yet supple and capable of surprising levels of qualification. But underneath the style is a desire for plain speaking and plain feeling. "Words change things," as Jim tells

Christine; she should know whether or not she is in love, just as she knows if she likes a certain variety of fruit. The novel's other notorious phrase, "nice things are nicer than nasty ones" (140), thus seems to be a simplistic reduction of large areas of life into two childlike categories, just as Jim divides humanity into those he likes and those he does not. Yet although the number of "nice" things remains unenumerated save for Christine's obvious niceness, the nastiness of life is continually defined: the work of an unnamed current poet, Christine if she sticks with Bertrand Welch, anything that Professor Welch might assign Jim to do, people during the Middle Ages, Bertrand's paintings, Christine's claim that being involved with an artist is different than being involved with an average person. Even though the "fairy-tale" plot of the novel ends with Jim running away with his Princess Charming under the benevolent eye of Fairy Godfather Gore-Urquhart, the lasting impression and chief pleasure of *Lucky Jim* is that the solution "to an environment bristling with people and things one thought were bad was to go on finding out new ways in which one could think they were bad" (129). It is the lesson that remains of the core of Amis's comic genius.

That Uncertain Feeling

Amis's second novel, *That Uncertain Feeling* (1955), begins with a characteristic narrative strategy: readers find themselves in the midst of an already ongoing conversation whose speakers and meaning will only become gradually clear. The narrator is telling someone that the "Bevan ticket . . . has expired."[2] British readers in 1955 would assume this to be a reference to Aneurin Bevan, Labour minister of health in the Atlee government, and chief advocate of the National Health Service. The explanation is much more mundane, however; John Lewis, a librarian, is explaining to a patron why she cannot borrow a book for a friend. This device shows Amis, a supposedly transparently realistic novelist, deliberately stimulating his readers' critical awareness at the outset of the story.

Unlike *Lucky Jim*, *That Uncertain Feeling* is a first-person narrative, which makes it all the easier to equate Lewis with Amis. They both work in the same location (at this time, Wales); they are both married and have young children; they are both devotees of science fiction; they both hate phony Welshness; they are both ardent lefties; and, most significant in terms of the plot, they both seem determined to probe the boundaries of marital fidelity. A major difference seems to be their occupations, but it turns out Amis has merely borrowed that of his best friend, Philip Larkin, from whom Amis also seems to have borrowed a characteristic manner (revealed in Larkin's letters to Amis) of hectoring himself when in difficulties: "That'll do, Lewis, that'll do, thank you. Give it a rest, can't you, Lewis?" (*That Uncertain Feeling*, 15).

Like Jim Dixon, John Lewis is stuck in a job he dislikes, and like Jim Dixon, Lewis is faced with a romantic dilemma. Yet he is much more politically aware and expressive than Dixon ever lets on. His wife, Jean, adjures him not to instigate among the upper-class people they will meet at a party, calling him "Karl Marx bloody Lewis" (*That Uncertain Feeling*, 26). Perhaps the chief difference between Dixon and Lewis is that whereas Dixon can never reveal his true feelings and must make faces to express his hidden emotional life, Lewis cannot hide them; he even practices making a stern expression in the mirror. Thus Jean can read him like a book: she knows as soon as she sees him with Elizabeth Gruffydd-Williams that he is attracted to her, and Jean knows immediately when he has made love to Elizabeth. And Lewis is just as sensitive; he almost instantly realizes that what he is doing with Elizabeth causes Jean pain.

The two moral poles of *Lucky Jim,* around which the intricacies of the plot are overlaid, love and work, are also at the center of *That Uncertain Feeling*. Lewis, although married, finds himself in the grip of a hormone-washed malaise that he continually attempts to particularize. At one point, he says it is a melange of "rootless apprehension, indefinite restlessness and boredom"; at another, it is compounded of "depression. . . . Boredom. . . . A slight tinge . . . of uneasiness and inert, generalised lust" (63, 98). The novel anatomizes the progression of this feeling into what Shakespeare called "lust in action" (Sonnet 129), with all the accompanying degrees of doubt, desire, anger, guilt, rationalization, and repentance. Amis shows how Lewis explains, defends, and even deludes himself in his affair with Elizabeth, but it is anything but a defense of Lewis's actions. Like Chekhov, Amis does not feel obligated to explain the difference between right and wrong to his readers; just as readers must make rational sense of his world in his initially confusing openings, he leaves it up to readers to decipher the moral dimensions of the plot.

Lewis's relationship with Elizabeth, like Dixon's with Christine, is hypergamic: a union of people from two separate classes. The word is used in both senses when Jean speaks of Elizabeth's "classy friends," and on the same page, Lewis remarks that Elizabeth has moved "out of our class" (*That Uncertain Feeling*, 24). At times Lewis seems to realize this, as when he comments on all the faux cultural items decorating the

Gruffydd-Williams household. It is also revealed to him in the actions of others. The Italian who helps with a stuck car instinctively finds Lewis friendly but shies away from the others in the upper-class party, and even Ieuan Jenkins, Lewis's rival for a promotion, sees that his new acquaintances are not Lewis's "sort" (141). When it seems that he and Elizabeth are about to consummate their affair, he has to jettison his preconceptions about her distasteful friends. But when Lewis feels angry with Elizabeth, he finds that the members of his own class are not really so bad after all: "[T]hat there was a lot to be said for them compared with the old privileged classes" (143).

This oscillation is mirrored in Lewis's own feelings about the affair. He begins by being aggressive with Elizabeth, at least in his own mind: "I'd show her. I'd teach her" (49), he thinks and then starts looking down the front of her dress deliberately. When Elizabeth tells him, "You're one of my sort" (54), she is not using the word in Jenkins's sense: it is a moral, not a social, distinction, as Lewis will come to realize. It is never entirely clear in Lewis's mind if his affair is a cause or an effect, even though he states, with the same generalizing force that accompanies Dixon's "nice" and "nasty" distinction, "It wasn't so much doing what you wanted to do that was important . . . as wanting to do what you did" (94). Yet one point, he declares that his fidelity was the result of "luck, not self-restraint" (105): in other words, he never met anyone attractive enough to inspire strong desire in him. Later, however, after the affair is over, he muses that "the bad effect in or on me was the sort that toted itself around looking for a cause" (229). By this point, Lewis is ready for reform.

What impels him to this crisis is the other moral crux of the novel, his attempt to be promoted to the sublibrarianship. Elizabeth's husband is the head of the promotion committee, and throughout the novel, Lewis fears that his relationship with Elizabeth will give him an unfair advantage over his colleague Jenkins, whom Lewis considers the best man for the job. However, as Jean reminds him, Lewis thus is forgetting his responsibility toward his own family. Even though he strongly dislikes Jenkins's wife, he still doesn't want to get the job if it means being underhanded. When he discovers the real reason for his getting the job—Elizabeth's husband wants to twit Lewis's boss by promoting a man his boss intensely dislikes—Lewis refuses not only the promotion but Elizabeth. In his mind, this "fiddling" to obtain the promotion for him equates to his being the right "sort" socially and educationally: both equally spurious reasons. This in turn leads to the realization that he would just as much have liked to have made love to another woman at the party as to Elizabeth. Now he sees what she means by being her "sort." Lewis ends the affair, also becoming the first Amis hero to get a deserved physical rebuke from his wife. They move back to Lewis's hometown, where he gets a job in sales at the colliery where his father worked. It is perhaps a "running away" (245), which Lewis certainly does when a young wife makes a pass at him at a party, but it is also a move into authenticity: he receives "a lovely, warm hug" (246) from his hostess, a somewhat outrageous figure whom Lewis nevertheless can appreciate. He has come to the understanding that "being moral and immoral at the same time, the thing was to keep trying not to be immoral, and then to keep trying might turn into a habit. I was always . . . going to get pulled two ways" (239–40). The theme remains an integral part of Amis's novelistic focus: the last phrase would be echoed in the title of his penultimate novel, *You Can't Do Both* (1994).

That Uncertain Feeling shows Amis trying, not entirely successfully, to find material outside his immediate circumstances. It contains in-jokes and references Amis would continue to use in his later career: L. S. Caton makes an offstage appearance, and the stridently adopted Welshness of figures such as Dylan Thomas is hilariously parodied in the character of Gareth Probert. But Amis is much more interested—and successful—in tracing the twists and turns of the male mind as it tries to justify itself to itself. "Feeling a tremendous rakehell, and not liking myself much for it, and feeling rather a good chap for not liking myself much for it, and not liking myself at all for feeling rather a good chap" (*That Uncertain Feeling,* 93): the convolutions of conscience, duty, and desire would remain one of Amis's central subjects.

I Like It Here

Many critics, Amis himself included, find *I Like It Here* his weakest novel: "[X]enophobic and slight" is one reference work's dismissal.[3] The novel betrays the difficulty with which Amis attempts to transform into fiction his visit to Portugal after winning the Somerset Maugham Award. The novel's hero, another Welshman, Garnet Bowen, shares even more of Amis's own traits and circumstances than do either of his predecessors: his family makeup (wife, two boys, one girl), his involvement with literature, his fear of flying, his affection for old Protestant hymns and for the fiction of Elizabeth Taylor, his contempt for Anglo-Saxon literature, and his habit when angry, of delivering, as Amis and

Larkin did in their correspondence, a fierce litany of complaints, each ending with the word "bum." Some parts of the novel do not cohere well; a commentary on Portugal's economic and political woes is awkwardly put into the mouth of a character who conveniently invites himself over to the Bowens' table just to deliver such judgments. Yet what ultimately makes the novel interesting is the depth of Amis's criticism of the recently promoted idea of a Great Tradition in literature, his defense of the tradition that it putatively supersedes, and his continuing investigation of the moral progress of human beings in the second half of the twentieth century.

Garnet Bowen knows more about literature and culture than either Jim Dixon or John Lewis, yet he hates to admit it, a seemingly strange failing in someone who makes his living on the outer fringes of literary life; Garnet is a supposed novelist turned supposed playwright who can get his characters on stage but can't think of anything for them to do when they get there. When he blurts out a fact about Edward Elgar, Garnet calls it a "moral failure"; his term for such conversation is "non-ironical cultural discussion."[4] This would seem to make him another in Amis's putative portrait gallery of philistines, save for Garnet's real and abiding affection for a certain kind of literature: Taylor's fiction, for example. Garnet is ultimately concerned with, as he calls it, "the nefariousness of people who made a living out of culture" (*I Like It Here,* 58). He is known for his integrity—his publisher friend Bennie Hyman jokes with him about it—and his wife, Barbara, unlike John Lewis's wife, continually reinforces it: to her, a regular job weakens one's integrity. Dropping names or genuflecting before critical shibboleths is the way Garnet thinks much of the work in the literary world is accomplished, and he refuses to go along with it. At one point, his integrity (given a strong jab by Barbara) places him in what can be termed a typical Amis crux: "To decide whether, and if so how far, self-interest conflicted with decency over this issue meant using his conscience as a precision instrument" (84). And, as with many of Amis's protagonists, Garnet's "instrument" proves at times to be much too crudely calibrated.

On one front, Garnet's war (with Amis's total approval) is with the whole tendency of model travel writing to invest any foreign part with charms, perils, and above all meanings that are impossible to discover at home. This applies whether the author, like D. H. Lawrence, is seeking some inner directness or simplicity or connection with nature otherwise lacking in people at home, or whether, like Graham Greene, he is looking for some forlorn outpost of seediness and ennui.[5] Garnet's protest against a bogus seeking for culture forms a large part of his "philistinism," and his protest against a spurious seeking for meaning forms a large part of his alleged "insularity." As though to show what an ultimate insularity would be like, Amis introduces an American who hates not only foreigners but all Americans as well and wants to retire to a small English village where he would only have to encounter one person other than his wife. Garnet, however, truly likes other people and tries to get along with even those, like his Portuguese landlord's motorcycling friends, with whom language is a barrier. Much of Garnet's bitching about life abroad is a burlesque, an exaggerated reaction similar to his fervent hatred of his mother-in-law.

On the other and ultimately more important front, Garnet's battle is against the pieties and hypocrisies of literary modernism. Hyman asks Garnet to investigate whether a manuscript his firm has received is actually the work of the famous modern master Wulfstan Strether, who supposedly had given up writing, and whom no one presently at the firm has ever seen or corresponded with. The author's name gives it all away: his sharing of last names with Lambert Strether, the hero of Henry James's novel *The Ambassadors* (1903), and even the comic transformation of his first name (a more tenable explanation than its being an allusion to an early Anglo-Saxon author). This seemingly ingenuous lamb is in reality an alpha wolf when it comes to ranking himself in the literary food chain. His novel *One Word More* (called more accurately by its prospective publisher *One Turd More*) is endlessly, convolutedly periphrastic in the style of the late James. Strether's bookcases hold only volumes by his supposed rivals: Jane Austen, George Eliot, Thomas Hardy, Joseph Conrad, and James; if one substitutes Lawrence for Hardy, these authors are the lineup, as has been pointed out, that F. R. Leavis offered in *The Great Tradition* as the best in English literature.

The climax to both the plot and the theme comes when Garnet and Strether visit the grave of Henry Fielding in Lisbon. When Strether declaims that he is a greater artist than Fielding, Garnet realizes that Strether must be the real thing because a poseur would have genuflected at Fielding's grave. Garnet, however, has different thoughts about the place of Fielding in the English tradition: "Perhaps it was worth dying in your forties if two hundred years later you were the only non-contemporary novelist who could be read with unaffected and whole-hearted interest, the only one who never had to be apologized for or excused on the grounds of changing taste." Fielding's milieu may have been "simplified," but his lasting worth rests in his ratifying of "the existence of a moral seriousness that could be made apparent without the aid of evangelical puffing and blowing" (*I Like It Here,* 167). The evangelism here probably refers more to Leavis than to Strether, but Amis makes his own point that moral seriousness need not be accompanied by a self-important and self-regarding earnestness.

In this novel, the "moral seriousness" revolves around Garnet's brief escapade with a Portuguese girl, Emelia (another Fielding allusion, this time to his last novel, *Amelia* [1752], and an ironic one because it involves a wife who rescues her husband), which ends with Garnet's being unceremoniously stung by an insect.[6] Garnet is not as conscience stricken as John Lewis is over his dalliance, but Garnet is happy that it led to nothing because it makes him realize Barbara's deep and abiding love for him. Even more morally distressing is Garnet's hesitation to get involved in a quarrel between Strether, whom Garnet really likes as a person (Strether is generous with drinks, always a good sign in Amis), and his chauffeur. This hesitation leads to Strether's getting injured, and Garnet later concludes that the injury occurred "because he had always been that sort of chap" (*I Like It Here,* 175), one who hesitates to become involved. In his reluctance, Garnet himself does turn out to be Jamesian.

But all in all, these are minor skirmishes; Garnet's most important epiphany concerns Strether's identity, which leads to what appears to be a more serious commitment to his own vocation. Garnet discards the earlier version of his play, *Teach Him a Lesson,* which involves a bunch of nasty people in nasty situations, the nastiest of whom is the hero. The new plot concerns "a man who was forced by circumstances to do the very thing he most disliked the thought of doing and found out afterwards that he was exactly the same man as he was before" (*I Like It Here,* 187), presumably a reference to Garnet's going abroad. Yet if he finishes his play, he is not the same man. But that would be because of his encounter with Strether, not his going abroad. As Fielding writes in defense of the comic in his preface to *Joseph Andrews* (1742), "Great vices are the proper objects of our detestation, smaller faults of our pity: but affectation appears to me the only true source of the ridiculous."[7] It is Amis's accomplishment that he can, as in his portrait of Strether, alloy pity within the laughter in his comic depiction. In the novels by Amis that would follow in the next decades, detestation would flow in as well.

Take a Girl like You

Take a Girl like You (1960), many readers agree, marks a major departure in Amis's early fiction. At the most obvious level, its plot revolves around the attitudes, mores, and concerns that would make up the decade later called "The Swinging Sixties." Yet Amis's stance toward the increase in personal freedom that the decade inaugurated is not what his readers of the 1950s might expect. His is an altogether darker vision, with its young male protagonist, Patrick Standish, engulfed at times by an almost Larkinesque fear of death; he is, on the whole, much more unappetizing and unappealing than Amis's previous heroes and can be called the first of Amis's portraits of the hero as a shit. The novel also introduces one of his most appealing female characters, Jenny Bunn, the good-looking schoolteacher whom Patrick pursues, and Amis even turns over more than half the narrative (14 of 25 chapters) to her point of view, the depiction of which is generally successfully handled. Jenny, who seems more than a match for Patrick's wiles, is defeated, however, when Amis concludes his narrative by having Patrick rape her. In defending Amis's choice, it is not enough just to point at the eighteenth-century models such as Samuel Richardson's *Clarissa* (1748–1749) that Amis followed in constructing his plot. In this novel, Amis deliberately draws a much darker picture of the way human beings treat each other, and an investigation of Patrick's entire character gives the reasons.

    The first view readers have of Patrick is from Jenny's point of view; she describes him as good-looking but "in a rather sissy way."[8] When he first hears the voice of Dick Thompson, her asinine landlord and a typical Amis foil, Jenny, watching Patrick, notices that a "spasm of pain or something crossed the man's face and he whispered a word or two to himself" (*Take a Girl like You,* 14). For the first time, we have an outer view of an Amis protagonist as he encounters the world. Patrick, like John Lewis, cannot hide his inner emotions; indeed, one of the more appealing of Patrick's character traits is his honesty. He cannot instinctively hide his loathing for those whom he despises, nor can he hide his bitterness when Jenny taunts him. Patrick, for instance, immediately dives for cover when a friend takes a shot in their direction; when Jenny mentions this, he gives her "a glare that made her feel cold all over for a second" (112). Patrick may think he is in love with her, but his instinctive reactions show the shallowness of that love.

    Indeed, Patrick is initially drawn to Jenny for the reason most men are: her physical attractiveness. Her beauty causes men to downgrade her morally; as Patrick says, with a significant allusion to the novel's title, "I should have thought a girl like you would be more up with things" (*Take a Girl like You,* 60). Because of her upbringing and birthplace (the north of England), Jenny is not "a girl like that," and Amis gives no indication in his narrative that he does not feel that this is exactly how it should be. Jenny is given every opportunity to defend her values, which she vigorously and sympathetically does. She is also quite capable of handling Patrick's brutish forwardness on their first date: in a phrase that presciently echoes women's concerns that would be expressed even more vocally in the years following 1960, she tells him, "When I say no I mean no" (59). For a time, Patrick respects her wishes. But the narrative indications all reveal that Patrick will not be put off forever. Deep into her relationship with him, she is vaguely disquieted: "[S]he could find nothing more, just something nasty, after her" (191). That something nasty is the part of Patrick that will not be put off, and it is significant that she applies to it Jim Dixon's chief pejorative term, "nasty."

Patrick is a typical Amis hero in his conflicts at work, and in his general dissatisfaction with not only society but the way human life seems to be constructed. A characteristic phrase, "Bastards' HQ" (41), sums up Patrick's view of those behind-the-scene presences who manage to inject the small and large screwups into life that make it at the least uncomfortable and at the worst existentially unendurable. Patrick, himself a schoolmaster, is spied on by his nemesis, Charlton; they are, like Jim Dixon and Bertrand Welch, mutually antipathetic. By the end of the narrative, Patrick is able to remove Charlton's threat by blackmailing his son with the help of the headmaster's daughter, with whom Patrick has been carrying on an affair. This is a far cry from Dixon's triumph over the falseness and hypocrisy of the Welches. An only child, Patrick shares with many Amis heroes a thirst for drink, a love of jazz (not too modern), and a strong libido. He generally feels superior to those occupying space in his world, such as his roommate, who is far too serious about everything, and Dick Thompson, the first leftie whom Amis portrays as being thoroughly ridiculous. The upper-class Julian Omerod, however, draws Patrick up; Julian seems to be morally much looser than Patrick, but appearances in this case will prove deceiving. All in all, Patrick is as iconoclastic as Jim Dixon; his placing of Beethoven, along with Dick Thompson and others, on a list for a hypothetical cricket team composed of those people he least admires probably got Amis in as much critical trouble as Dixon's "filthy Mozart" did.

Even Patrick has to admit that his present life has worn down his previous idealism in many areas. At one point, he wonders what happened to the young student who was truly interested in the classics and scholarship, and this thought leads directly into a fugal meditation on his own death: "[A] gradual loss of consciousness followed by dreams of water and mud and the struggle to breathe, dreams superseded by identical dreams, a death prolonged for ever" (*Take a Girl like You*, 271). Many of Patrick's psychological fears seem to be connected to guilt over his present conduct. His condition he attributes to "insecurity and remorse and feeling guilty about Jenny and so on" (272). In his youth, what he calls his "blackberrying-Delius" days, he was a romantic about love, but now, involved with Jenny, "He was in too much of a situation with her—adult, real, mutual, involving conscience, choice, action—for his mind to treat her as it liked" (215). This seems one of the strangest rationalizations in defense of sexual adventurousness ever offered, but Patrick is a past master at taking his own moral pulse and finding himself healthier than he might appear to a more objective observer. Like other Amis heroes, he constantly performs a moral calculus on his conduct: "Conscientiousness inspired him to leaf rapidly through his memory: he had felt very much like that at the time, hadn't he? Check" (155). Yet such calculations, however specious in their real significance, can never totally hide the hollowness often at the core of Patrick's actions.

   Patrick is most afraid of turning into what he most hates: that moral creature he calls "a bastard." When he first sleeps with an empty-headed model, he finds himself impotent and thinks: "He hoped that if he ever saw himself as a bastard, instead of just seeing himself as seeing himself as a bastard, he would be drunk or in bed with a woman at the time" (*Take a Girl like You*, 231). Actually, this turns out to be true, because his bastardy is forever sealed when he drunkenly rapes the even more drunk Jenny, who cannot defend herself. Yet the morning after his nonperformance with Joan, he finds himself able to function with her, and he then calls his conscience a "propaganda-ministry": he comes up with the rationalization that his initial impotence was due to booze and his love for Jenny, and his later success to his image of himself as "a rakehell, but with heart" (236). Later he refers to his second night with Joan as "morally unimpugnable fun" (273), which shows precisely how much further morally Patrick has yet to go. Yet Patrick is capable of real guilt and its accompanying moral insight; when he makes love to Sheila, his headmaster's daughter, who has shown up at his apartment on the night he and Jenny were first to make love, the act leaves him "feeling more ashamed and humiliated than he had ever felt in his life" (279). This leads to his conclusion about himself and Jenny that "there was not much left of that elaborate structure of love and obligation and restraint which the two of them had been struggling to assemble and which he had begun to believe was bastard-proof" (279). At some level, he realizes that the bastard against whom he has to proof his relationship with Jenny is himself.

This theme of being a bastard is intimately bound up with Patrick's inability to make his sexual desires and needs conform to his own and society's expectations. When the old peer Lord Edgerstoune talks about the death of physical desire, it drives Patrick outdoors. He then utters what appears to be a prayer to God, which begins, "I'm sorry, I know I'm a bastard, but I'm trying not to be"; the ensuing chain of qualifications and hedgings is called "this familiar regressive series" (243–44).[9] It is a series of justifications that leads to only one conclusion. Patrick's descent culminates in his rape of Jenny at Julian's party. When Julian, who really is a rakehell with a heart—and a conscience—objects to Patrick, "But fairness," Patrick can only lament, with complete accuracy, "Oh Christ. I am a bastard." But his words immediately following show whom he ultimately blames this on: "Oh Christ. Right, this is your lot, Jack" (304). God has constructed the universe so that creatures suffer and die, sometimes horribly (the subject of the savage poem "To a Baby Born without Limbs" in *The Anti-death League,* whose diction is repeated here); God has also constructed things so that the same creatures become so confused by their sexual nature that they end up becoming moral bastards. Amis himself elsewhere called these problems "those subtler engines from Jehovah's army of maleficence, the pains incidentally accruing from sexual love, marriage, and the begetting of children" (*What Became of Jane Austen,* 220). To Patrick, his deed is a consequence of being a human being; whether he accepts his own blame and responsibility for it will show how deep his bastardy goes.

Luckily, Jenny is around to inject needed distance into Patrick's self-pitying portrayal of himself. She uses the same phrase for him as he has applied to the freeloading Dick Thompson: "Mr. Eat-All-Sup-All-Pay-Nowt" (*Take a Girl like You,* 310). Patrick refuses to accept responsibility for his actions. But she still loves him, and in an ending perhaps not fierce enough for all readers' liking, she accepts Patrick as he his, telling herself, "She must learn to take the rough with the smooth, just like everybody else." Yet when Patrick tells her that it was unavoidable that her ideals would be shaken, considering her appearance, she rejoins, "But I can't help feeling it's rather a pity" (317). It is also a pity that two people who do love each so deeply in their own ways must finally come together in this way. Amis has previously shown the confluence of their ultimate hopes about life in their complementary dreams: Jenny's vision of rural happiness (110) and Patrick's urban dream (137). Yet an insistent subtext runs underneath, promising that modern life will not match anyone's dreams; it is distilled in the proclamations that a drunken seaman occasionally makes outside Jenny's window. "What [people] do is their nature" (316) is Jenny's ultimate lesson, one she will have to live with.

All in all, although parts of *Take a Girl like You* are as funny as anything Amis had done up to that point (the scene in which Patrick quotes T. S. Eliot's "East Coker" to himself as he leaves Joan, for instance), the novel also points in the directions that Amis's fiction would increasingly take over the next few decades: unappealing, even distasteful heroes, a preoccupation with morbidity and mortality, and an increasing awareness of the incongruous ways in which human aspirations do not match reality, often the result of conflicting desires. It also shows, by the divided nature of the narrative, that merely because Amis adopts a point of view does not mean that he totally endorses the focus character's thoughts and actions. This becomes increasingly important in narratives where there is no Jenny through whom to view the main character's bastardy. That Amis would return much later in his career to depict Patrick and Jenny's life a few years down the road in *Difficulties with Girls* (1988) shows perhaps that he felt that to leave them in such a suspended situation at the end was too harsh: he never continued Jim and Christine's life together, for instance. For Amis, this particular modern fairy tale's 1960 ending of a conditional "they lived happily ever after" would have to be answered more explicitly.

One Fat Englishman

If Patrick Standish is the first step in Amis's portrayal of the hero as bastard, then Roger Micheldene, the main character in *One Fat Englishman* (1963), represents the near completion of that journey. Almost nothing about Roger is appealing or in any way admirable. An English publisher visiting America on business, he is snobbish and selfish, hates children, hates America, and combines a contempt for women with a desire to sleep with as many of them as possible. In one sense, the plot of *One Fat Englishman* resembles that of Garnet Bowen's play *Teach Him a Lesson*: "[A] nasty man . . . and the nasty practical joke played on him by his nasty friends with nasty consequences" (*I Like It Here*, 96). There can be little doubt that Amis shares many of the same feelings toward Roger as readers must. Roger is insufferably rude to waiters and servants, a trait that Amis despised, and Roger is prejudiced against Jews and blacks, biases that Amis abhorred even more. Then why place Roger as the central character in a supposedly comic novel?

One reason that has been given is that Amis liked placing opinions that he dared not make in his own persona in the mouths of reprehensible characters. Take, for instance, Roger's internal evaluation of another character's fatuous speech: "To be sure about nonsense he had to be able to classify it, assign it to a family tree of liberal nonsense, humanist-humanitarian nonsense, academic nonsense, Protestant nonsense, Freudian nonsense and so on."[10] This sounds very close to Amis's own position, if not in 1963, then a very short time afterward. Yet at a party, Roger loudly projects his dislike for John F. Kennedy, and when a guest drives him home, he tells Roger, quite correctly, "Why don't you go back to your island and stay there?" (*One Fat Englishman,* 108). In almost every instance in the novel, readers must evaluate the moral and ethical aspects of the situation for themselves, with the added confusion of the moral focus residing in the central reflective character, with all the consequent attendant sympathy, as well as having bits of the author's personality and biography thrown in to add to the muddle. Roger's grandfather, for instance, made his fortune in the crockery trade, much as did Amis's own grandfather, with the important difference being that Roger's background is thus upper-class, with all its snobbery, for which Roger blames his own father. Indeed, at one point, he almost accuses Nigel Pargeter, a young Englishman whom he meets in America, of being a middle-class climber—much like Willie Maugham had accused Kingsley Amis. Like Amis, Roger loves eighteenth-century fiction. Yet he can think of his bête noire, the young novelist Irving Macher, as a "Yid scribbler" (24). And Amis seems to like America more than Roger does, yet what is one to make of Amis's naming all his fictional American colleges—Budweiser, Schlitz, Ballantine—after beers? The question raised by such statements is a legitimate one: Are these the embittered complaints of a contemptible character, or are some of them authorially endorsed?

Questions persist when Roger's conduct is examined. In a memorable self-judgment, he is somewhat proud of his moral shortcomings: "Of the seven deadly sins, Roger considered himself qualified in gluttony, sloth and lust but distinguished in anger" (8). Much of that anger is directed at the women he finds himself lusting after. At one point, he wants to hit Helene Bang, a married woman whose seduction forms the main part of Roger's quest, but he refrains on considering that such a course would make it much less likely that she would sleep with him. Roger is the first of a long line of Amis heroes who refer in their thoughts to women as a group by the third-person plural pronoun "they" without immediately identifying its antecedent: "Letting them enter one's base of operations was to be avoided whenever possible" (87). It is particularly in this aspect of his code of conduct that Roger presages much of the controversy that would later embroil Amis's depiction of the conflicts between men and women.

In religion as well, Roger shares some of Amis's feelings about God, with the significant qualification that Roger is Catholic. Like Amis, Roger feels that to view the creator of this particular universe as a God of love denies the evidence of suffering and death: "[I]f it is it's a pretty odd kind of love" (92). When Roger prays at night, he does not ask for forgiveness or help in becoming a better person; rather, like Patrick Standish, he accuses God of making him the way he is and then putting him in situations where he cannot control himself. "You know what I'm like and yet you keep on at me" (53). These attitudes are comic exaggerations of Amis's own theological positions. In these prayers, as in many other instances, Roger acts like a child, a fact that a priest whom Roger meets soon points out to him. Colgate is one of those modern clerics whose faith has seemingly been undermined by current ideas and for whom Amis usually has nothing but contempt. In one of the most uncomfortable scenes in all of Amis's works, after Roger is gnawed at by sexual shame, he tracks Colgate down, apparently to have Colgate hear his confession. Instead, however, Roger angrily accuses God of creating the occasions of sin, including liquor and women, and in a fierce parody of both baptism and Christ's adjuration to the apostles to become "fishers of men," he dunks Colgate's head into a fish tank. Granted, Colgate deserves some of the satire Amis aims at him, but he does seem to be genuinely concerned with Roger's soul, which, if it were to be saved, would make him a much better human being, no matter what one's belief in the afterlife is. This one plot strand exemplifies the problems throughout the novel of locating the author's moral stance, and consequently where readers' should be.

In the end, however, even Roger cannot prove to be a total bastard. At first, he seems a true monster of selfishness, much as the Anglophile American Strode Atkins (whom Roger immediately hates) is. According to Strode's wife, with whom Roger has a brief dalliance, for Strode, "What he's not doing doesn't exist" (*One Fat Englishman,* 86). Yet near the end of Roger's visit, some of his egotism begins to crumble. When Mollie Atkins shows up his rudeness, he finds himself feeling, "unusually for him, a mixture of feelings. One of them resembled agitation" (153). This leads directly to his confrontation with Colgate. Later, Helene runs away for a short fling with Irving Macher, and Roger confronts them. For the first time, Helene is able to talk openly and honestly with Roger about her feelings for him, and indeed about her own feelings. Amis, outside of the novels that involve Jenny Bunn, rarely adopts a female narrative stance, but he almost always allows his female characters to speak the truth to his male characters, often with a resoundingly deflationary message. Helene tells Roger that she has slept with him because then "I feel less sorry for you, you bug me less, I stop feeling responsible for you" (185). Helene is also able to make generalizations about men's behavior, as she explains what attracted her to her husband. "Then I met someone who looked at me sometimes when he was making love to me, didn't keep his eyes shut all the time the way the rest of them did. He knew I was there. From start to finish. So I married him" (186).

When Roger bids farewell to the Bangs and to America as he departs by ship, he actually feels like crying, although he is not as aware of himself in another, more constructive way to realize that perhaps he had started to love her. After they have left him, he realizes that he has an ocean voyage before him, during which he will have an opportunity to pursue more females, but "something in him was less than enthusiastic about this course of action." Characteristically, he resists that urge: "Better a bastard than a bloody fool" (192).

That phrase, although it could stand as a motto for many of Amis's later characters, also reveals perhaps why Amis made Roger a Roman Catholic. One author to whom Amis has been constantly compared is Evelyn Waugh, usually on the grounds of working in the similar genres of comic fiction and the contingent territories of British society. Yet if one looks at Waugh's early central characters, from Paul Pennyfeather in *Decline and Fall* (1928) to Tony Last in *A Handful of Dust* (1934) to Guy Crouchback in the *Sword of Honour* trilogy (1952–1961; coll. 1965), they can usually be classified as "bloody fools." Waugh's "bastards," such as Basil Seal, are often only foils for these naive and tenderhearted lovers. Later heroes, such as Charles Ryder and Dennis Barlow, as Malcolm Bradbury points out, are precursors of the Amis hero. Roger Micheldene, on the other hand, will not be conscience ridden by priests or ensnared by women; a character more unlike, say, William Boot in

Scoop (1938) would be hard to imagine. Another Catholic novelist to note in this context is Graham Greene, about whom Amis wrote a now lost study and whose negative "anxiety of influence" on the early Amis has been noted by several critics. The small dollop of guilt that Roger feels near the end of the novel is nowhere near the existential weights that bear down the heroes of *The Power and the Glory* (1940), *The Heart of the Matter* (1948), or *The End of the Affair* (1951). In a sense, Amis's "bastard" heroes are answers to both Waugh's and Greene's suffering believers; readers do not come away from *One Fat Englishman* asking themselves about Roger Micheldene, "Do such people exist?" as might be the case with Crouchback or Greene's Scobie in *The Heart of the Matter*. Yet this does not prevent Roger from suffering, as has been pointed out, a fate similar in kind, if not duration, to that of Waugh's Tony Last, who must read Dickens to a madman in the middle of the Brazilian jungle: Roger will be accompanied on his journey back to London by the insufferable Strode Atkins. Both Waugh and Amis would at times agree that for their heroes, whether fools or bastards, sometimes, to paraphrase Marlowe's Mephistophilis, "This is hell, nor are [they] out of it."

The Egyptologists

Written in collaboration with Amis's close friend and ideological soul mate Robert Conquest, *The Egyptologists* (1965) is on the surface a slight production. Mercifully retitled from the original *Mummy Knows Best,* the novel (and one suspects that gruesome title) was Conquest's idea; Amis came up with much of the plot, as well as new incidents and characters. That plot would provide another arrow in the quivers of his feminist critics. A small group of men supposedly meet every Thursday night (and travel on occasional weekend excursions) to investigate their amateur enthusiasm, the study of ancient Egypt. It soon becomes apparent that almost none of these men knows anything about or cares anything for ancient Egypt, so as a British paperback breathlessly asks on its back cover, "But what in fact is the Society for?"[11] The breathlessness is quite unnecessary, however, for the same back cover's paragraph title gives the game away: "The Adultery Club."

Yet the mysterious and deliberately vague opening pages of the novel are an expansion of Amis's usual technique of beginning a novel or a chapter in the midst of a dialogue that does not identify its speakers until a page or two on, thus forcing the reader to make a conscious attempt to understand this world. The three main characters are named merely the President, the Secretary, and the Treasurer, and they are never further specifically named. (An allusion or two to the President's cheapness with liquor lets us know we are in an Amis novel, as well as revealing something about the President's character.) As a matter of fact, these three remain more distinguishable as individual characters to the reader than the other named members of the club, who all tend to merge into one mass; this is one the novel's failings and does not seem to be a deliberate effect.

In the way that the novel parades Amis's popular literary enthusiasms—science fiction, the spy novel, the mystery—it points toward his next major novel, *The Anti-death League*, which also treats these subjects, but at a more integral level. *The Egyptologists* is shot through with knowing references to science fiction. The classical detective story also is alluded to with approval several times. Most of these allusions function on the level of in-jokes. The spy-novel aspect, however, is much more fully harmonized into the plot of the novel, perhaps because Amis was also occupied with his studies of James Bond at this time. Forced to lead double lives, these men constantly remind each other that they are spies, duplicitous to all they meet. "Security" is talked about a lot, and the Secretary has devised a list of rules that the members must follow to ensure the secrecy of their organization. Of course, such secrecy sooner or later engenders paranoia, with which the society is rife; one of the fears is "that their opponents are equally well organized, but on a much vaster scale, and have just set in motion against them the whole apparatus of the State" (*Egyptologists*, 42). In one case, this is exactly what happens when one of their members loses an instruction sheet, and it is brought to the attention of MI5. In perhaps an allusion to G. K. Chesterton's *The Man Who Was Thursday* (1908), one of Amis's favorite works, some of the members suspect their organization is being used as a facade by *another* group: "[T]here's some sort of inner ring with a different purpose that's using the Society as a blind or a front" (43). Someone brings up the possibility that this group may be homosexual (one of the members actually is), thus conflating this "spy" ring with the Cambridge spies of the 1930s. There are also references to more mundane spy novels, such as to Ernst Stavro Blofeld, the villain of Ian Fleming's later Bond novels.

Another enthusiasm of Amis's at this time that makes its appearance in the novel (as well as in his next) is the army, which forms the model for many all-male organizations. Of course, the characters feel as if they are in a war, the war between the sexes, to use a term widely employed at the time of the novel and before. Yet in the end, after following the plots and counterplots, the deceptions and the discoveries, a reader may come to the same conclusion as one of their wives does: "[T]hey're a pack of great big schoolboys, every one of them. Scratch a man and find a child" (*Egyptologists*, 75).

This is one of the few generalizations about the opposite gender allowed women in the text. Usually the males are doing the categorizing, which carries, one suspects, a deliberately inflammatory subtext, even for 1965. "Not that, being women, they took much notice of what they drank—they came for the chatter" (*Egyptologists*, 69) is fairly mild; the President's comment about why women couldn't wear a bra that unfastened in both the back and front is more incendiary: "They'd go *insane*, the poor little dears . . . fathoming the procedure afresh each time. It would mean having to count up to two" (131). Furze, the general factotum, is the worst of the lot; in this secret cell of revolutionaries, he is the Danton. To him, all women are concerned about is the constraint of freedom, and being in total control: "That'd be something like a world, though, that would—half the ladies in prison where they belong and the other half looking after them" (135). Furze is admittedly an extreme case; when the society is inevitably disbanded, he decides to become a lighthouse keeper, a job for which is he eminently suited.

So why do these men form this society in the first place? Most of them wish to escape a wife generally described as a harridan or virago. Yet the President, who holds his office not from leadership ability but because he came up with the idea for the society, has a young and attractive wife, and the Treasurer's wife seems nice enough, except, as he complains, she "never . . . said anything in the least bit interesting or amusing or original" (*Egyptologists*, 109). Most of the members think that their problem lies in the institution of marriage. Many readers, though, would agree with placing the blame on a gender but would shift it on to the members' shoulders, and as the reversal at end of the novel shows, perhaps Amis and Conquest would half agree.

Like other Amis novels, *The Egyptologists* ends with the revelation that the female characters have not been so blind as they first appeared, nor have they been as ignorant, in all senses of the word, as their spouses first supposed. The Secretary, the Robespierre of this revolution, has been all along indulged by his wife, who lets readers in on the knowledge early in the novel when she tells him, "Anything you like to take up or mess about with or what-have-you is all right with me" (*Egyptologists*, 77). The President's wife suspects something is going on and, during her investigations, has an affair with another member of the club. When he protests at her display of sexual appetite, she rounds on him with "I'm being unemotional, cynical, just *using* sex. Like a man, in fact" (127). To top it all off, the Treasurer, who has generally been presented as more levelheaded, gets the most serious surprise. His wife, the "unoriginal" and "unexciting" one, has been carrying on an affair for as long as he has. When he displays incredulity about the source of her knowledge, she answers sarcastically with the brutal language she knows he employs in his head, "By using my tiny little mind, mate" (205). Indeed, all the tomfoolery he and the others employed in constructing their cover stories or "legends" was totally unnecessary; she never worried much about the stratagems she herself had to employ because "it was easier for me than for you, because you thought I might be listening and I knew you weren't" (206). The novel ends with the Treasurer staring at a real statue of Nefertiti and still not getting it: "Why are you what you are?" (207). What do women want, indeed? To use the idiom Amis's female characters often employ: if you don't know now, mate, then you'll never.

I Want It Now

Amis's last mainstream novel of the decade, *I Want It Now* (1968), at first sounds as if it will primarily be concerned with the images and attitudes that that decade brought into prominence and fame. The dregs of Carnaby Street are visible through cab windows; partygoers are attired in mod outfits as if for a masquerade; and, most important of all, the title of the novel is a demand that the heroine, Simona Quick, makes of the hero, Ronnie Appleyard, at their first meeting and refers to the sexual act. In hindsight, the 1960s have been cursed as a decade of instant gratification during which youth wholeheartedly renounced the premise of delayed gratification on which responsible adulthood has insisted for so long. Yet Simona's (or Simon's, to use the name by which she is most widely known) demand is, in the wider context of the novel, a symptom of her particular affliction, which Ronnie later diagnoses as "somebody who doesn't know what she wants."[12] Perhaps in the final analysis that was the main problem of the decade, but Amis does not seem very interested in making Simon's a global malaise.

Rather, Amis is once again, to use his terms of reference, concerned with the moral progress of a self-proclaimed "shit"—in this case, Ronnie Appleyard—through the upper reaches of Anglo-American society. At the age of 36, Ronnie is the host of an issues-oriented television talk show, *Insight;* he is driven, ambitious, a master of his medium, hypocritical, and he only postures as a leftie, a spokesman for "the intelligent and independent-minded young" (*I Want It Now,* 11) because at this time such a stance will get him further in his career. In Ronnie's inverted moral schema, "integrity" is defined as his refusal to have the more entertainment-oriented TV host Bill Hamer on *Insight* (the inner and stronger reason being compounded of professional jealousy and pride). Like many people in not only the 1960s but the subsequent decades that Amis as well as his son Martin would fictionally dissect, Ronnie chiefly pursues, as he frankly admits to himself, "Fame and money, with a giant's helping of sex thrown in" (14).

Yet Ronnie's pilgrimage will not be the circular round that Roger Micheldene traverses through his own secular inferno. Once again, as in *Lucky Jim* and *That Uncertain Feeling,* Amis is interested in hypergamy, males linking up with females of a higher social class and status. Simon will one day be incredibly rich; her mother, Lady Julliette Baldock, having made two very financially advantageous matches (her third, with "Chummy" Baldock, was made for the title only), now vacations in the Greek isles with the fictional counterparts of Niarchos and Onassis and has mansions in England and America as well. Despite Simon's androgynous name and appearance, Ronnie thinks she has "the most attractive face he had ever seen" (*I Want It Now,* 26).

Yet when on first bedding Simon he learns that she is sexually frigid, he tries to kick her out of his flat so that he can bed a more willing partner, who is contemptuously (and quite characteristically for Ronnie) referred to only as "fat Susan." But as soon as he learns that Simon is a presumptive heiress, "cash registers" sound in his mind (*I Want It Now,* 47). Ronnie has tried once before to marry for money, but the equine appearance of his fiancée, plus her desire to enjoy connubial relations, caused Ronnie to call off the match; he blames his current state of domestic penury on "the deficiencies of his character" (38)—another moral inversion—in not being able to be duplicitous during such a marriage.

Yet, as happens in *Lucky Jim,* Ronnie's saga turns into a version of the Cinderella (or Cinderfella) story, for as he awakens the physically frigid Simon, he awakens his own moral and emotional self (the fairy tale of Sleeping Beauty in Simon's context is also explicitly referred to in the novel). Ronnie's own diagnosis of his progress owes something to the vocabulary of the times, as well as his own desire to never appear too good to himself: "[H]e had started enjoying being nice to Simon, started using tenderness as an end in itself, got hooked on the bloody stuff, in fact" (*I Want It Now*, 225). It is chiefly in this realm of love that Ronnie feels redeemed; as he says in his last and perhaps overobvious confession to her: "But because of you I've had to give up trying to be a dedicated, full-time shit. I couldn't make it, hadn't the strength of character. Which is a pity in a way, because when you fall back into the ranks of the failed shits or amateur shits or incidental shits you start taking on responsibility for other people" (254). Because of love, Ronnie's point of view toward everything changes.

Ronnie's most significant change of heart, however, occurs in his attitude toward the rich. Circumstances readily show that the rich are indeed different than you and me (the Hemingway-Fitzgerald dispute over the accuracy of this statement is specifically alluded to), particularly in the penny-pinching ways in which their households are run. At first Ronnie finds this "Stilton-paring" "sweet" (*I Want It Now*, 76), but as he is further subjected to its constraints by his position as a not-rich guest, as he falls further in love with Simon, and as he sees how this penuriousness translates itself into rudeness to servants and menials, he begins to rebel. This rebellion culminates in his confrontation with Lady Baldock on national television, a meeting that Bill Hamer has manipulated. Ronnie flatly states, "If you're rich, you can afford to abandon reason, justice and good manners whenever you feel like it" (235)—all mortal sins to Amis, particularly the first. Ronnie's subsequent public renunciation of Simon's fortune ensures that he will never see a penny of it, but he nevertheless makes off into the London streets with his now-awakened Sleeping Beauty back in cinders, to mix together the main fairy tales governing the plot.

Perhaps *I Want It Now* shares some of *The Anti-death League*'s optimism about love: in another sense, the novel echoes Beauty and the Beast, or, to use the novel's categories, Beauty and the Shit. Depending on the reader's mood, Ronnie's change of heart concerning Simon can seem natural or strained. The one incident in the novel that does seem far-fetched is when the totally illiberal Ronnie tells off the blatantly racist Student Mansfield. Amis's description of the eruption of liberal sentiment in Ronnie is humorous, but in the end one feels the truly liberal Amis (at least in the racial area) is merely getting his own back for all the racist remarks he heard when visiting the South around this time. Similarly, the satire against the upper classes is at times hilarious (particularly about their meals), but some of it seems overtendentious, and the upper-class names (Baldock, Van Pup, the Upshots) are sub-Wodehouse. Some touches, however, are right on the money, so to speak. Several times Amis uses the technique of reproducing the speech of a character whom another character cannot for accentual reasons understand in syntactically lucid but semantically ridiculous sentences. He refuses to "translate" these and leaves it up to the reader to decipher them. Once more Amis makes the reader actively work to understand the text on the lexical level, as well as on the level of plot and morality. Yet on the whole, *I Want It Now* is a novel in which everyone gets what he or she deserves, except for perhaps the reader.

Girl, 20

Girl, 20 (1971), Amis's first novel of the decade that followed the 1960s, is perhaps a more damning indictment of the excesses of the previous decade than anything he wrote during it. The novel also marks a transition from the relative optimism about the possibility of happiness in *The Anti-death League* and *I Want It Now* to the darker attitudes and endings that would color several of his next mainstream novels, particularly *Jake's Thing* and *Stanley and the Women,* and in turn mark him for some as a misogynistic reactionary. Yet *Girl, 20* is a carefully plotted and modulated moral examination of why men and women were increasingly entering emotional relationships based on false premises, and why the so-called freedom promised by the decade of liberation was, in many ways, an *ignis fatuus* that for some would lead to destruction and death.

The novel's focus is, as many critics have pointed out, one of Amis's finest creations, Sir Roy Vandervane, a sort of British Leonard Bernstein, an irredeemably leftist composer-conductor of the second rank in both roles. By this point in Amis's novelistic career, such a political orientation in an Amis character marks him or her as a fatuous trend follower at best, or a moral imbecile at worst. Yet matters are not as simple in Amis novels as even some of his political admirers might suspect. For one thing, Roy's bête noire, the newspaper editor Harold Mears, who hates Roy for both his politics and his choice of girlfriend—Mears's 17-year-old daughter—is just as irretrievably right-wing and yet is no better (probably a tad sight worse) in his dealings with the world. "Shitty" is the pithy summary of his behavior by one of his reporters.[13]

More important is the tremendous verbal and behavioral vigor Amis gives Roy. To mark Roy's conversation as reflective of his character, and to amuse the reader, Amis imparts to Roy's speech a "slurring policy" (*Girl*, 35), which is, to use an anachronistic term, more politically correct (in an older time more "matey"), more in tune with youth. Thus, a "sonata" becomes in Roy's mouth a "snarter" (40), and Amis characteristically leaves it up to his reader's intelligence to decipher these elisions, which in turn adds to the humor. In the same vein, Roy's euphemisms for swearing, what he uneuphemistically calls his "fuckettes" (43), are witty and amusing. Roy takes terms whose political (or artistic) import he despises, such as "sporting spirit" and "Christian gentleman," and interjects them in his conversation instead of shorter Anglo-Saxon terms. Thus when he prefaces his statements with bursts such as "Puck-like theme" (65) or "Socialist Gestapo" (109), it takes readers a few seconds to orient themselves in the lexical wonderland into which they seem to have stumbled and realize that Roy has just said the equivalent of "balls" or "bugger off."

Roy's revolutionary attitudes often shade into the ridiculous. He refuses to perform Berlioz's *Harold in Italy* because it is based on a poem by Byron, who died fighting for Greek independence, and the current rulers of Greece are right-wing. These attitudes are also, the novel strongly suggests, hypocritical as well. As Tom Wolfe pointed out in "Radical Chic" (1970), his seminal essay on the upper echelons of art consorting with the "revolutionary proletariat," the vulgar accoutrements of wealth are cognitively dissonant with an egalitarian, supposedly reformist political agenda. According to Roy's close friend Douglas Yandell, the narrator of the novel, Roy makes up for this disparity by doing small penances. For instance, Roy's night at an expensive seat at the opera, followed by a rich dinner, must be preceded by a subway ride and walk to get there. Even though Roy calls the main choice of his time whether "you're a have person or a be person" (*Girl*, 67), it's fairly clear that no matter what Roy *is,* he will not give up what he *has*. Even more disturbing to Douglas, who is a music critic, is the way in which Roy's artistic interests follow in the footsteps of the political. Roy's undertaking a Mahler symphony cycle is "trendy," but "far, far better" than the bastard child of rock and classical music that Roy hopes to perform (56). Called *Elevations 9,* it is a self-admitted reference to "Revolution #9," the Beatles' exercise in contemporary music, with a bawdy reference to an aroused male organ thrown in. As was the case for many Beatles fans, Douglas hopes that Roy will "get back" to his own musical roots, but even after Douglas's attempted sabotage of the premiere of *Elevation 9* by smearing Roy's bow with butter, and the even more catastrophic destruction after the concert of Roy's beloved Stradivarius by a band of hooligans, Roy refuses to give up courting youth.

Of course, the most serious example of Roy's youth courting is his involvement with Sylvia Mears, who is even younger than the title of the novel suggests. That title comes from Roy's comment to Douglas about the aphrodisiacal effect of seeing such a phrase in a newspaper advertising column indicating the age of the woman therein offering her services. Sylvia's attractiveness for Roy is almost entirely grounded in sex, and also in that she is not currently married to him. It cannot be anything in her character, which is constantly demonstrated in episodes of what Douglas rightly calls "moral vandalism" (*Girl,* 150). Roy remarks that the freedom with which the Zeitgeist has imbued her makes her so desirable; he comments to Douglas that a wife will not perform certain sexual activities, but a girl, whatever her age, "will do that for you, and other things besides" (79). And it is precisely in this freedom that almost all of the novel's problems originate.

Not only the age, but also the way children are raised, is free, and here are the seeds for disaster. Roy tells Douglas that Sylvia's parents, despite their political orientation, "give her a lot of freedom" (*Girl,* 76). The end result of such freedom is seen in the barbarism of many of her actions, such as nearly killing Roy's wife, Kitty, when confronted by her. But the real casualties in the book are Roy's own children, particularly Penny, and Roy's younger son, the six-year-old Ashley. Douglas concludes that Roy is an "agreeable" person to be with because of his "system of total permissiveness towards himself" (130), but such permissiveness percolates throughout his whole life, and its results can be seen in Ashley's reply to Roy after being mildly reprimanded: "Shut your trap, you fucking monkey-face" (36). At least Roy is getting what he deserves, though it doesn't bother him overmuch, but at the end of the novel, Douglas learns that Ashley, in the never-ending tantrum that forms his life, has permanently crippled the Vandervanes' inoffensive little dog.

Whereas Ashley's destructiveness is directed at the world around him, Penny's is directed entirely at herself. She still lives at home, she tells Douglas, because "It's free" (*Girl,* 29), and she probably does not mean "free" only in a financial sense. A lack of parental affection, manifested in the absence of any boundaries or rules of behavior, has turned Penny into an affectless, apathetic wanderer. In her, the pun of their last name—wander vainly—is most hauntingly embodied. Even the physical enjoyment of sex has subsided into a morass of ennui for her. Douglas is urged by several characters in the novel, including Roy, to attempt to "reach" Penny, but in the end, she proves irredeemably lost. When, at the end of the novel, Douglas finally sees her enthusiastic, the cause turns out to be her taking up heroin, which she knows will soon kill her. In the most ironic and chilling ending to any Amis novel, Penny can finally happily proclaim, "We're all free now" (253).

Yet *Girl, 20* is more than just the tribulations of the house of Vandervane. Its other central character is the narrator, Douglas Yandell. He shares some of Amis's own prejudices; both, for instance, despise the music of Miles Davis. Yet Douglas is essentially apolitical; when Harold Mears censors his column by cutting out any reference to a musician's country of origin if it happens to be communist, Douglas thinks about resigning, but he never will because he simply doesn't care. He shares his girlfriend, Vivienne Copes, with another man, and that arrangement doesn't disturb him much either. Douglas initially goes to the Vandervanes' ostensibly to commiserate with Kitty, and really because he is physically attracted to the statuesque Penny, but when she turns out to be involved with a black artist, Gilbert, Douglas accepts that as well, along with Penny's subsequent offer to sleep with him for helping her with Roy. Nothing disturbs his equilibrium until he witnesses the debacle of *Elevation 9*, which, even though it turns out exactly as poorly as he had connived at, leaves him "overwhelmed with feelings of anticlimax and defeat" (*Girl*, 226). Douglas's only real passion is music: he doesn't care about how Roy is destroying his family or children a tenth as much as he does about what Roy is doing to music.

At the end of the novel, as with so many Amis protagonists, Douglas learns exactly what he has been missing, and the initial bearer of this information is, as in those other cases, a woman whom the hero has never really *seen*. Vivienne leaves him to marry, of all people, Gilbert, because at least he cares about her enough to change her behavior—and significantly enough, vice versa. When Vivienne finally walks away from him, Douglas correctly assesses her as "strong-looking in a sense that had not struck me before" (*Girl*, 241). It is too late, however, for Douglas, and he doesn't have a chance of helping Penny, whose problems not even the industrious Gilbert could crack. Douglas's most important revelation occurs when he sees what Ashley has done to Furry Barrel, the Vandervanes' dog: he feels "as if something dismal had happened right in the middle of my own life and concerns, something major, something irretrievable, as if I had taken a fatally wrong decision years before and only now seen how much I had lost by it" (251). His fatal flaw is not to care enough about anything except music, and even that in a desultory fashion—he plans on finishing the biography of Weber he is working on in time for Weber's bicentenary, 16 years in the future. In one of the most effective passages of the novel, Douglas is waiting for Roy, Sylvia, and Penny in a trendy, overloud basement bar made up to look like a Great War battlefield. Douglas finds himself with a feeling that had occurred to him as a child, "a fusion of boredom and discomfort," which then becomes "a solipsistic despair, a progressive and apparently irreversible loss of belief in anything not here and not now." He concludes, almost correctly, "This place is hell, in fact" (148). Yet it, as well as Douglas's future after having lost Vivienne and never being able to help Penny, is not the fierce inferno reserved for such slaves of appetite as Roger Micheldene or the acrid circle reserved for cynics such as Jake Richardson; this is Dante's first infernal circle, meant for those who never made a choice, never made up their minds. It is, to use a word Amis would probably have despised, more existential, but nevertheless just as painful as those increasingly bitter circles Amis would investigate in his next mainstream novels. Deciding whose future is more appealing, Roy's or Douglas's, may appear to be a Hobson's choice, but at least Roy, however hypocritical, will be able to bellow "random noise considered as art" (216) when confronted with a world that does not conform to his dreams. Douglas has no dreams at all.

Ending Up

For most of his career, Amis had been flirting with that comic mode, black humor, that came to prominence in the 1960s (and that his son Martin would so steadily mine in his own career). But none of those flirtations would prepare readers for the acerbity of the conclusion of *Ending Up* (1974). The novel also introduces the subject of old age, which Amis, by now in his early fifties, seemed to be more and more concerned with, and would form an important subtext in three of his subsequent novels (*Jake's Thing, The Old Devils,* and *The Folks That Live on the Hill*). Also, like the last two of those novels, *Ending Up* is what has been called an "ensemble" novel: instead of focusing on the experiences of one individual, like many of his novels from *Lucky Jim* to *One Fat Englishman,* or on what might conventionally be called a "couple," as in *Take a Girl like You* or *I Want It Now,* Amis takes as his subject a group of people, thrown together either by proximity or friendship. Such situations reveal the mastery with which Amis is able to handle narrative flow and the subtle transitions in point of view and free indirect discourse involved in such a situation. In fact, he often has fun with it, as when describing various interpretations of a character's facial expression: a character looks "in a way the doctor saw as indicating concern and Marigold herself as pretended concern hiding utter indifference, but in fact amounted to pretended concern hiding hostile curiosity."[14]

The novel, at first reading, seems relentlessly gloomy and bitter, as if Amis were reinforcing every stereotype about the perils of old age; one of the younger characters thinks at one point, "The idea of sex in any relation to the old, any relation at all, was obscene" (*Ending Up*, 40). The five septuagenarians forced into living with each other, primarily for financial reasons, in the archly named Tupenny-hapenny Cottage, seem bent on proving Sartre's adage in *No Exit,* "Hell is other people," and add an important codicil: it is probably more hellish when they are older. Bernard Bastable, the most unsavory of the lot, has reached the point in his life where all he desires or can do is "pass the time" (73). Like many Amis heroes, he is exceptionally exact and scrupulous in his speech, constantly pointing out the clichés and euphemisms with which conversation is spotted, but usually for no better reason than to exhibit his exasperation with the world and those creatures in it with whom he lives. It has been a half decade since he has been capable of feeling any positive emotion about any other human being, and even longer than that about his unprepossessing sister Adela. Nor does he feel anything for another inhabitant of the cottage, his old batman, Derrick "Shorty" Shortell, with whom he had a physical relationship some 30 years before, for which he was drummed out of the army. Shorty is an alcoholic who performs many of the chores at the cottage, and, in certain situations, proves himself to be basically fair and honorable.

Adela is the glue that holds the cottage together. Because of her appearance and the tone of her voice (its volume and brassiness belying the concern she often feels), she has never married, and she often grates people the wrong way. She can sometimes divine the truth behind appearances: for instance, that the pain in Bernard's injured leg is inversely related to the relish with which he regards a prospective task, and, as the narrator tells us, "Adela was unsardonically aware of the regular shifts in the condition of her brother's leg" (*Ending Up,* 82). The "unsardonically" points to a key feature of Adela's character: she is good-natured in the moral sense of the term. The narrator seems to approve of her actions, no matter how they are regarded by the other characters. When discussing her motivation for putting up Christmas decorations, the narrator points out that even though few would enjoy them, "That did not mean that doing as much was negligible or ridiculous or hypocritical" (132).

Adela is even nice to the second most unpleasant inhabitant of the cottage, her old friend Marigold Pyke. Marigold's most noticeable habit, as is the case with many of Amis's less admirable characters from Bertrand Welch to Roy Vandervane, is linguistic; in her case, an affected infantile rhyming duplication, in which the word "blacks," for instance, becomes "blackle-packles" (*Ending Up,* 128). Another sure sign of her moral placement by Amis is her racism; her previous mention of blacks is in a comment about the likelihood of their eating dog food. (Bernard, we discover on the same page, is—no surprise—anti-Semitic.) Yet the narrator is scrupulously evenhanded in his depiction of Marigold's motivations and conduct. For example, at one point, Marigold tactlessly extols the joys of having children in front of the childless Adela, and one of the characters remarks to himself on Marigold's seeming cruelty. The narrator feels compelled to add, "To be fair, the risk of also hurting Adela did not cross Marigold's mind" (53). Indeed, by the end of the novel, Marigold has become an object of pity herself as she begins to succumb to what was at the time called senility. This fate seems harsh even for someone so persistently foolish as Marigold. She decides not to leave the cottage and to put up with Bernard's and Shorty's insults so that she can at least be told about her now forgotten life with her husband: a selfish reason, but a pitiable one nonetheless.

The fifth inhabitant of the cottage, Bernard's brother-in-law, George Zeyer, is also mentally afflicted, in his case with nominal aphasia, the inability to remember the names of things. A substantial amount of the verbal comedy in the novel involves George's attempts to describe something without saying its name (characteristically, Amis leaves it to his readers to decipher what George is talking about). It is almost as if George is playing a kind of parlor game, and at the Christmas party memorably described near the end of the novel, the characters indeed play such a game, "Call My Bluff," which Bernard and Marigold use as the opportunity to hurl verbal harpoons at each other. And by this point, George has been able substantially to overcome his ailment; in fact, his overindulgence in nouns now threatens to swamp his conversation, as Bernard harshly tells him.

Yet even Bernard has an excuse of sorts for his behavior: he has been diagnosed as having three months to live. At first, this news seems to transform Bernard: he acts kindly toward his sister and begins drinking again. But both liquor and kindness have lost their appeal for Bernard, and he quickly becomes even worse than before. The only way to pass the time is to become involved in juvenile pranks that, more often than not, do not work, or even backfire on him. Whereas, for example, before he did not feel the necessity of hiding his flatulence and its result from his opponents, now he undertakes what he calls "Operation Stink," letting off a stink bomb in the bathroom after Marigold has used it, hoping thus to embarrass her. Other projects are even more reprehensible: making the other inhabitants of the cottage get rid of George's dog, his only remaining source of affection, or drenching Marigold's cat with water from a squirt gun.

The climax of the novel is even more fatal than that of *Hamlet;* in a dark comedy of errors, all the inhabitants of Tupenny-hapenny Cottage die, one deservedly perhaps, and one mercifully, and some—perhaps all—ironically. The ultimate irony is that the bodies are discovered by Bernard's son, who is seeing his father for the first time since infancy. The ending reinforces the fear that one younger character hysterically expresses about the prospect of growing old, which he sees enacted before him at the cottage: "They can't help it . . . they've got nothing to look forward to it's just got to be accepted you'll be like it yourself one day you'll be out of here soon oh Christ" (*Ending Up,* 145). We shall all end up there, Amis seems to be saying, and the bodies strewn across the scene hide some of the more profound terror and pity Amis has presented earlier. Bernard hoped that his diagnosis would have at least made him appreciate the beauties and pleasures of everyday life, but that enjoyment, like that of liquor, is denied him. He is even denied a summing-up, "that he would have been able to look back on his life and—not find a meaning in it, which he had never hoped for, but see it as a whole" (164). That old age prevents such an eventuality is the blackest humor in *Ending Up.*

Jake's Thing

Amis's last novel of the decade brought to a head the charges that had been more mutely following him since the period of *The Egyptologists* and *One Fat Englishman:* that he was a misogynist, or if not that, then a novelist who at the least created "misogynist characters with whom the author appears to identify himself."[15] Actually, the broader charge—that Amis and his main male characters were one and the same—had been dogging him since Maugham's comments on *Lucky Jim.* And in the case of *Jake's Thing,* a novel about a man whose feelings about women cause him to embrace his loss of libido, such an identification seemed all too easy. On a broader front, Jake Richardson shares many of Amis's more widely known and notorious opinions: about trendy restaurants, about noise in pubs, about the way service-based businesses think only about their own ease of operations (he even uses the same phrase, "easier-for-them items"), about the lowered standards of education at all levels, and in general, imprecations and warnings about "the steady progress towards more sophisticated awareness which had come to fuck up (so it seemed to him) most kinds of human behaviour in the last however many years it was."[16] Thus when Jake breaks into philippics against women, it seems logical to assume that Amis must share these opinions. A closer examination of the novel, however, reveals that as is his practice, Amis carefully constructs a character whose misogyny, his most obvious trait, is only a part of a greater psychological condition, or in Jake's case, malaise.

A more rewarding point of comparison is to note, as several critics have, that Jake Richardson is an older version of Jim Dixon, as their names suggest (Dixon/Dickson/Richardson). Like Jim, Jake is learned, and also like Jim, Jake is at times contemptuous of learning. Like Jim, Jake is enraged by many of the situations and people he meets in the world. Unlike Jim, he has learned to control his rage somewhat and does not have to make secret faces to himself to vent it. Unfortunately, he has gotten slipshod in recent years about hiding his true feelings, and his faces become all too apparent to those around him. Given the narrative stance of the novel (free indirect discourse from Jake's point of view), readers are only aware of this when Jake becomes so. Brenda, his wife, is best at reading him, but after others have pointed out his all too obvious disdain to him, Jake is forced to admit, "I'm not as good as I used to think I was at disguising my feelings, especially when they're feelings of contempt, hatred, weariness and malicious hilarity as they are most of the time these days" (*Jake's Thing,* 223).

Much of that contempt, and the novel's comedy, centers on the various treatments Jake is forced to undergo to cure his loss of libido. Most of them involve some form of humiliation for Jake, and his attempts to explain that none of them seem to be helping him are met with various levels of incomprehension. As Jake asks his hilariously ignorant psychiatrist, "What makes you think that what's deep down is more important than what's up top?" (*Jake's Thing,* 266). Yet Jake's ultimate situation is not tragic: he will be able to live with the results of their failure. Kelly, a young girl whom Jake tries to help (and fails), is more profoundly affected. When she unsuccessfully tries to commit suicide during a weekend therapeutic workshop, Jake is the only one who feels any guilt or responsibility. The guilt and shame that his therapists have been trying to make Jake feel as the cause of his problem are, in actuality, the very emotions they should be feeling over the inefficacy of their work.

Jake's "thing" is not merely his growing aversion toward women. It is a larger problem, seemingly connected to the fact that Jake is growing old and doesn't have much of a vocation to do anything, not even his current occupation of being a don at Oxford. He has published several works in his field and, although not overvaluing them through pride, feels compelled to rip out a copy of an article he wrote because several students have written in comments about its validity. Because he has no religious faith, he views the basic problem of the rest of his life as "how to see to it that the period between now and then should be as comfortable and enjoyable as could realistically be expected" (*Jake's Thing*, 100). Yet anything beyond the mere creature comforts of drink or watching the telly seem to be receding from Jake's grasp. Early in the novel, Jake looks out on his neighborhood and tries to recapture the sense of "curiosity" and "expectation" he had when he first moved there, but it is gone: "What was before him left him cold, and he didn't mind" (33). At the country house where the workshop is being held, Jake gazes at the scenery and enjoys it, at the same time thinking it "not so grand, he felt, as the same scene would have looked to him five or ten years ago" (256). Even with that most English of hobbies, puttering around in the garden, "he couldn't be fucking bothered" (268), as Amis bluntly transcribes it. Jake's underlying "thing" is partially explained by the other allusion contained in his name: his full Christian name is Jaques, a name that he shares with the melancholy wanderer in the forest of Arden in Shakespeare's *As You Like It*. The world delights not Jake, to adapt a phrase the equally melancholy Prince of Denmark uses in another play of Shakespeare's, nor—more infamously—do women.

Jake's loss of interest is most markedly symptomized by his loss of sexual desire but also enters all other phases of his marriage. Nonetheless, Jake does have feeling for Brenda and does want to save his marriage, but not enough. The point is made in two delayed revelations during the course of the novel: at its midpoint and at the end, when Brenda reveals she is leaving Jake for her friend Alcestis's semimoronic husband, Geoffrey, who at least is interested in Brenda. She knows that Jake has been ignoring her at a level perhaps less intimate, yet even more important, than the sexual when he stopped telling her about things: "Why should I live with someone who thinks I'm as bloody unrewarding as that?" (*Jake's Thing*, 273). After Brenda has left, he again tries to recapture some of the feelings they had felt for each other, but like those about his neighborhood and the country landscape, these feelings too have fled.

Beyond the contextualization of Jake's misogyny within the larger framework of his entire character, Amis lets several other characters comment more objectively on Jake's attitudes, most notably Damon Lancewood, a homosexual English (his subject as well as his nationality) don. "From the way you go on," Lancewood tells Jake, "most people would say you were the one with the thing about women" (*Jake's Thing*, 120). But in the end, these counterbalances might not appear as vigorously mounted—or supported—as Jake's lengthy diatribes against female perfidy. One can note that the paragraph-long charge that leads up to Jake's refusal to be "cured" of his libido loss ends with the mopping-up phrase "and lots of other things like that," which in a sense deflates the preceding charges, as well as the overtly stated qualifying phrase "all according to him" (286). One can also point out (and this perhaps cuts both ways) that Jake is much less of a "shit" than, say, Roger Micheldene; Jake is genuinely interested in, and kind to, various characters ranging from a madwoman he meets on a bus to Kelly and Ivor, people he meets at the workshop. Whatever the exculpations and conditions one might make about Amis's "misogyny" in *Jake's Thing* and even more infamously in his next novel, one fact remains: the power with which the charge resonates testifies to Amis's abilities and strengths as a novelist, as well as his weaknesses. Of course, it also testifies to his genuine nonconformist core; the more trouble he caused, the more intransigent he appeared to become. And perhaps, as some have claimed, the whole issue arose from his personal life at the time. Ultimately, though, Amis seems to be suggesting that Jake's real "thing" might be something all will have to face as they grow older in a faithless, dishonest world.

Stanley and the Women

Stanley and the Women (1984) is certainly the most problematic of Amis's novels. It, more than any of his others, caused the reversal of his critical reception, and his image became widely transformed from that of a witty and trenchant observer of social manners into that of an embittered, misogynistic polemicist. The novel's notoriety supposedly delayed its appearance in America, causing several publishers to reject it because of its depiction of women. *Stanley and the Women* cannot easily be defended, as can *Jake's Thing,* as being the sum of the projections of a main character slowly subsiding into a melancholic old age. Yet, as is the case with other novels by Amis, the easiest, most straightforward assumptions about the conclusions of the novel overlie another layer of meaning.

Amis's narrative habit of initially mystifying the reader at the beginning of his works is at its peak in *Stanley and the Women*. For its first two-and-a-half pages, the novel seems to be a third-person narrative about a 38-year-old assistant literary editor named Susan. It is even written in the style of a typical novel about such a character, a style remote from Amis's own: "The sitting room on the first floor had a low ceiling and a rather awkward shape, but she had done her best to turn it into an attractive place with carefully chosen lamps and bright rugs and cushions."[17] This parody continues until a sentence about Susan's "distinctive" facial features, the adjective defined as "meaning less good versions of it somehow never seemed to show up, and the obvious word always had a lot to be said for it, quite enough in this case" (*Stanley and the Women,* 10). This change into a knottier rhythm, which matches the progressions and mental qualifications of a typical Amis narrator, prepares the reader for the appearance of the real first-person narrator, Stanley Duke, in the next sentence. The unsettling lack of a steady narrative focus in these first few pages should prepare us for a certain indeterminacy in what will follow.

Stanley and Susan seem to share a happy marriage. Although they are not from the same class background, they appear to live happily together. Most of Stanley's negative feelings about women are initially reserved for his first wife, Nowell, for whose arsenal of conversational and behavioral dirty tricks Stanley is no match. And Stanley eventually becomes ready to tar, at least in general, all women with his complaints against Nowell: "[T]he Eternal Woman once more looked out of Nowell's eyes" (*Stanley and the Women,* 210). When it comes to particulars, Stanley refrains from thinking about Lindsey Lucas, an old flame, that way, or even Susan, at least until the end of the novel.

Indeed, almost every other male character, major and minor, consistently looks on women as enemies. Attending a party on a boat in the Thames, Stanley comes across a man repeatedly kicking a step; the man explains to Stanley that he is "working off" his frustrations about his wife's "being a little bit provoking. . . . You know, feminine" (*Stanley and the Women,* 162). A police officer who returns Steve, Stanley's son, after he has caused a fracas at a Middle Eastern embassy tells Stanley that at least in that part of the world, "They do seem to have gotten the women problem sorted out nice and neat" (200). Harry Coote, Stanley's boss, refuses to get married, preferring a habitual relationship with a prostitute to living with a woman. The male doctors in the novel are even more outspoken, no matter what their social class. The elegant Dr. Nash at first hints that he thinks all women are mad but later reveals, "They're all too monstrously, sickeningly, terrifyingly sane" (249). And Stanley's old friend Dr. Cliff Wainwright, who comes from the same lower-middle-class neighborhood as Stanley, agrees with Nash's initial hypothesis: "Mad as a hatter. Like the lot of them" (251). He even gets into an extremely unpleasant defense of wife beating: "Nobody ever even asks what the wife had been doing or saying" (253). This all leads to Stanley's dour conclusion about relationships between the sexes: "[I]f you want to fuck a woman she can fuck you up. And if you don't want to she fucks you up anyway for not wanting to" (254). If these indictments were all there was to the novel, then it would merit the charges of being mean-spirited and unfair, that Amis has stacked the narrative deck. But is this really the case?

The theme of madness runs throughout the novel. The dislocating shift of narrative focus at the beginning of the novel, obviously intentional in a novelist as careful as Amis, is reminiscent of madness. Steve suffers from acute schizophrenia, which becomes manifested in his hearing voices and in wild paranoid fantasies about Jews and Israel. Could it be that all the male characters in the novel are similarly paranoid? Admittedly, Trish Collings, Steve's doctor at the hospital, is another negative female portrayal, but she is also in the novel to satirize once again the irresponsibility of the psychiatric profession. Most of the major misogynists in the novel can be shown to be all too human in their own failings. Even Stanley can see, for example, that his boss's reluctance to be married is grounded in cheapness (a mortal sin in Amis's world), not in any real objections to women qua women. Nash, for all his surface impressiveness, is a fairly hollow figure. He has written a book on literary madness (strike one, for Amis), he inveighs at one point about "all these vile rights of the individual" (74) (strike two), and, worst of all, he doesn't seem to care very much about Steve's condition, even after Stanley has exhaustively described Collings's spurious treatments (he's out). There are also hints that Nash's own marriage is extremely unpleasant.

When Nash finally bursts into his diatribe against women at the end of the novel, even though it might seem authorially endorsed, the fact remains that Nash is also somewhat of a charlatan. Cliff Wainwright's case is different, in that he does not seem to be incompetent, but we are reminded too that he is in an unhappy marriage, and he comes from the same social background as Stanley. Even his defense of wife beating is coupled, by him, with a defense of racial prejudice, which Amis never even remotely condoned, and the distastefulness of which thus is intended to be connected to Cliff's justification of spousal abuse.

What about Stanley himself? As the illustration on the original dust jacket seems to bear out, he is surrounded on all sides by disagreeable females—Susan; her mother, the supercilious Lady Daley; Trish Collings; and Nowell. Is Stanley thus an innocent victim? For most of the novel, Susan is a sympathetic figure, and she tries to help Stanley as he copes with his son's mental illness. She begins to change as Stanley becomes more concerned about Steve than her, even to the point of not removing a knife Susan has found in his room, a course of action for which the police officer also criticizes Stanley. Although his marriage seems to be functioning fairly well, Stanley thinks nothing of starting an affair with Lindsey once again (which he consummates after Susan leaves him), or going to the boat party in search of an unattached female. Thus when Susan does break down, she is not entirely without reasons, especially because Stanley cannot seem to handle his son's condition (insisting to Cliff and Nash that another therapist care for and medicate Steve seems beyond Stanley's powers). Whether Susan lies about Steve's attack on her with a knife is never finally established, but even if she does so, it seems to be the only way to get through to Stanley how much the situation with Steve is upsetting her. Stanley's unspoken accusation that she has faked the attack causes her brutal outburst against him and echoes what her snobbish mother feels about Susan's marriage. But Stanley, who resembles other Amis protagonists in the scrupulosity with which he examines his own motivation, has to admit to himself, "But what was absolutely bleeding certain and inescapable was that I could have been weighing up the chances, which was the same as I could easily have been, which meant I might even have been going to be foul to her" (*Stanley and the Women,* 219). Stanley is similarly honest in that he is not entirely sure he is without blame for Steve's illness, no matter how much he overtly denies it to Nowell and Dr. Collings: "I would always feel I had had some hand, somehow, in bringing about his condition" (224). And no matter how much Nowell and Dr. Collings unfairly gang up on Stanley in the blame game, there is also Steve's testimony: "You're getting rid of me, aren't you?" he asks Stanley on being sent to the hospital (73). Stanley is also truthful enough with himself to feel guilty about that as well.

As Eric Jacobs has pointed out, Stanley and Amis share much the same social background and upbringing, and it is tempting to see in Stanley's hypergamic second marriage, to Susan, an analogy to Amis's own second marriage, to Elizabeth Jane Howard. Yet if one follows those assumptions, then how can Stanley's ferocious attitudes toward his first wife, Nowell, be reconciled with Amis's much gentler feelings for Hilly Bardwell? Jacobs gets around this by claiming that it is Nowell, not only Susan, who is the Jane Howard figure in the novel, but that's having it both ways. Certainly Amis's personal life did have some effect on the tone of certain passages in the novel, and perhaps on its overall effectiveness. Also, Amis seems to be twitting critics of *Jake's Thing* with even more outrageous declarations by his male characters. But it seems to me that there are enough hints under the surface of the story that *Stanley and the Women* is not an outright indictment of women; rather, it is another instance in Amis's oeuvre of readers having to peer through and behind the narrative of a very human and fallible protagonist to see where the truth of the matter lies. Stanley and Susan might yet be reconciled, but if that is not a happy ending, then it is the fault of both parties.

The Old Devils

Amis's next work marked the recovery of much of his critical reputation, and the beginning of a period of industriousness in his career that would be extinguished only by his death. *The Old Devils* won the Booker Prize as best novel for 1987 and was widely seen as a return of his old powers of social observation and moral complexity, all pointed by a witty mordancy. And on the surface, *The Old Devils* does seem to be somehow more "genial" than any of his later novels. Yet all the old Amis interests are there, including those that had caused his critical disfavor, such as the war between the sexes, along with ongoing battles against hypocrisy and sham, whether national, artistic, or personal, as well as some newer subjects, such as the desuetudes of old age. What then precisely caused this reversal of fortune?

It is tempting to attribute the glow that suffuses the otherwise sometimes bitter events of the plot to Amis's final removal from his relationship with Elizabeth Jane Howard and his return to an accommodation with his first wife, Hilly. But the change in attitude and tone is in reality more a change of perspective; *The Old Devils,* like *Ending Up* and the later *The Folks That Live on the Hill,* is what might be called an "ensemble" novel, with a large cast of characters among whom the narrative focus and attending indirect discourse shift, so that writer and reader are not locked into one point of view. In a sense, it becomes easier to view them from the outside, somewhat more "objectively," and the reader does thus not fall into the all too easy habit of identifying narrator (or narrative focus) with the author.

For instance, Alun Weaver, whose return to his Welsh hometown precipitates the events of the plot, is almost a "typical" Amis main character: male, conceited, an antifeminist womanizer, and an artist manqué. If Alun had narrated or been the prime focus of the novel, readers might have been tempted to identify him with Kingsley Amis: both are only children, share a love of early jazz, and dream about being the object of Margaret Thatcher's undying love. Yet because we see Alun most of the time from the outside, we know that when, like so many other Amis protagonists, he makes a standard accusation against women, "They always took it out of you for doing anything on your own, without them, however innocent, like glancing at a newspaper" (with a characteristic use of the pronoun "they" without a direct antecedent), we know that he is just being an old hypocrite.[18] When he protests to his wife, the levelheaded and stable Rhiannon (Amis's best female character since Jenny Bunn), that a woman psychologically outnumbers a man four to one, she immediately calls him out on it: "You outnumbered. That'll be the day" (*Old Devils,* 57). His friends, among whose wives Alun is generally cutting a fairly wide swath, tell him, "We see through you, chum" (110). By this time, the reader does too. Alun is insufferably rude to waiters and cabdrivers. His literary productions are easy to judge. One of his friends, Charlie Norris, frankly tells Alun that his new novel is no good, too influenced by the figure of the dead poet Brydan (another swipe by Amis at the reputation of Dylan Thomas). Yet throughout this frank appraisal of Alun's misdeeds, his character remains appealing. His response to a "professional" Welshman's invitation to visit America is hilarious. Although Alun does seriously let down his old friend Charlie in revenge for his honest literary evaluation, Alun does have the honesty to admit to himself and Rhiannon the gravity of his offense: "It's the worst thing I've ever done" (243). Even the manner of his death is humorous and oddly noble, while at the same time grotesque: he drops dead of a stroke after learning that another old friend, the incredibly penurious Garth Pumphrey, intends to charge his friends for the liquor he serves them inside his own home. When Alun offers to pay for the first round they have been served, Garth testily protests, "They were my freely offered hospitality. Good God, man, what do you take me for, some kind of Scrooge?" (259). Somehow dropping dead seems the only appropriate response to that level of selfish obtuseness.

Peter Thomas, Rhiannon's old lover (old in both senses here), is, like most of the other friends, locked into an unsatisfactory marriage, although his is almost totally loveless. His wife, Muriel, knows that she was Peter's third choice among women he wanted to marry, and that knowledge colors their whole relationship. They have not even touched each other for a decade; their sex life has been blasted since she asked him once during lovemaking "how much longer he was going to be" (*Old Devils,* 121). Thus Peter's conclusion about marriage, that men's heart attacks could be attributed to their wives' "steady winding them up with anxiety and rage" (122), although resembling a typical Amis protagonist's antifeminist complaint, seems more understandable in the circumstances of his particular marriage. And Muriel herself utters an even more general condemnation of the opposite sex (adopting from the other side the use of the unreferenced "they"): "They're all shits. . . . And the ones who pretend not to be are the worst of the lot" (197). Thus Peter becomes the main focus of sympathy in the novel, along with Charlie and Rhiannon, and when he and Rhiannon are able to get together at its end, it seems like, to use a phrase of Peter's about another happy occurrence, "reading a communiqué announcing a catastrophic defeat of the shits" (265).

Of course, the forces of nature and hypocrisy cannot be held forever at bay, and the novel also delineates the unpleasantness of old age and the shams with which human beings attempt to deceive themselves. The main reflector these last "stages of man" is Charlie (in many ways a melancholy successor to Jaques Richardson), for whom "the most noticeable characteristic of the past, as seen by him, at least, was that there was so much more of it now than formerly with bits that were longer ago than had once seemed possible" (*Old Devils,* 70). Like Amis himself, Charlie cannot bear to be left alone, suffering when meanly left so by Alun "an attack of depersonalization" (242). Old age means that time must be endured.

All in all, *The Old Devils,* while remaining characteristic of Amis in its subjects and characters, also reveals a deepening of his powers of analysis, sympathy, and overlying (or is it underlying?) humor. The novel is a triumph of his method, which is, to use Charlie's advice to Alun, a refutation of "a whole way of writing that concentrates on the writer and draws attention to the chap, towards him and away from the subject" (224), a repudiation that forms the basis of Amis's animus against everything from Dylan Thomas to literary modernism to Charlie Parker to Raymond Chandler to the New Wave in science fiction. The old ways, in the hands of an old master, can seem, when handled this skillfully, the best.

Difficulties with Girls

Difficulties with Girls (1988) is Amis's only sequel to one of his own novels. In it he returns, after an absence of 28 years in the real world, to the 7-year-old marriage of Patrick Standish and Jenny Bunn, whose tumultuous courtship was chronicled in *Take a Girl like You*. As long as the novel concentrates on Patrick and Jenny, it generally succeeds. Two subplots, however, are less successful. Amis's first version of the novel involved homosexuality, and this aspect of the novel is preserved in the story of Eric and Stevie, homosexual partners who live next door to Patrick and Jenny in a new block of flats in London. Another neighbor, Tim Vatcher, is a solicitor whose sexual problems (premature ejaculation, as far as one can tell from the hints in the text) have led him to a therapist—no points for guessing that Amis has made the therapist into a fraudulent nincompoop—who advises Tim to explore homosexuality, with predictably disastrous results. As always in Amis's books, these characters are handled with almost scrupulous fairness, but on the whole, all their "difficulties with girls" (the phrase is Tim's), whatever the girls' gender, do not mesh as successfully as Amis perhaps hoped they would with the main plot.[19]

Patrick and Jenny now live in London, which, except for a few pub and house interiors, is not described in any great detail. The novel, despite its setting in the past, is not in any sense a "historical" novel. The details, however, of Patrick's new position as a publishing executive are presented in depth, and Amis once again has an opportunity to delineate the *lex talionis* that rules the London literary world: the poet who pursues grants and fellowships; the petulance when mutual back-scratching in the form of favorable reviews is not practiced; the publishing of a line of poetry books not because the works deserve it but to impress other publishers. Patrick's boss, Simon Giles, is first presented as being incredibly cheap when he throws a party, so it comes as no surprise to readers familiar with Amis's moral calculus that Simon is also a trendy leftie.

The main focus of the novel is on Patrick and Jenny's marriage, and as readers already familiar with them might have guessed, it has not been entirely successful, mainly because of Patrick's sporadic infidelities, coupled with Jenny's miscarriage of the baby that prompted the marriage in the first place. By this point in their lives, they know each other and themselves too well to be traumatically disillusioned by these circumstances. Jenny, for instance, is able to produce the peculiar brand of doublethink that durable love requires: "[S]he went on thinking he was the most wonderful man in the world long after she was sure he was not" (*Difficulties with Girls,* 7). She endures Patrick's affairs, which is not to say that she condones them or is unhurt. On the other hand, Patrick realizes that his behavior is ultimately destructive but does nothing to stop it. He ruefully recognizes that in his own circumstances, experience is no teacher at all: "You lived and learned, there was no question. At least where other people were concerned you did. When it came to yourself there was a strong case for saying you just lived" (135). Patrick is a past master at placing all these admissions, however true, swiftly out of his mind and moving on to the next incipient disaster.

That disaster nearly turns out to be a brief fling with a next-door neighbor, Wendy Porter-King, who, while harboring romantic delusions about their relationship, can quickly cut Patrick down to size; as she tells him when he moves to break it off, "It's easier work turning moral on someone when you've fucked them a bit" (*Difficulties with Girls,* 183). Patrick's main problem is that he confesses this transgression to Jenny, a ploy that she realizes is Patrick's way of gaining exculpation. By confessing, he moves the burden off himself and on to Jenny, without any thought of her feelings. To top it all off, Patrick comes up with a scheme for Jenny to have an affair with an old friend of his, Oswald Hart, so that, as she tells him, "You wouldn't feel so bad about going to bed with whoever's going to come after Wendy" (237). Patrick cannot understand that she will not sleep with Hart because she is married to Patrick. During their climactic argument, she uses the works of two literary figures to nail down her case against Patrick. One is Somerset Maugham, who wrote about the possibility of actually loving someone without ever having to express that love sexually. "Love without going to bed. What an idea," she sarcastically tells Patrick (238). She also throws Patrick's own annotations in Henry Fielding's *Tom Jones* against him. Patrick has somewhat smugly underlined a passage in it by the narrator concerning Tom's sexual adventures: "Though he did not always act rightly, yet he never did otherwise without feeling and suffering for it" (239). Jenny realizes correctly that Patrick uses this line to explain and condone his own conduct.[20] Patrick has come close to destroying her love for him, which might be better anyway because, she tells him, "Then you could be a shit to your heart's content" (239).

By now the experienced reader of Amis knows that a decisive point has been reached, as the main female figure in the novel realizes exactly what the main male figure has been doing, whereas the male figure doesn't have a clue as to her knowledge. Although this situation can often lead in Amis to a dissolution of the relationship, Jenny and Patrick are saved by an *infantus ex machina:* Jenny finally becomes pregnant. Considering Patrick's track record, the chances of their "living happily ever after" are decidedly mixed, although there is the slight chance that Patrick could actually be "growing up at last" (*Difficulties with Girls,* 264). The evidence for that is the immediate and decisive way he turns down Simon Giles's plans to move into Patrick's building so that Patrick could sexually fulfill Simon's wife, who has become physically demanding ever since reading some of the sexual "how-to" books his firm publishes. Whether Patrick will change is ultimately answered by Jenny, who muses, "She was going to have him all to herself for at least three years, probably more like five, and a part of him forever, and now she could put it all out of her mind" (276)—a temperate and tempered conclusion to this modern fairy tale. *Difficulties with Girls* perhaps does not mesh thematically as other novels by Amis do (*Girl, 20* for one), but it answers one of the primal concerns of fiction lovers, what happens to the characters after the story is over, in this case, with a realistic yet somewhat melancholy prospect.

The Folks That Live on the Hill

The hill referred to in the title of Amis's last and perhaps best "ensemble" novel is Shepherd's Hill, an area of London that is called a "quasi-village."[21] Unlike the London in *Difficulties with Girls,* Shepherd's Hill is meticulously, and often acerbically, described, from the traffic jams, to the new businesses moving in, to the cacophony of accompanying sounds and noises that increasingly make urban life dolorous for the sensitive, which most of Amis's main characters are, at least aurally. The foci of this neighborhood are its pubs, particularly the King's, and the local post office, run by two Asian brothers, commonly called Charles and Howard, whose choric comments on the passing scene add significantly to the novel's bittersweet humor. When the brothers remark on the condition of England as it enters the last decade of the twentieth century, their caustic conclusions are contested by no one, not least of all the author, or any of his stand-ins.

The folks in the title center on Harry Caldecote, who in many ways is a characteristic Amis protagonist. A retired librarian (very faint echoes of Philip Larkin here), some—but certainly not all—of the circumstances of his life echo Amis's. Harry has been married and divorced twice and is now living in a household run by a widowed sister. Thus Harry with Clare, like Amis with Hilly, is able to enjoy companionship and understanding without the complications of a sexual relationship. Like almost any Amis protagonist, he is hyper-correct in his views of grammar. He hears the elisions of everyday speech in an exact yet comic way: "A dime breed. Dine out like the dinosaurs" (*Folks,* 35). He uses exactly the same phrase as Patrick Standish does to comment in code that the actions of another person are outlandishly offensive (at least to him): "You're not a bloody American, are you?" (200). Harry's opinions about women are strong, and some would say strongly sexist, and, as is customary in Amis, marked by the use of the referentless *they:* "If you let them have the last word, no matter what as long as it's the last and a word, then they're happy" (98). He is also at times remarkably thick; for instance, he has never noticed, or even cared to ask, if his quasi mistress actually enjoys sex (no marks for guessing that she doesn't).

In general, Harry leads what he thinks is an unreflective life; for him, the unexamined life is worth living. To a certain extent, he knows what he is: "[A] dried-up old frump from the Irving Club," he calls himself at one point (*Folks,* 175). At several places in the narrative, we see him as others see him, and it is not a flattering view. Harry gets into a snobbish little fit with a minicab driver and is immediately corrected. When he is able to act somewhat democratically, he tells himself that "he wished he had a wife to convey to him that he was ever so slightly marvellous for not minding" (69). If this were all there was to Harry, then one would suspect that some rude recognition scene, like Jake Richardson's, awaited him.

What makes Harry different from Amis's other semiblind protagonists is his good nature and desire to help others, even if they are not closely related to him—in a word, his *caritas.* As he puts it early on, "I keep feeling responsible for people and there doesn't seem to be anything I can do about it, I'm sorry to say" (*Folks,* 12). Harry's sympathetic nature is instinctual; when he hears that Fiona, his niece by marriage, is once again in deep trouble because of her alcoholism, he "felt as if he had been thrust out of a great door on to a desolate hillside" (37). He tells Clare, "You know how I hate doing that" (159), when she adjures him to look at a situation from someone else's point of view. Yet when trying to convince his ex-stepdaughter's ex-husband to leave her alone sexually—she has left him because she is a lesbian—Harry is able to come up with exactly the right sympathetic image to show the man how unwanted his advances are. Harry tries to convince Fiona that she can change, that she is not fated by ancestry to self-destruction; he enables his brother, Freddie, to publish his poetry so that he can make some money to become slightly independent of his voraciously domineering wife, Désirée; he lends a sympathetic ear to his ex-stepdaughter, Bunty, and her ex-husband, Desmond, in their still turbulent relationship with each other and others; he refuses a highly remunerative position in America to continue to live in London with Clare, and, by default, be on hand to care about and for his "folks."

Amis is able to treat other characteristic themes and subjects in this novel. One that seems to have a particular hold on him at this time is the publishing of bad poetry, a subject he also touches on in *Difficulties with Girls* and *The Russian Girl* (1992), as well as the earlier story "Dear Illusion" (1972). Another favorite subject is the gradation of morality, usually discussed in a style that mirrors the thought process behind the decision. Harry tells Desmond about unconscious motivation: "We do quite enough we know the reasons for without having to start worrying about what we do that we don't know the reasons for, in other words when we do something for a reason we don't know about it's the same morally as not doing it for that reason" (*Folks,* 100). That makes everything quite clear, if read out loud. Another subject of Amis's later novels is the ruminations accompanying old age. Harry looks at the garden of the house where he grew up: "[A] place where childhoods and adolescences were got through like so many terms of military service, or were they just the scene of a string of vague but luminous wonders, bits of emotions, some of it glad, some of it miserable, remembered when the occasion was long forgotten?" (167). What is interesting here is that in the first section, Harry seems to be agreeing with Larkin's antiromantic judgment in his poem "I Remember, I Remember," but in the second part, he admits the possibility of a quasi-Wordsworthian remembrance of things past, both good and ill. Amis also seems to make some concessions in the war between the sexes. When Clare tends the bloody and bedraggled Fiona, the narrator comments on "the superiority and seniority of the sex that has always had to do the rough work, the real work, the clearing up of the sick and the shit and the afterbirth and the dead bodies while the men think and create art" (229). If these thoughts are actually meant to be connected with Clare, then the last clause must be taken ironically; given that the only art to which we are exposed in the novel is Freddie's, perhaps the phrase is ironic, no matter whose it is.

The new element in this novel is the tenderness that pervades the reflections of the main characters, particularly Clare, about the nature of love. Harry is tempted to shout, at one point, "that nobody *just happened* to love anybody" (*Folks,* 31), which is not merely a protest against a cliché. If love grows into mere companionability, then even that is not to be shunned. As Clare muses about her dead husband, "What she missed above all was not him actually being there but herself expecting him back from work or anywhere, him coming in and the two of them starting to talk" (57). She later tells Harry that they both have come to realize "how important it is to be used to someone" (221). In a sense, this realization might seem a retreat, a defeat, yet there is not a hint of that in the text. Howard declares that Harry lives unconsciously, "In a dream, goes about in a dream, like so many of them" (191). But what gives this dream its reality, as well as its generosity, is the acceptance of the small pleasures that life can bring, as well as trying to ameliorate its vicissitudes, and protesting its inanities. "You've got a stake in Mrs. Thatcher's Britain," Harry tells Freddie at the end of the novel, not without a large modicum of irony (246). These "folks" might not indeed end up inheriting England, but at least they will take care of each other.

We Are All Guilty

This novella (1991) is perhaps Amis's most tendentious work of fiction. In a brief foreword, he claims of the novel's young protagonist, about whom Amis had written a teleplay in the 1970s, that "I cared more about him than any of my previous male characters that I can remember."[22] This may well be the case, for the characterization of Clive Rayner is the best part of what is otherwise a predictably characteristic philippic against the prevailing sociological Zeitgeist, which has abolished personal guilt and responsibility in favor of indicting a person's environment—societal, familial, religious—for any crimes he or she commits. Many of Amis's straw villains make an appearance, including a vacuously nattering social worker and a suavely modern clergyman. What makes the novella worth reading is the dull integrity with which Amis invests Clive, making this art instead of merely a tract.

The work begins almost conventionally, with a standard description of Clive's neighborhood—a tip-off that Amis here is not working in his usual fictional territory, the relationships between human beings as chiefly represented in their speech, whether external or internal. All the same, Amis generates a suitably blunted voice for depicting the world as perceived by Clive through indirect discourse: "By the time they went outside it was dark, but most of the shops had lights on and there were buses and stuff" (*We Are All Guilty*, 22). As his mother tells him, Clive is a bit thick. He is an example of the representative youth in the latter days of Mrs. Thatcher's Britain, unemployed, almost unemployable, and with no desire ever to be employed. What saves Clive at first, perhaps for himself and certainly for the reader, is his complete lack of self-pity over his circumstances.

Yet the petty crimes necessary to support himself, along with a general boredom and hopelessness that he feels, soon lead to the central events of the novel, Clive's breaking into a warehouse, and the subsequent accidental paralyzing fall of a night watchman. As Clive moves through the bowels of the criminal justice system for his crime, he is repeatedly told not to feel so bad about what happened; the clergyman who bails him out of jail advises him that "your sacred duty is to learn to forgive yourself, to get rid of those feelings of shame" (*We Are All Guilty*, 50). His social worker even more blatantly tells Clive that he is not in any way culpable: "It's society that's guilty. . . . We are all guilty" (60). Clive's heroism lies in his refusal to believe it. But no one will blame Clive, not even his formerly Calvinistic stepfather (perhaps the least plausible conversion in the story) or the victim of the crime himself. Clive wants to accept responsibility so that he can ask for forgiveness, but no one will let him, nor is there anywhere to turn. He goes back to the church in search of it, and there are faint echoes of Larkin's poem "Church Going" when Clive tells the clergyman that he doesn't know exactly why he returned to the church: "It's like I've forgotten, only there's nothing to remember" (91). The England of *Russian Hide-and-Seek* is here already.

What balances Amis's presentation is the virulence he gives to the other side of the argument, as voiced by the policemen who arrest Clive and taunt him as he goes through the judicial process. While everyone else is all forgiveness, they offer none: "You're scum, the pair of you, and you'll never hear about it, except from me" (*We Are All Guilty*, 37). After such knowledge, what forgiveness, indeed? The novel ends with a hint of redemption as Clive spread-eagles himself against a wall in a surprising use of Christian symbolism by Amis. As he finally goes home, the dawn promises "a beautiful day" (93), but readers still must wonder what kind of future is in store for Clive and the others. If he can build on his acceptance of his own burden, then perhaps society can fend for itself.

The Russian Girl

Although the novel takes place after the fall of the Soviet empire, the eponymous heroine of *The Russian Girl* (1992) comes from a nation that is for all intents and purposes indistinguishable from its tyrannical predecessor. Nevertheless the novel is much more successful than Amis's previous foray into Russian subjects, *Russian Hide-and-Seek,* mostly because Amis takes the advice of one of his own characters and writes a novel, not a political statement, and novels concern themselves with, in one character's words, "the life and death of individuals, or growing up and falling in love and getting married and being bereaved, or loss and grief and pain and remorse and courage and any of that old embarrassing stuff."[23] This is not to say that Amis does not ride various hobbyhorses, such as the sorry state of education, during the course of the novel. For instance, the protagonist, Richard Vaisey, is a Russian scholar who is fighting a losing battle to keep the study of Russian works in their original language in his school's curriculum. Trendy leftists also come in for a few knocks, as usual, this time in the person of Sir Stephen—one wants to fill in Spender, but the character's last name is never given, and Amis carefully makes his Sir Stephen an architect, not a poet. But on the whole, Amis concentrates on the perennial subjects that make the novel a novel: the conflicts that various characters have not only with their environment but chiefly with each other.

Indeed, the main plot, as several of Amis's do, resembles a fairy tale. In one respect, it is the story of the prince's (along with the princess) escape from the clutches of an evil witch—in this case, the ironically named Cordelia, Richard's wife. She is one of Amis's most memorable creations, a monster of affected selfishness. She has her own distinctive accent, which Amis transcribes every once in a while, to devastating effect (one of her imprecations is "Vug of, uzzhaul" [*Russian Girl,* 75]). Even so, Cordelia is allowed some sympathy in her portrayal. Her voice, as she explains, she adopted after she realized no one paid any attention to her. But even when she complains that Richard's leaving her has hurt her deeply, one is not sure whether this is all an act. And the actions she takes in revenge after Richard does leave her for "the Russian girl" (the phrase is Cordelia's) leave little doubt that her attempts to gain sympathy are as manipulative as any of her other actions. Like Susan in *Stanley and the Women,* Cordelia throws Richard's class origins in his face when he leaves.

The question that many of the characters in the book, as well as its readers, immediately want to ask is, why did Richard marry Cordelia in the first place? Sexual attractiveness is a large component of the answer, but just as important is Richard's unwillingness to engage with life on any meaningful level. That he and Cordelia have not had any children only serves to remind him about what he terms "the appalling underpopulation of his life" (*Russian Girl,* 227). What brings him alive is meeting the poet Anna Danilova, who from the beginning represents to Richard a way out: "[H]e was attracted to Anna Danilova at almost the precise moment that he had seen in her a threat to his ordered set of beliefs and secure life" (43). If Richard leaves Cordelia, he will have to sacrifice his comfortable life, because most of their money is Cordelia's. Yet many actions in his life now become truly volitional, as he feels after he and Anna have made love for the first time: "What had been new was how single-mindedly and totally he had acted as he wanted, and not out of habit or memory or with some indefinable but largish part of him otherwise engaged" (137). This is not to say that Richard undergoes any Lawrentian liberation. Like many other Amis characters, Richard makes frequent examinations of his conscience and often finds himself wanting, particularly in the area of personal honesty. "A little voice in his mind, more than one, murmured to him with questions, allegations, accusations, but to no avail—theoretical, conditional" (64). What makes Richard different from other Amis characters is that although these voices often make him feel like a shit, he is basically not a shit to begin with. He can regret the end of his marriage to Cordelia, "not for the life they had had together but for all they had not had" (289).

What prevents this fairy tale from an immediate happy ending, besides the thornbushes Cordelia throws in their path, is Anna's occupation—she is a poet, and an egregiously bad one. Once more, Amis takes up the subject of bad poetry and bad poets, but like Edward Potter in "Dear Illusion" and Freddie Caldecote in *The Folks That Live on the Hill,* Anna is portrayed sympathetically. Nonetheless, Amis hilariously reproduces some of her verse, which is awful. Richard's problem is how to tell her his evaluation, and initially he cannot. In this respect, the plot resembles a folktale Richard recalls "about the boy who won the goose or the sorcerer's ring by giving the wrong answer to the vital question, whatever it had been" (*Russian Girl,* 36). Here the boy wins a princess by giving his own wrong answer, by lying, which leads to the first moral quandary of the book: Why doesn't Richard tell her his true opinion of her poetry before he sleeps with her? Eventually Anna does learn something of the truth, and she vows never to write again, the possibility of which "horrified him more than any possibility that had occurred to him so far" (260). Even bad poets must feel free to write. Thus Richard lies again, which not only causes him to feel like a shit many times over but means the surrender of his professional self-respect. Even when they are living together near the end of the novel, Anna's work has not improved. Anna can, however, see through Richard and knows what he truly thinks of her work, and as she tells him, "But that lie told me how much you loved me, and it means I'll always love you" (293).

The expected end of any fairy tale is that they lived happily ever after, only in the case of Richard and Anna, one can only wonder. Crispin Radestky, Cordelia's ex-brother-in-law, functions as fairy godfather and gets Richard a job as an interpreter, so that Richard and Anna can survive without Richard's having to persist in academia. Yet can any long-term relationship exist in which one partner utterly despises the work that the other's vocation creates? One thread that runs through the novel is the ultimate importance of the writer's calling; as one character puts it, "being a writer is much more important to the person, to the writer, than being anything else is to the person being it" (*Russian Girl,* 169–70). Yet these are the words of a writer who has gone from producing political statements disguised as novels to writing spy thrillers about a Czarist secret agent (based on Amis's own ideas for a television show). Even Richard takes the destruction of all his notes for a book on Lermontov with surprising equanimity. Yet one suspects that being a writer was extremely important to Amis; one only has to look at his production during the last decade of his life. The glow with which *The Russian Girl* ends might not last long into the future, but while it exists, it is real and fierce.

You Can't Do Both

To anyone at all familiar with Amis's own life, *You Can't Do Both* will immediately seem above all else an autobiographical work. Both Amis and the novel's hero, Robin Davies, grow up as the sole focus of their parents' attentions; Amis does give Robin an older brother and sister, but they are not around for Robin's most formative years, especially puberty. Both their fathers read detective novels, have renounced the faiths of their youth, and take an inordinate interest in their sons' personal affairs, particularly in their sex lives. Both Amis and Robin love jazz, attend a solid school in London, go up to Oxford on a scholarship, serve in World War II, marry their pregnant girlfriends (who are very young when first met), embark on teaching careers in provincial universities, and are not particularly monogamous. Amis puts in some key differences; both Robin's parents die much earlier in his life than Amis's did, and Robin is a classics scholar, albeit one with tastes resembling Amis's: Robin, for instance, wants to subtitle Xenophon's *Anabasis* "How to Fuck Up a Good Story."[24] Yet to read *You Can't Do Both* exclusively autobiographically would be a mistake; it is rather an exploration of how someone very much like Amis came to be the way he is. The largest reason for that would seem to be his father.

Thomas Davies intrusively examines every area of his son's life; even at the age of 14, Robin is asked about his morning bowel movements. His father is most dictatorial when it comes to Robin's personal life and friends. The novel's title refers to an incident when Robin accepts a friend's invitation to tea on the same day his family is supposed to go out in the evening. Even though Robin protests that there is plenty of time to attend both events, his father insists, "You can't do both" (*You Can't Do Both*, 27). This unreasonable demand fires Robin's rebellion. When Jeremy Carpenter, the son of his mother's friend (who is thus parentally acceptable even though he is gay), introduces Robin to the works of W. H. Auden, D. H. Lawrence, William Blake, and Homer Lane, Robin is able to accept their message without totally buying into their works. As Jeremy puts their message, "You can't have too much of a good thing" (69). Later on, he will admit to Robin that "all that sacredness-of-desire stuff was just queer propaganda" (159). But at the moment, it fits in with an important aspect of Robin's personality, one that is always ready for any opportunity. As his brother tells him, "Good old O. O. Davies Dad used to call you, standing for Options Open" (220). For Robin, these options are usually sexual.

The other way in which Robin's father is so influential is because he refuses to inculcate in Robin any belief in organized religion because of the way he was raised; "he had God and the prophets shoved down his throat when he was a youngster" is the way his mother puts it, using the same phrase Amis does of his own father in *Memoirs* (*You Can't Do Both*, 42). Thus Robin, using some of Amis's own previously stated reasons, argues fiercely with a cleric about the existence of God: "He can't exist without being a shit, and I wouldn't dream of saying flatly he doesn't exist, just that the world and everything in it are indistinguishable from a world et cetera in which he doesn't exist" (172). The problem then arises that without such a belief, it becomes almost impossible to enforce a set of moral precepts, a failing for which Thomas Davies asks deathbed forgiveness of Robin. Raised in such an age, Robin's own motto becomes "you never know" (209).

Thus Robin has few internalized barriers to compel morality. Robin's brother tells him that one reason enforcing monogamy is "reluctance to feel a shit." He adds a qualifier that almost certainly applies to Robin: "I realize some people don't mind feeling a shit and some may even like it" (*You Can't Do Both*, 227). Robin's capacity for feeling guilt or even admitting it is extremely limited. His reluctant process of conscience inventory is described with a striking metaphor: "With the deliberation of some shitty Dickens mercer turning through swatches of cloth at a rotten old textile fair, he set about examining his motives" (161). Yet even though he is not particularly fond of any scrupulosity, Robin almost cannot help himself. On the one hand, he is trying to live up to (or down to) his own era's image of what a man should do, which leads to some convoluted moral reasoning. "It had even occurred to him that sticking firmly to one girl could be unethically used to obtain exemption from the sometimes gruelling task of promiscuity" (149).

Nevertheless, Robin is strongly attracted to Nancy Bennett, and while this attraction has a strong sexual component, it also clear that in his own way, Robin loves her, even though he is reluctant to admit even the possibility to himself. At the moral center of the book, his refusal to let Nancy go through with an abortion, Robin acquits himself through his love for Nancy, but he never states it as such consciously to himself. At one point, he looks up the meaning of the word *curettage*, the scientific name for the procedure, and the description causes him "to gasp and swallow for a minute or so while moisture issued from his eyes" (*You Can't Do Both*, 235). The use of indirect discourse from Robin's viewpoint will not allow the narrator to employ the simple phrase "He cried." Even though Robin ends up doing the right thing by marrying Nancy, he still remains a selfish sod; when his mother tells his in-laws, "Look after number one, that's all you can trust him to do" (275), it is not for rhetorical effect. She means it.

At some points, Robin feels as if he is in a novel. Nancy becomes pregnant after the two have unprotected sex immediately after Robin learns about his father's terminal illness. Later Robin muses that his need for sex at that particular moment was like something from "a deep, irremediably pissy book by D. H. Lawrence out of Bernard Shaw and celebrating the dark gods of the abdomen and the bleeding Life Force" (*You Can't Do Both*, 198). Later on, when we see Robin teaching in a "literally redbrick building" (291), it is after he has been sitting in his office making faces; now the novel is *Lucky Jim*. When Robin goes to London to conduct one of his many affairs, the novel (hero as unfaithful shit) could be anything from *One Fat Englishman* to *The Green Man*. And when Nancy surprises Robin at the hotel, the possibilities range from *The Egyptologists* to *Jake's Thing* (hero as unfaithful shit getting a well-deserved and totally unexpected comeuppance). What makes *You Can't Do Both* different is what accompanies Nancy's revelation, an action that Jean Lewis performs in *That Uncertain Feeling:* a backhanded slap by Nancy to Robin's face. Echoing the title of the novel, she tells him, referring to their family, "You can have the three of us, or you can have everyone else. Not both" (305). In a sense, this scene is, as Eric Jacobs contends, Amis's apology to Hilly Bardwell, but it also caps Amis's entire novelistic career as far as the theme of marital infidelity goes. We are no longer in *Lucky Jim,* and this is no normal fairy tale. Whether that slap can turn a frog into a human being is unresolved. That it should is pretty plainly—and finally—evident.

The Biographer's Moustache

Amis's last novel (1995) was evidently inspired by Eric Jacobs's researches into Amis's own life. But, as could be predicted, Amis's fictional musings on the problems faced by biographers and their subjects is far removed from such postmodern works as Vladimir Nabokov's *The Real Life of Sebastian Knight* (1941) or Steven Millhauser's *Edwin Mullhouse* (1972). The novel is even fairly far removed from Amis's own autobiographical novels such as *You Can't Do Both* in that none of the characters is particularly identifiable in any way with the author. The only similarities between Jimmie Fane, the biographical subject, and Kingsley Amis are their general age (Jimmie is slightly older) and that both started their careers as poets but became better known as novelists. Jimmie's background is far more upper-class, he has been married four times, has published only 6 novels (as opposed to Amis's 22), and is an unregenerate snob. Like Amis, Jimmie is particular about language, but in persnickety ways that Amis did not countenance.[25] Gordon Scott-Thompson is both unambitious and somewhat undersexed, or so at least he feels. The latter matter marks somewhat of a departure in an Amis protagonist. Yet we are fairly certain that in *The Biographer's Moustache* we are in what could be called late Amis-land. Gordon gets on a bus, for instance, that is "apparently reserved for winners and runners-up in some pan-European repulsiveness contest."[26]

The subject of the novel, however, is a characteristic one: class snobbery. The title facial hair, according to Jimmie, marks Gordon as a member of the middle class. Jimmie was born into the upper classes and is always trying to ascend into higher realms (he quotes Evelyn Waugh on snobbery with approval)—thus his assiduous bum kissing at his club and his disparaging remarks to Gordon. The same class loyalty is true for Gordon. When Gordon later calls Jimmie "that toffy-nosed old twit" (*Biographer's Moustache*, 220), Gordon is using a middle-class phrase that Robin Davies's father has abbreviated to "TNT" (*You Can't Do Both*, 113). In this muted but no less heated class war, the trophies are Jimmie's and Gordon's women. Gordon has an affair with Joanna, Jimmie's wife, an action Jimmie has warned Gordon against, solely on grounds of their differing classes. Jimmie battles against Gordon by getting him and his quondam girlfriend, Louise, invited to a weekend at the Duke of Dulwich's (Amis is never subtle in the names he provides for his aristocratic characters), in the hopes that the duke will make a pass at Louise. The duke does, and he and Louise are eventually married, a true example of hypergamy, as Louise tells Gordon, but it is not really a triumph for Jimmie because Gordon was never that involved with Louise to begin with (in this respect, Gordon resembles Douglas Yandell, the narrator of *Girl, 20*). Gordon has nonetheless fallen in love with Joanna, but she breaks off their relationship on what seems to be the very sensible grounds of their age—she is in her fifties, Gordon in his forties. Their relationship does seem to be a genuine one, based not only on physical attraction—Gordon is not all that undersexed—but also on emotional tenderness. As Joanna tells Gordon, "A hug says more than a fuck any day" (*Biographer's Moustache*, 121).

The other main conflicts in the novel involve integrity. One subplot revolves around the present circumstances of Madge Warner, an old girlfriend of Jimmie's, whom he threw over for his first wife, who was much more well-off and well connected than Madge. Gordon is able to wrangle some money out of Jimmie via Joanna to make Madge's last years more comfortable. Even more important is the issue of why Gordon has chosen to write about Jimmie Fane. There is no question here of identification between writer and subject or literary transference; as a literary journalist, Gordon has selected a writer who appears to be a fit subject for a revival, which could benefit both subject and writer in both pocketbook and reputation. Almost everyone queries Gordon on the point of what he really thinks about Jimmie's works. Gordon's private appraisal of Jimmie's oeuvre is not overwhelmingly positive. Thus it is extremely unlikely that Gordon, or "Mr. Valiant-for-Sodding-Truth" (*Biographer's Moustache*, 125), as Joanna calls him, will be favorable about Jimmie's works, or his life, when it comes to that, even though some of the revelations that Gordon learns are not particularly shocking, particularly for the 1990s. Yet Jimmie, when presented with an excerpted article that reveals his character faults, gives it his full approval because "These days the public *like* to think of an artist as a shit" (250). Jimmie, however, will not allow publication of an accompanying article critical of his work. But by this time, it has all become moot; Gordon has given up his task because his subject has become so unappealing to him, particularly in the way Jimmie almost revels in Gordon's revelations. As Gordon tells him, "You're not a reluctant shit and certainly not an unconscious shit, you're a self-congratulatory shit" (267).

On first reading, Amis's last novel can feel like somewhat of a letdown; at the end, nothing is concluded for Gordon except that he has learned about the hazards of writing about someone you neither admire nor respect. But on reflection, that is precisely what Amis is trying to get across. After musing about his middle-class childhood and upbringing in *You Can't Do Both,* Amis shows in his last novel, as he did in his first, a representative of the "lower orders" battling the pretentiousness and artificiality in modern society. But now the weight of experience is behind him. At one point, Gordon is almost ironically referred to as the standard-bearer for "a whole dismal army of buck-toothed scholarship boys" (*Biographer's Moustache,* 269). But, as Madge Walker tells him, "It's character that counts, the way one was born" (224). It is also, one might add, the middle-class virtues that are instilled during childhood and adolescence that sustain one throughout life, virtues such as "consistency of character, logical behaviour, reliability, sense of duty," which become, as Gordon says, "moral qualities" (201). In *Lucky Jim,* these virtues are not considered as Jim Dixon makes his triumphal fairy-tale escape to London, but without them, his escape will be neither pleasant nor long lasting. Gordon has no such prospect before him, yet his future might be just as favorable. Earlier in the book, Gordon tells his editor that his work on Jimmie will show how "decent writing" (28) can succeed despite its unpalatable subject matter. Now Gordon needs a decent subject for both his own life and any life he may write.

Chapter Five
Thinking about Amis

When Kingsley Amis died, one hoped that some kind of perspective could be gained from which it would be possible to view his career without the intervention of personal or political passions. Opinions about him, however, were as divided as they were during his life. Paul Gray, in Amis's obituary in *Time,* declared that "the British decades between 1955 and 1995 should in fairness be called the Amis era."[1] Yet a month later, D. J. Taylor observed, "We don't want a new Amis. We had our doubts about the old one."[2] The problem of placing Amis is much as he described the problem of placing Kipling, whose literary merits "are not yet enough appreciated, disentangled enough from the characteristics of the 'figure' " (*Rudyard Kipling,* 114). Even if the years since Kipling's death have not afforded enough time for objectivity, the attempt must nevertheless be made in Amis's case. Few dispute Amis's significance as a writer: his influence as a prose stylist in both his novels and his critical works has been widespread (although recently comic novelists in England have been described as the children of Martin, not Kingsley, Amis). But as Amis himself would have contended, the ultimate question is not whether Amis was important. Rather, was he good?

Reasons for this question's being answered in the negative can be grouped in two broad categories. The first is one originally noted by David Lodge and Malcolm Bradbury. Broadly speaking, Amis can be located in the "realist" tradition of British novelists, as opposed to the "experimental" tradition, which reached its height in the great modernists such as Virginia Woolf and James Joyce. Richard Bradford, among others, has shown that Amis cannot be pigeonholed as a mere premodernist comic realist; his methodology is more complex than that. Nevertheless, as John Rodden has shown in *The Politics of Literary Reputation* (1989), "experimental" writers, broadly speaking, are regarded more highly and thus taught much more widely than "realistic" writers such as George Orwell.[3] The second reason is linked to the first. Amis is primarily a comic novelist, and the prejudice against comedy as a mode worthy of merit extends from the academy to the Academy Awards. Consider the authors extolled by F. R. Leavis in *The Great Tradition.* Can anything be more impossible to imagine than a comic novel by Joseph Conrad or George Eliot? Leavis's snide expulsion of Fielding from this tradition is well known and probably inspired Amis's own pledge of allegiance to Fielding in *I Like It Here*. Many modern advocates of Amis have successfully argued that Amis's fundamental seriousness is inextricably linked with his comedy; as Bradford says, Amis's style "is serious *because* it is funny."[4]

Although the question of the ultimate value of comedy cannot be answered here, it is closely linked to an attack that has been made against Amis by a wide range of critics. According to D. J. Taylor, for instance, Amis "robbed the English comic novel of . . . a moral sense"; his chief crime is a "want of moral seriousness" (Taylor, 63–64). The language here betrays its Leavisite origins.[5] Even though critics such as John McDermott have argued that Amis is a moralist (McDermott even subtitling his study of Amis *An English Moralist*), the point does not seem to have sunk in, and it is worth making again: Amis is worthy of study—good, if that is the necessary term—precisely because of his fundamental moral seriousness, which he manages to engage in "without," as Garnet Bowen thinks of Fielding, "the aid of evangelical huffing and blowing" (*I Like It Here,* 167). As Amis once unabashedly stated, "I've always been a moralist."[6] The original title for *That Uncertain Feeling* was *The Moral Man.* Clive James, one of Amis's most perceptive readers, says that Amis "is so plainly a moralist."[7] Amis declared that "the prime literary subject" is "relations between human beings" (*Amis Collection,* 179), and it is in these relations and the ensuing choices that morality lies.

In his fiction, Amis begins with the basic elements of the morality play, and of the commedia dell'arte, for that matter—character types. Dale Salwak speaks of "an Amis archetype,"[8] and Amis himself talks about "my favorite types" (James, 23). They include a wide array (this list is not meant to be all-inclusive): the Hero-Shit (John Lewis and Garnet Bowen, mild; Patrick Standish, Roger Micheldene, Ronnie Appleyard, Roy Vandervane, Maurice Allington, Jake Richardson, Stanley Duke, Alun Weaver, Jimmie Fane, these last shading into what James calls the "supershit" [22]); the Hollow Man (Douglas Yandell, Richard Vaisey, Gordon Scott-Thompson); the Gorgon (Margaret Peel, Lady Baldock, Sylvia Korocheno, Nowell Hutchinson, Désirée Caldecote, Cordelia Vaisey); the Learned Fraud (the Welches, Dr. Best, Trish Collings); the Long-Suffering Woman, often a mother (Jean Lewis, Barbara Bowen, Helene Bang, Catherine Casement, Rhiannon Weaver, Nancy Davies); the Sympathetic Gay (Max Hunter, Colonel Manton, Damon Lancewood, Jeremy Carpenter); the Upper-Class Fairy Godfather or Brother (Gore-Urquart, Julian Omerod, Chummy Baldock, Crispin Radetsky); the Naif (Jenny Bunn, Peter Furneaux, Brian Leonard, Hubert Anvil, Harry Caldecote), this type shading into the Holy Fool (Tim Vatcher, Freddie Caldecote); the Trendy Clergyman (Father Colgate, Tim Sonnenschein, Robin Foster); the Weak Father (Tobias Anvil, Mr. Furneaux, Sergei Petrovsky). Often enough, the plot that moves these characters, particularly in the case of a happy ending (*Lucky Jim, I Want It Now, The Russian Girl*), is that of a fairy tale. Amis also often centers his works around one vice, as happens in the morality play, such as anger in *One Fat Englishman* or selfishness in *The Green Man*. All these relatively crude fictional tools seem to promise a very unsubtle result, which, of course, is precisely what comedy is often arraigned as being. What makes Amis's novels worthy of further study is the way he makes these fairly broad ingredients and plots, combined with a realistic mode, into the complex products that are his often misunderstood novels.

Amis's main tool is the indeterminate point of view he adopts in his novels. The free indirect discourse, as well as first-person narration, destabilizes the readers' relationship with the main characters. This destabilization is often presaged by the narrative uncertainty with which so many of his novels and chapters begin. Where are we? Who is speaking? In the case of *Stanley and the Women,* who is narrating? Once readers must cognitively place themselves within the terms of the plot, they are faced with the further, and much more difficult, problem of deciding how to take the characters. As Martin Green says, Amis "insists there is no comfortable position for the reader to assume to his subject-matter."[9] Much of the argument about Amis's fiction, whether by its detractors or its advocates, is about how we are to take these characters. Amis further complicates the process by seeming to endorse some of the views that his characters voice. Or does he? In his essay refuting such an identification with his main characters, "Real and Made-Up People," Amis claims that his heroes are "vehicles of . . . self-criticism"; they enable the novelist "to see more clearly, and judge more harshly, his own weaknesses and follies. . . . he may be helped to acquire tolerance for them in others" (*Amis Collection,* 5). This declaration is not, pace Richard Bradford, ironic or comic (Bradford, 31). It seems entirely sincere. Amis thus implicitly asks his readers "to see more clearly and judge more harshly" his characters' flaws. This is the real underlying meaning of the question that the speaker poses at the end of Amis's poems "Aberdarcy: The Main Square" and "Aberdarcy: The Chaucer Road": "What about you?" (*Collected*

Poems, 105, 116). Morality implies a judge, and such judgment, at least since Jesus' admonitions about first stones, implies a two-way judging. And because there is no Last Judge either divine or narrative in Amis's fiction, outside and beyond the plot, readers have to judge. Not only do we judge these characters, we judge ourselves, because we will share in some of the vices as well as the virtues the characters exhibit. As Amis puts it, he hopes "the reader will perhaps accommodate the writer in the same parallel process of self-discovery" (*Amis Collection,* 5).

The problem with any discussion of morality in fiction, whether the moral tradition Leavis discusses in *The Great Tradition* or morality in Amis's novels, is that the term becomes relatively imprecise once its theological ramifications have been removed. How, for instance, is Jane Austen's morality like that of D. H. Lawrence? (Emma Woodhouse, meet Oliver Mellors.) This imprecision leads to nebulous talk about "moral seriousness" and countercharges of evangelism. Amis—or Leavis, for that matter—rarely talks about sin. For Amis particularly, the difficulty is as George Orwell described it: "The real problem of our time is to restore the sense of absolute right and wrong when the belief that it used to rest on—that is, the belief in personal immortality—has been destroyed."[10] This is the fear that William Amis revealed to his son (as Robin Davies's father did to him)—that his refusal to countenance his son's religious education meant that his son's moral education and development were stunted and imperiled. This is the real absence at the core of Amis's fiction, and perhaps another reason for his antitheism. How do we live a moral life not only without the rewards and punishments of religion but without evidence that the universe is structured morally? In this *aporia* lies the darkness that lies at the heart of so much of Amis's fiction after 1960, the darkness that gives rise to his comic infernos. Meaning may be absent from life, but it can be given to art.

The other main reason that makes Amis a major writer—and belies his label as a simple realist—is his obsession with words. On the one hand, it led to his greatest weakness, his dismissal of any work that uses words for their own sake, instead of as bearers of articulate meaning. This bias was inextricably linked with the connection of culture and class in his mind, which goes back to his days at Oxford, where he first received the impression that the proper study of literature was the property of some exclusive club—lower-middle-class applicants from suburban London need not apply. When listening to a group of American academics at Princeton name-drop cultural figures of the late 1950s, he grumbled "Bloody Oxford!" sotto voce.[11] To Amis such affectations were bound up with the literary use of words for their sound or associations, not their meaning, and drew attention to the writer, not the subject. Thus for Amis *Lolita* is not bad because of its subject matter, pedophilia, but because its author is logophilic, entranced with the use of words for their sounds, as shown in Humbert's indefatigable alliterating, even when the subject is his wife's dead body. Such a critical attitude is perhaps defensible, but one gets the impression that at times Amis had such fun in adopting it (describing John D. MacDonald as a better writer than Saul Bellow, for instance) that the mask soon fitted so well it was impossible to remove. His reactions to the fiction of his son Martin, a true word lover and player, were supposedly not as harsh as often reported.

In his own fiction, Amis's respect for the syntactic value of words is almost absolute. Characters are judged not only by their acts but, as critics have pointed out, by their speech, which is closely interrogated for its meanings, often by the central character. Clichés are dissected and ridiculed, figures of speech exploded. In portraying his characters' thoughts, Amis uses language as a tool to describe not only their motivations but their rationalizations, their self-exculpations. "This familiar regressive series" (*Take a Girl like You*, 244), as Patrick Standish's thoughts are called, often leads to the moral vacuum at the center of the character's motivations, a vacuum increasingly associated with death, which is why so many of Amis's heroes (Patrick Standish, Maurice Allington, Dai Evans, and Robin Davies, for instance) find themselves hurrying to a sexual encounter after meeting or thinking about death.

But even in linguistic matters, Amis revealed, if not a capacity to change, then a willingness to see the other side. At the beginning of his career, words are supreme. In *Lucky Jim*, when Christine tells Jim that he has said what she means, only "in different words," Jim replies, "Words change the thing" (144). But such certainty fades with time. In *The Russian Girl*, Richard Vaisey thinks that if Anna's poetry reading succeeds, "It would encourage the notion that there could be a sphere of meaning beyond language" (105). Of course there is such a sphere, one that Richard enters when he falls in love with Anna and lies about his opinion of her poetry. In *You Can't Do Both*, Robin and Nancy share clichés just before she is to undergo an abortion, and Robin then thinks, "It was as if words had been the wrong idea from the start" (249). Sometimes words are not enough, and the word can never change the thing. Jimmie Fane, in Amis's last novel, *The Biographer's Moustache*, is the first linguistically precise Amis character who is also portrayed as a snob and pedant—in Amis's term, a "wanker." (The other slang meaning of the term "wanker" should be recalled here.)

Amis was a Victorian in his work habits, a lover of the eighteenth century in its fiction, and found his subject matter in the twentieth century. He was an empirical realist whose works could at stretches be cognitively puzzling. Like many British authors before him (Rupert Brooke and George Orwell, for instance), he started on the Left and moved gradually to the Right, much farther than any of his predecessors. He had no religious beliefs, yet he regretted his loss and was able to regard perhaps the most religious twentieth-century British author, G. K. Chesterton, as a personal favorite. He was a moralist in his fiction whose personal life was, at times, anything but moral.[12] He was brutal in print to equals and superiors, courteous in real life to those to whom he did not have to be. He prized reason and yet often found himself prey to irrational fears. Above all, he was an entertainer who at all times made his readers think, not only on the intellectual but on the moral level, and for that reason, in an age of increasing irrationality, both mental and moral, he deserves to be studied and above all appreciated.

Notes and References

Preface

    1. This volume is entirely original, in the sense that I consulted Philip Gardner's otherwise fine study only after I had completed the bulk of my own. Certain observations nevertheless became duplicated, and for these the award of originality must go to Professor Gardner.
    2. This was the purpose of Amis's friend Paul Fussell in his study *The Anti-Egotist* (1995), but Fussell's knowledge of Amis's personality focused his field too narrowly.
    3. If my discussion of Amis's poetry seems proportionately small, it is because the subject is solidly handled in Jerry Bradley's "Kingsley Amis," in *The Movement: British Poets of the 1950s*, TEAS 502, ed. Kinley Roby (New York: Twayne, 1993), 26–43.

Chapter One

    1. Kingsley Amis, *What Became of Jane Austen? and Other Questions* (New York: Harcourt Brace Jovanovich, 1971), 192; hereafter cited in the text as *What Became of Jane Austen*.
    2. Kingsley Amis, *Memoirs* (New York: Summit, 1991), 6; hereafter cited in the text.
    3. Amis's adult attitude toward religion, particularly Christianity, was too combative to be called merely agnostic. When the Russian poet Yevgeny Yevtushenko asked Amis if he believed in God, Amis gave the infamous answer, "It's more that I hate him" (*Memoirs*, 237). Basically he agreed with William Empson and those who held that because of the manner in which He appeared to allow suffering to go on in the world, "the traditional God of Christianity [is] very wicked" (*What Became of Jane Austen*, 216).
    4. Eric Jacobs, *Kingsley Amis: A Biography* (London: Hodder and Stoughton, 1995), 49; hereafter cited in the text.
    5. Kingsley Amis, *Collected Poems: 1944–1979* (New York: Viking, 1980), 103 (emphasis added); hereafter cited in the text.
    6. Andrew Motion, *Philip Larkin: A Writer's Life* (New York: Farrar Straus Giroux, 1993), 69; hereafter cited in the text.
    7. Kingsley Amis, *Socialism and the Intellectuals* (London: Fabian Society, 1954), 1; hereafter cited in the text.
    8. Philip Larkin, *Selected Letters of Philip Larkin, 1940–1985*, ed. Anthony Thwaite (New York: Farrar Straus Giroux, 1992), 759; hereafter cited in the text.

9. Quoted in Blake Morrison, *The Movement* (London: Methuen, 1980), 81; hereafter cited in the text.
10. W. Somerset Maugham, "Books of the Year," *Sunday Times*, 25 December 1955, 4.
11. Kingsley Amis, "The Day of the Moron," *Spectator*, 1 October 1954, 408.
12. Lindsay Anderson, in Tom Maschler, ed., *Declaration* (London: MacGibbon and Kee, 1957), 166.
13. During a series of hallucinatory dreams after an operation in 1982, Amis thought he saw the manuscript of a work by himself, Kenneth Tynan, and one of his sons. Later he figured the subject of such a collaboration could have been a musical about George Orwell.
14. John Osborne, *Look Back in Anger* (New York: Bantam, 1959), 104.
15. Paul Johnson, "Lucky Jim's Political Testament," *New Statesman*, 12 January 1957, 36.
16. Conquest began a subsequent planned project, *Peach Key* (an obscenity in Bulgarian), in 1960. Amis last looked at this tale of men running away from women in October 1993 but decided against completing it.
17. Andrew Lycett, *Ian Fleming* (London: Weidenfeld and Nicolson, 1995), 445; hereafter cited in the text.
18. When Amis briefly summarized the plot to Margaret Thatcher on meeting her around this time, she shot back, "Get yourself another crystal ball!" (*Memoirs*, 318).
19. After Amis's death, an unseemly row broke out over the editorship of Amis's letters between Martin Amis and Eric Jacobs, who threatened to publish a diary he kept during Amis's last illness.

Chapter Two

1. Many of the chapters in *Memoirs* had first appeared in Amis's collection *What Became of Jane Austen? and Other Questions* (1970). It is interesting to compare the different versions of some of these chapters. For instance, the conclusion to the essay on Yevtushenko is much more lenient when rewritten after the fall of the Soviet Union.
2. Kingsley Amis, *On Drink* (New York: Harcourt Brace Jovanovich, 1973), 41; hereafter cited in the text.
3. Kingsley Amis, *Every Day Drinking* (London: Hutchinson, 1983), 74.
4. Kingsley Amis, ed. *Harold's Years* (London: Quartet Books, 1977), 7.
5. Kingsley Amis, *An Arts Policy?* (London: Centre for Policy Studies, 1979), 1; hereafter cited in the text.
6. Kingsley Amis, *The Amis Collection: Selected Non-fiction, 1954–1990* (Harmondsworth: Penguin, 1991), 59; hereafter cited in the text as *Amis Collection*.

NOTES AND REFERENCES

7. Margaret Drabble, *Angus Wilson* (London: Secker and Warburg, 1995), 482.
8. Kingsley Amis, *Rudyard Kipling* (London: Thames and Hudson, 1975), 22; hereafter cited in the text.
9. Kingsley Amis, *The King's English* (London: HarperCollins, 1997), 177; hereafter cited in the text.
10. Kingsley Amis, *Collected Short Stories,* rev. ed. (London: Hutchinson, 1987), 110; hereafter cited in the text.
11. Kingsley Amis, *Mr. Barrett's Secret and Other Stories* (London: Hutchinson, 1993), 22; hereafter cited in the text as *Mr. Barrett's Secret.*
12. Kingsley Amis, ed. *The Amis Anthology* (London: Arena, 1989), 344; hereafter cited in the text.
13. D. J. Enright, ed. *Poets of the 1950's: An Anthology of New English Verse* (Tokyo: Kenkyusha, 1955), 17.
14. Kingsley Amis, ed. *The Pleasure of Poetry* (London: Cassell, 1990), 129; hereafter cited in the text.
15. Paul Fussell, *The Anti-egotist: Kingsley Amis, Man of Letters* (New York: Oxford University Press, 1994), 151.
16. Kingsley Amis, ed. *The New Oxford Book of Light Verse* (New York: Oxford University Press, 1978), viii.
17. Kingsley Amis, ed. *The Faber Popular Reciter* (London: Faber, 1978), 15; hereafter cited in the text.
18. Robert Conquest, ed. *New Lines* (1956; reprint, New York: Macmillan, 1967), xv.
19. Kingsley Amis, *A Frame of Mind* (Reading: University of Reading School of Art, 1953), 18; hereafter cited in the text.

Chapter Three

1. John Clute and Peter Nichols, *The Science Fiction Encyclopedia* (New York: St. Martin's, 1993), 28; hereafter cited in the text.
2. Kingsley Amis, ed. *The Golden Age of Science Fiction* (Harmondsworth: Penguin, 1983), 18; hereafter cited in the text as *Golden Age.*
3. Kingsley Amis, *New Maps of Hell* (New York: Harcourt, Brace, 1960), 26; hereafter cited in the text.
4. Sometimes this slant also skews Amis's interpretations. If Gulliver is, as Amis claims, "a pretty ordinary human being," then why does he get so taken in and over by the society of the Houyhnhms, which Amis describes as "a loveless, lifeless hell" (*Golden Age,* 12, 13)?
5. Frederik Pohl, in *Science Fiction of the 50's,* ed. Martin Greenberg and Joseph Olander (New York: Avon, 1979), xii.
6. Kingsley Amis, *The Alteration* (New York: Caroll and Graf, 1988), 26; hereafter cited in the text.

7. Kingsley Amis, *Russian Hide-and-Seek* (Harmondsworth: Penguin, 1981), 17; hereafter cited in the text.
8. George Orwell, *Nineteen Eighty-Four* (New York: Signet, 1961), 220.
9. In Douglas C. Greene, *John Dickson Carr: The Man Who Explained Miracles* (New York: Otto Penzler, 1995), 370; hereafter cited in the text.
10. John Dickson Carr, *The Three Coffins* (New York: Charter, n.d.), 160; hereafter cited in the text.
11. W. H. Auden, *The Dyer's Hand and Other Essays* (New York: Vintage, 1968), 151.
12. Kingsley Amis, *The Riverside Villa Murders* (Harmondsworth: Penguin, 1984), 18; hereafter cited in the text.
13. Kingsley Amis, *The Crime of the Century* (New York: Mysterious Press, 1989), vii; hereafter cited in the text.
14. Kingsley Amis, *The Green Man* (Chicago: Academy Chicago, 1986), 4; hereafter cited in the text.
15. Interestingly enough, in 1966 Henry Treece, a New Apocalyptic poet and historical novelist, published a novel entitled *The Green Man*. In this case, the title character is none other than Hamlet—or more specifically, Saxo Grammaticus's Amleth, prince of Jutland. Amleth himself is the Green Man, a fertility figure and a "more human" version of the King of the Wood, the Druid sacrificial king associated with the oak tree, who had to die when his reign was finished.
16. Kingsley Amis, *The James Bond Dossier* (New York: Signet, 1966), ix; hereafter cited in the text.
17. Here Amis is not quite accurate. He declares twice that Bond recognizes among artists only Botticelli and Da Vinci, but in *Moonraker,* for instance, Bond also makes allusions to Dali and Marie Laurencin.
18. Kingsley Amis (writing as Robert Markham), *Colonel Sun* (New York: Harper and Row, 1968), 65; hereafter cited in the text.
19. Kingsley Amis, *The Anti-death League* (New York: Ballantine, 1967), 289; hereafter cited in the text.

Chapter Four

1. Kingsley Amis, *Lucky Jim* (Harmondsworth: Penguin, 1992), 72; hereafter cited in the text.
2. Kingsley Amis, *That Uncertain Feeling* (Harmondsworth: Penguin, 1985), 7; hereafter cited in the text.
3. Margaret Drabble, ed., *The Oxford Companion to Literature,* rev. 5th ed. (Oxford: Oxford University Press, 1995), 25.
4. Kingsley Amis, *I Like It Here* (Harmondsworth: Penguin, 1968), 143, 144; hereafter cited in the text.

NOTES AND REFERENCES

5. *I Like It Here* is, as critics such as Norman Macleod have pointed out, partially a commentary on Greene's fiction and travel writing.

6. Another correspondence lies in Fielding's *The Journal of a Voyage to Lisbon* ([London: Penguin, 1996], 107), in which he calls Lisbon "the nastiest city in the world," a Dixonian judgment.

7. Henry Fielding, *Joseph Andrews* (Harmondsworth: Penguin, 1977), 30.

8. Kingsley Amis, *Take a Girl like You* (Harmondsworth: Penguin, 1962), 13; hereafter cited in the text.

9. This phrase forms the title of the best study of Amis's fictional uses of language.

10. Kingsley Amis, *One Fat Englishman* (New York: Summit, 1989), 20; hereafter cited in the text.

11. Kingsley Amis and Robert Conquest, *The Egyptologists* (London: Panther, 1975); hereafter cited in the text.

12. Kingsley Amis, *I Want It Now* (New York: Harcourt, Brace and World, 1969), 132; hereafter cited in the text.

13. Kingsley Amis, *Girl, 20* (New York: Summit, 1989), 16; hereafter cited in the text as *Girl.*

14. Kingsley Amis, *Ending Up* (New York: Penguin, 1976), 79; hereafter cited in the text.

15. Peter Parker, ed., *Readers' Guide to Twentieth Century Authors* (New York: Oxford University Press, 1996), 20.

16. Kingsley Amis, *Jake's Thing* (Harmondsworth: Penguin, 1980), 256, 71; hereafter cited in the text.

17. Kingsley Amis, *Stanley and the Women* (London: Hutchinson, 1984), 8; hereafter cited in the text.

18. Kingsley Amis, *The Old Devils* (New York: Perennial, 1988), 73; hereafter cited in the text.

19. Kingsley Amis, *Difficulties with Girls* (Harmondsworth: Penguin, 1989), 74; hereafter cited in the text.

20. One cannot help but think that Amis includes this reference to Fielding to somehow clarify or qualify the enthusiasm shown for Fielding's brand of fiction in *I Like It Here.*

21. Kingsley Amis, *The Folks That Live on the Hill* (Harmondsworth: Penguin, 1991), 193; hereafter cited in the text as *Folks.*

22. Kingsley Amis, *We Are All Guilty* (Harmondsworth: Viking/Reinhardt, 1991), 7; hereafter cited in the text.

23. Kingsley Amis, *The Russian Girl* (Harmondsworth: Viking, 1992), 169; hereafter cited in the text.

24. Kingsley Amis, *You Can't Do Both* (London: Hutchinson, 1994), 212; hereafter cited in the text.

25. For instance, Jimmie taunts Gordon with his pronunciation of *tissue* as "tish-you" instead of "tiss-you." In *The King's English,* Amis recommends

Gordon's, not Jimmie's, version. Jimmie is, to large extent, a "wanker," to use Amis's terms in that book: "prissy, fussy, prim, priggish" (*King's English*, 23), but not completely: both Amis and Jimmie complain about the spread of the glottal stop.

26. Kingsley Amis, *The Biographer's Moustache* (London: Flamingo, 1995), 70; hereafter cited in the text.

Chapter Five

1. Paul Gray, "The Irritable Young Man: Kingsley Amis, 1922–1995," *Time*, 6 November 1995, 87.
2. D. J. Taylor, "The Amis Legacy," *New Statesman and Society*, 15 December 1995, 64; hereafter cited in the text.
3. This hierarchy extends to genres as well. Drama, poetry, and fiction are taught, and more ephemeral, topical genres, such as the personal essay or criticism, are hardly taught at all. No full-length study of Amis, for instance, goes very much into *New Maps of Hell* or *The James Bond Dossier*.
4. Richard Bradford, *Kingsley Amis* (London: Edward Arnold, 1989), 106; hereafter cited in the text.
5. See the attacks on Amis by the Leavises in their *Dickens the Novelist* (New Brunswick, N.J.: Rutgers University Press, 1979), 141, 157. Not only was Amis a "pornographer," in this view, he was a Henry Gowan, the dilettante painter in Dickens's *Little Dorrit* (1857).
6. Dale Salwak, "An Interview with Kingsley Amis," *Contemporary Literature* 16 (Winter 1975): 6.
7. Clive James, "Profile 4: Kingsley Amis," *New Review* 1 (July 1974): 21; hereafter cited in the text.
8. Dale Salwak, *Kingsley Amis: Modern Novelist* (New York: Harvester-Wheatsheaf, 1992), 49.
9. Martin Green, *The English Novel in the Twentieth Century* (Boston: Routledge and Kegan Paul, 1984), 153.
10. George Orwell, *The Collected Essays, Journalism, and Letters*, vol. 3, ed. Sonia Orwell and Ian Angus (New York: Harcourt Brace Jovanovich, 1968), 100.
11. Russell Fraser, "Lucky Jim As I Remember Him," *Southern Review* 32 (1997): 783.
12. Fraser recounts how his friendship with Amis survived Amis's propositioning of Fraser's wife.

Selected Bibliography

PRIMARY SOURCES

Novels

Lucky Jim. London: Gollancz; New York: Doubleday, 1954.
That Uncertain Feeling. London: Gollancz, 1955; New York: Harcourt, Brace and World, 1956.
I Like It Here. London: Gollancz; New York: Harcourt Brace, 1958.
Take a Girl like You. London: Gollancz; New York: Harcourt, Brace and World, 1960.
One Fat Englishman. London: Gollancz, 1963; New York: Harcourt, Brace and World, 1964.
The Egyptologists (with Robert Conquest). London: Cape; New York: Random House, 1965.
The Anti-death League. London: Gollancz; New York: Harcourt, Brace and World, 1966.
Colonel Sun [Robert Markham, pseud.]. London: Cape; New York: Harper, 1968.
I Want It Now. London: Cape, 1968; New York: Harcourt, Brace and World, 1969.
The Green Man. London: Cape, 1969; New York: Harcourt, Brace and World, 1970.
Girl, 20. London: Cape, 1971; New York: Harcourt Brace Jovanovich, 1972.
Ending Up. London: Cape, 1973; New York: Harcourt Brace Jovanovich, 1974.
The Riverside Villa Murders. London: Cape; New York: Harcourt Brace Jovanovich, 1973.
The Alteration. London: Cape, 1976; New York: Viking, 1977.
Jake's Thing. London: Hutchinson, 1978; New York: Viking, 1979.
Russian Hide-and-Seek: A Melodrama. London: Hutchinson, 1980.
Stanley and the Women. London: Hutchinson, 1984; New York: Summit, 1985.
The Old Devils. London: Hutchinson; New York: Summit, 1987.
The Crime of the Century. London: Hutchinson, 1988; New York: Mysterious Press, 1989.
Difficulties with Girls. London: Hutchinson, 1988; New York: Summit, 1989.
The Folks That Live on the Hill. London: Hutchinson; New York: Summit, 1990.
We Are All Guilty. Harmondsworth: Viking/Reinhardt, 1991.

The Russian Girl. London: Hutchinson, 1992; New York: Viking, 1994.
You Can't Do Both. London: Hutchinson, 1994.
The Biographer's Moustache. London: Flamingo, 1995.

Short Stories

My Enemy's Enemy. London: Gollancz, 1962; New York: Harcourt, Brace and World, 1963.
Collected Short Stories. London: Hutchinson, 1980; rev. 1987.
Mr. Barrett's Secret and Other Stories. London: Hutchinson, 1993.

Poetry

Bright November. London: Fortune Press, 1947.
A Frame of Mind. Reading: University of Reading School of Art, 1953.
Kingsley Amis: No. 22. The Fantasy Poets. Oxford: Fantasy Press, 1954.
A Case of Samples (Poems 1945–1956). London: Gollancz, 1956; New York: Harcourt, Brace and World, 1957.
The Evans Country. Oxford: Fantasy Press, 1962.
A Look around the Estate (Poems 1957–1967). London: Cape, 1967; New York: Harcourt, Brace and World, 1968.
Collected Poems, 1944–1979. London: Hutchinson, 1979; New York: Viking, 1980.

Nonfiction

Socialism and the Intellectuals. Fabian Tract 304. London: Fabian Society, 1957.
New Maps of Hell: A Survey of Science Fiction. London: Gollancz, 1961; New York: Harcourt, Brace, 1960.
The James Bond Dossier. London: Cape; New York: New American Library, 1965.
Black Papers on Education. Manchester: Critical Quarterly Society, 1968–1975.
Lucky Jim's Politics. London: Conservative Political Centre, 1968.
What Became of Jane Austen? and Other Questions. London: Cape, 1970; New York: Harcourt Brace Jovanovich, 1971.
On Drink. London: Cape, 1972; New York: Harcourt Brace Jovanovich, 1973.
Rudyard Kipling and His World. London: Thames and Hudson, 1975; New York: Scribner's, 1976.
An Arts Policy? London: Centre for Policy Studies, 1979.
Every Day Drinking. London: Hutchinson, 1983.
How's Your Glass? London: Weidenfeld and Nicolson, 1984.
The Amis Collection: Selected Non-Fiction, 1954–1990. London: Hutchinson, 1990.
Memoirs. London: Century-Hutchinson; New York: Summit, 1991.
The King's English: A Guide to Modern Usage. London: HarperCollins, 1997.

SELECTED BIBLIOGRAPHY

Works Edited by Amis

Oxford Poetry 1949. With James Michie. Oxford: Blackwell, 1949.
Oscar Wilde: Poems and Essays. London: Collins, 1956.
Spectrum (I)–V. With Robert Conquest. London: Gollancz, 1961–1965; New York: Harcourt, Brace and World, 1962–1967.
G. K. Chesterton: Selected Stories. London: Faber, 1972.
Tennyson. Harmondsworth: Penguin, 1973.
Harold's Years: Impressions from the "New Statesman" and the "Spectator." London: Quartet, 1977.
The Faber Popular Reciter. London and Boston: Faber, 1978.
The New Oxford Book of Light Verse. Oxford and New York: Oxford University Press, 1978.
The Golden Age of Science Fiction. London: Hutchinson, 1983.
The Great British Songbook. With James Cochrane. London: Pavilion/Michael Joseph, 1986.
The Amis Anthology. London: Hutchinson, 1988.
The Pleasure of Poetry: From His "Daily Mirror" Column. London: Cassell, 1990.
The Amis Story Anthology: A Personal Choice of Short Stories. London: Hutchinson, 1992.

SECONDARY SOURCES

Bibliographies

Gohn, J. B. *Kingsley Amis: A Checklist*. Kent, Ohio: Kent State University Press, 1976.
Salwak, Dale. *Kingsley Amis: A Reference Guide*. Boston: G. K. Hall, 1978.

Interviews

Barber, Michael. "The Art of Fiction LIX: Kingsley Amis." *Paris Review* 16 (Winter 1975): 39–72.
James, Clive. "Profile 4: Kingsley Amis." *The New Review* 1 (July 1974): 21–28.
Salwak, Dale. "An Interview with Kingsley Amis." *Contemporary Literature* 16 (Winter 1975): 1–18.
———. "Kingsley Amis: Mimic and Moralist." In *Interviews with Britain's Angry Young Men*. San Bernadino: Borgo, 1984. An expansion of the previous item.

Books and Parts of Books

Bradbury, Malcolm. " 'No, Not Bloomsbury': The Comic Fiction of Kingsley Amis." In *No, Not Bloomsbury*, 201–18. New York: Columbia University

Press, 1988. Best single essay on Amis's novelistic career up to *The Old Devils*. Places Amis in the English tradition of comic realism.

Bradford, Richard. *Kingsley Amis*. London: Edward Arnold, 1989. Excellent study of Amis's fictional techniques and his place in literature, but weakened by a refusal to recognize the moral aspects of his work.

Bradley, Jerry. "Kingsley Amis." In *The Movement: British Poets of the 1950s*, 26–43. New York: Twayne, 1993. Solid discussion of the main themes in Amis's poetry.

Fussell, Paul. *The Anti-egotist: Kingsley Amis, Man of Letters*. New York and Oxford: Oxford University Press, 1994. Sound but ultimately unsatisfying depiction of Amis as a complete writer, written by a personal friend.

Gardner, Philip. *Kingsley Amis*. Boston: Twayne, 1981. Many good insights.

Green, Martin. "Kingsley Amis: The Protest against Protest." In *The English Novel in the Twentieth Century*, 133–67. Boston: Routledge and Kegan Paul, 1984. Some good points, but his description of Amis's career as moving from social realist to the "ruling class's jester" is absurd.

Jacobs, Eric. *Kingsley Amis: A Biography*. London: Hodder and Stoughton, 1995. Useful study of Amis's life; too reliant, however, on connections between the writer and his characters.

———. "The Authorized Biography." In *The Literary Biography*, ed. Dale Salwak, 130–36. Houndsmill: Macmillan, 1996. The advantages and dangers of writing the title work.

Lodge, David. "The Modern, the Contemporary, and the Importance of Being Amis." In *The Language of Fiction*, 243–367. New York: Columbia University Press, 1966. Seminal essay on the way Amis's use of language places him in the English literary tradition.

Macleod, Norman. "*This Familiar Regressive Series*: Aspects of Style in the Novels of Kingsley Amis." In *Edinburgh Studies in English and Scots*, ed. A. J. Aitken, et al., 121–43. London: Longman, 1971. Excellent study of the characteristic ways in which Amis uses language in depicting his characters' thoughts to reduce the "seriousness" of the humor.

McCabe, Bernard. "Looking for the Simple Life: Kingsley Amis's *The Antideath League*." In *Old Lines, New Forces: Essays on the Contemporary British Novel, 1960–1970*, ed. Robert K. Morris, 67–80. Rutherford, N.J.: Fairleigh Dickinson University Press, 1976. Emphasizes Amis's seriousness as a comic writer, using the title novel for proof.

McDermott, John. *Kingsley Amis: An English Moralist*. London: Macmillan; New York: St. Martin's, 1989. Debatable in individual judgments, but overall an impressive achievement, particularly in separating the writer from his characters.

Miller, Karl. "Kingsley and the Women." In *Authors*, 118–32. Oxford: Oxford University Press, 1989. Sensitive discussion of the narrator's place and Amis's use of "ventriloquism" in *Difficulties with Girls*.

SELECTED BIBLIOGRAPHY

Moseley, Merritt. *Understanding Kingsley Amis.* Columbia: University of South Carolina Press, 1993. Brief but useful overview, concentrating on the novels.
Rabinowitz, Rubin. "Kingsley Amis." In *The Reaction against Experiment in the English Novel, 1950–1960,* 38–63. New York and London: Columbia University Press, 1967. Valuable analysis of Amis's fictional tenets and his place in tradition as revealed in his occasional writings and early fiction.
Roberts, G. O. "Love and Death in an English Novel: *The Anti-death League* Investigated." In *A Festchrift for Edgar Ronald Seary,* ed. A. A. Macdonald, et al., 200–214. St. John's: Memorial University of Newfoundland, 1975. A solid reading of the main themes of the novel.
Salwak, Dale. *Kingsley Amis: Modern Novelist.* New York: Harvester-Wheatsheaf, 1992. Lucid and well-researched study of Amis's development as a novelist.
———. "Discovering Kingsley Amis." In *The Literary Biography,* ed. Dale Salwak, 80–85. Houndsmill: Macmillan, 1996. How the author's *Kingsley Amis: Modern Novelist* was written.
———, ed. *Kingsley Amis in Life and Letters.* New York: St. Martin's, 1991. Solid collection of essays about Amis's life and work.

Articles

Fraser, Russell. "Lucky Jim As I Remember Him." *Southern Review* 32 (1996): 783–92. Reminiscences, pleasant and unpleasant, by an old friend.
Hamilton, Kenneth. "Kingsley Amis, Moralist." *Dalhousie Review* 44 (1964): 339–47. One of the first essays to note that Amis's focus is moral and grounded in class awareness.
Hopkins, Robert. "The Satire of Kingsley Amis's *I Like It Here.*" *Critique* 8 (Spring–Summer 1966): 62–70. The novel satirizes F. R. Leavis's *The Great Tradition* and the author as so-called angry young man.
Hutchings, W. "Kingsley Amis's Counterfeit World." *Critical Quarterly* 19 (Summer 1977): 71–77. Sees *The Alteration* as a mostly successful use of genre fiction.
Macleod, Norman. "A Trip to Greenland: The Plagiarizing Narrator of Kingsley Amis's *I Like It Here.*" *Studies in the Novel* 17 (1985): 203–17. Unconvincing reading that posits *The Third Man* "as a source" for Amis's novel.
McDermott, John. "Kingsley and the Women." *Critical Quarterly* 27 (Autumn 1985): 65–71. Defines the title problem of *Jake's Thing* as accidie and persuasively maintains that the novel is not misogynistic.
Skinner, John. "Novelist as Mimic: A Sociolinguistic Study of Kingsley Amis." *Lore and Language* 8 (1989): 3–17. Excellent study from a linguistic standpoint of Amis's reproduction of his characters' speech.

Teachout, Terry. "A Touch of Class." *New Criterion* 7 (November 1988): 8–17. Defense of Amis vitiated by political tendentiousness and errors.

Voorhees, Richard. "Kingsley Amis: Three Hurrahs and a Reservation." *Queen's Quarterly* 79 (1972): 38–46. Disjointed essay that deplores Amis's forays into genre fiction while praising his first three novels.

Watson, George. "The Coronation of Realism." *Georgia Review* 41 (1987): 5–16. Argues that the emergence of Amis, along with those of William Golding and Iris Murdoch, marked the return to realism in English fiction at the accession of Elizabeth II.

———. "I Was Kingsley Amis." *The Hudson Review* 59 (1997): 610–18. Valediction about Amis's importance.

Wilmes, D. R. "When the Curse Begins to Hurt: Kingsley Amis and Satiric Confrontation." *Studies in Contemporary Satire* 5 (1978): 9–22. Interesting analysis of the narrative stance in Amis's novels as an aspect of satire.

Wolcott, James. "Kingsley Ransom." *New Yorker,* 30 October 1995, 52–57. Initially a defense of Amis against hostile British reviews and interviews surrounding *The Biographer's Moustache,* it grows into an effective evaluation of Amis's entire career.

Index

"Aberdarcy: The Chaucer Road," 142
"Aberdarcy: The Main Square," 142
"Abide with Me" (hymn), 32, 46
"Affairs of Death," 38
"Against Romanticism," 45
Aldiss, Brian: "Outside," 32; as participant in "Unreal Estates," 50; *Trillion Year Spree,* 47–48
Allen, Walter, as critic of the Movement, 15
Allsop, Kenneth, 28
"All the Blood within Me," 36
Alteration, The: as alternate history, 53–57; as comic inferno, 54; inspiration for, 53; wins Campbell Prize, 21; writing of, 21
Amis, Kingsley: attitudes towards communism, 4–6; attitudes towards education, 10–12, 27; attitudes towards his son's fiction, 23; attitudes towards politics, 16–17, 27; attitudes towards religion, 2, 40, 143, 147n. 3; attitudes towards sex, 3, 31–32; B. Litt. thesis, 7–8; conflicts with father, 2–3; connection with Angry Young Men, 16–17; connection with the Movement, 14–16; death of, 23; dependence on women, 3; education at City of London School, 4–5; education at grammar school, 4; education at Oxford, 5–8; first marriage, 7, 17–19; on genre fiction, 47; on ghost stories, 68–69; grandparents, 1; later feelings towards parents, 3; lectures in Prague, 20; linguistic concerns, 143–45; love of jazz, 5; love of Wales, 9; military involvement, 4, 6, 8–9, 33–35; moral concerns, 141–43; on mystery stories, 62; narrative methods, 142; parents, 1–3; on poetry, 41–44; powers of mimicry, 1, 4, 5, 14; psychological maladies, 2, 22, 69, 123; second marriage, 19, 21–22; on short stories, 32; teaching career at Cambridge, 11–12; teaching career at Princeton, 10; teaching career at Swansea, 9–10; teaching career at Vanderbilt, 12; use of distinctive character types, 141–42; work habits, 2; writings on food, 22, 25–26; years after second divorce, 22–25
Amis, Martin: argument over editing Amis's letters, 148n. 19; attitude towards Vietnam War, 17; birth of, 9; influence of, 140; visits father in later years, 23
Amis, Rosa Annie (nee Lucas): cosseting of Amis, 3; encouragement of Amis as writer, 3; religious background, 2
Amis, Sally: birth of, 11; visits father in later years, 23
Amis, William: attitudes towards religion, 2; conflicts with Amis, 2–3; Englishness, 1; literary influence on Amis, 2, 6; reading habits, 2
Amis Anthology, The, 42, 43
Amis Collection, The, 43
Amis Story Anthology, The, 32–33
Anderson, Lindsay, as critic of Amis's anti-intellectualism, 16
Anderson, Poul, "Sister Planet," 52
Angry Young Men, 16–17
Anti-death League, The: autobiographical aspects, 81–82; as satire on psychology, 82; as spy novel, 80; theological speculations, 81, 82; writing of, 20
Arendt, Hannah, 10
Arts Policy?, An, 27
Ash, Paul, "The Big Sword," 50
Ashley, Kenneth, 41
Asimov, Isaac, 49, 50
Astounding, 49, 51, 52
Auden, W. H.: Amis's admiration for, 36, 41; as critic of detective story, 64; as editor of *The Oxford Book of Light Verse,* 42; influence on Amis's early verse, 44
Austen, Jane: as author in Great Tradition, 91; *Mansfield Park,* 29

Ballard, J. G., "The Voices of Time," 51, 52
Bardwell, Hilary (Hilly): importance in Amis's life, 7, 23–24; meets Amis, 7
Bateson, F. W., 7, 44
Belloc, Hilaire, "Ha'nacker Mill," 42
Bellow, Saul, Amis's disdain for, 23, 144
Berkeley, Anthony, 65
"Beowulf," 44
Betjeman, John, 25, 36
Bierce, Ambrose, "An Occurrence at Owl Creek Bridge," 33
Biographer's Moustache, The: autobiographical aspects, 136–37; class conflict in, 137–38; connection to *Girl, 20*, 137; connections to *The King's English*, 30; linguistic aspects, 137, 144–45; sexual conflict in, 137–38; writing of, 23
Bixby, Jerome, "It's a *Good* Life," 52
Blackmur, R. P., 10
Black Papers on Education, 12, 27
Blake, William, 134
Blunden, Edmund, 42
"Bobby Bailey," 46
Bone, Gavin, 6
Book of Bond, The: design of, 76–77; writing of, 20
"Bookshop Idyll, A." *See* "Something Nasty in the Bookshop"
"Boris and the Colonel," 39
Boucher, Anthony: "Barrier, The," 50; "Quest for St. Aquin, The," 32, 52
Bowman, Ruth, attitudes towards Amis, 5
Bradbury, Malcolm, 140
Bradford, Richard, as critic of Amis, 140, 141, 142
Bradley, Jerry, as critic of Amis's poetry, 147n. 3
Braine, John, 25, 56
Bright November, publication by Fortune Press, 13, 44
Brooke, Rupert: political stance, 145; as World War I poet, 15
Browning, Robert, as subject in "Mr. Barrett's Secret," 39
Budrys, Algis, 52
Burgess, Anthony: *1985*, 58; as subject in *Memoirs*, 25; *Wanting Seed, The*, 57

Byron, Lord: 42; as model for Bond, 74, 78

Campbell, John W., Jr.: award named after him, 57; as editor of *Astounding*, 49
Carr, John Dickson: Amis's evaluation of, 2, 62–64, 65; *Hollow Man, The* (U.S. title: *The Three Coffins*), 63–64, 66, 68–69, 71; introduction to, by Bruce Montgomery, 5, 63; postmodern aspects, 63–64; praises *Lucky Jim*, 63
"Captain Nolan's Chance," 39
Case of Samples, A, 45
Caton, R. A.: as "L. S." Caton, 13, 80, 89; as publisher of The Fortune Press, 12–13, 45
Causley, Charles, as editor of *Poetry Please*, 42
Cecil, Lord David, as Amis's dissertation adviser, 7–8, 25
Chandler, Raymond, 62, 124
Chaucer, Geoffrey, 28
Chekhov, Anton, 87
Chesterton, G. K.: as favorite of Amis, 16, 44, 62, 65, 145; *Man Who Was Thursday, The*, 102
Christie, Agatha, *The ABC Murders*, 67
Clarke, Arthur C., 50; "The Nine Billion Names of God," 52
Clifton, Mark, "Sense from Thought Divide," 50
Clute, John: as critic of *New Maps of Hell*, 47; as critic of *Spectrum V*, 50–51; on golden age of science fiction, 52
Coles, Frank, 8
Collected Poems, 43, 44
Collected Short Stories, 33–38
Colonel Sun: Bond as Byron, 78; as characteristic Amis, 79; as improvement on Fleming's Bond, 78; use of "Fleming effect" in, 77; writing of, 20
Conquest, Robert: author of pastiche of "The Vicar of Bray," 43; co-author of *Peach Key*, 148n. 16; collaboration on *The Black Papers on Education*, 27; collaboration on *The Egyptologists*, 19; collaboration on *Spectrum*, 50; editor of

# INDEX

New Lines, 44; friendship with Amis, 17, 22, 25, 28
Conrad, Joseph, 91, 141
"Court of Enquiry," 35
Crime of the Century, The: alternate ending, 68; postmodern aspects, 67; as thriller, 67; writing of, 21, 67
"Crisis Song," 46
Crispin, Edmund. *See* Montgomery, Bruce

"Darkwater Hall Mystery, The," 38
Davie, Donald, 1, 14, 15
Day-Lewis, Cecil, 1
"Dear Illusion," bad art as subject, 36–37
Delany, Samuel, 53
Delius, Frederick, 4
Dick, Philip K., *The Man in the High Castle,* 55
Dickens, Charles, 28
Dickson, Carter. *See* Carr, John Dickson
Difficulties with Girls: homosexual subplot, 124; as sequel to *Take a Girl Like You,* 97, 124; sexual conflicts in, 125–26; writing of, 22
Doyle, Arthur Conan, 38, 62
Dozois, Gardner, editor of *The Year's Best Science Fiction,* 50
Drinkwater, John, 41

Egyptologists, The: allusions to military, 102–3; connections to genre fiction, 102; narrative method, 101–2; sexual conflict in, 103–4; writing of, 19, 101
Eliot, George, 91, 141
Eliot, T. S.: "East Coker," 97; as originator of "objective correlative," 82
Elgar, Edward, 90
Ellingham, Rev. C. J., 4
Empson, William, as critic of religion, 147n. 3
Ending Up: as black comedy, 111, 114; as ensemble novel, 111; linguistic concerns, 112–13; narrative method, 111–12; old age as subject, 111; writing of, 21
Enright, D. J., editor of *Poets of the 1950's,* 41

"Evans Country, The," 46, 142, 144
Every Day Drinking, as repetitive, 26

Faber Popular Reciter, The, 43
Fast, Howard, "The Large Ant," 51
Fielding, Henry: as comic realist, 141; as subject in *I Like It Here,* 91–92, 151n. 6; *Tom Jones,* 125–26, 151n. 20
Fenton, James, 43
"Festival Notebook," 46
Fleming, Ann, attitudes towards Amis as Bond writer, 20, 77
Fleming, Ian, *The Man with the Golden Gun,* 19, 77
Francis, Dick, "Twenty-One Good Men and True," 33
Fraser, Russell, on difficulties of being Amis's friend, 152n. 12
Folks That Live on the Hill, The: autobiographical associations, 23, 127; bad art as subject, 128; characteristic hero, 127; love as subject, 127–28, 129; old age as subject, 128; setting of, 126–27; sexual conflict in, 128; writing of, 22
Forster, E. M., 32
Fortune Press, The, 12–13
Fowler, H. W., *Modern English Usage,* 31
Frame of Mind, A, 45
Freeman, R. Austin, 2
"Friends of Plonk, The," 37
Fuller, Roy, 12, 36
Fussell, Paul: *Anti-Egotist, The,* 147n. 2; as critic of *The Amis Anthology,* 42; as critic of *Memoirs,* 25; as critic of *On Drink,* 26

Galaxy, 51, 52
Gale, George, friendship with Amis, 11, 25, 28
"Garden, The," 45
Gardner, Philip, as critic of Amis, 147n. 1
Ginsberg, Allen, 36
Girl, 20: as comic inferno, 111; ironic freedom as subject, 109–10; linguistic exuberance, 107–8; noncommittal narrator, 110–11; political aspects, 108–9; as turning point, 107; writing of, 21

Godwin, Tom, "Mother of Invention," 51
Golden Age of Science Fiction, The, as apparent anti-New Wave anthology, 50–51
Gollancz, Victor: Amis's attitudes toward, 20; publishing *Lucky Jim,* 14
Graves, Robert: influence on Amis, 11, 18–19, 41, 45; influence on the Movement, 18; as subject in *Memoirs,* 25
Gray, Paul, as writer of Amis's obituary, 140
Gray, Thomas, "Elegy Written in a Country Churchyard," 39, 41, 43
Green, Martin, as critic of Amis's narrative method, 142
Greene, Douglas C., as critic of John Dickson Carr, 64
Greene, Graham: Amis's lost study of, 13; birth year, 1; as Catholic novelist, 101; as critic of *Colonel Sun,* 77; excellence as novelist and story writer, 32; as model for *I Like It Here,* 90, 151n. 5
Green Man, The: appearance of God in, 72; fear of death in, 6, 46, 72, 144; as ghost story, 70–73; main character as shit, 70–72; as morality play, 142; writing of, 21
Grierson, Francis, 2

Hammett, Dashiell, 62
Hardy, Thomas, 91
Harold's Years, 28
Heinlein, Robert, 49, 50
"Here Is Where," 45
Hopkins, Gerard Manley, obscurity of, 44
"House on the Headland, The": as combination of genres, 40; connections to Fleming, M. R. James, 38
Housman, A. E., as tragic poet, 42
Howard, Elizabeth Jane: as character in Amis's fiction, 37, 81–82; collaborates with Amis, 21; divorces Amis, 22; meets and marries Amis, 19
"Huge Artifice, The," 46
Hughes, Ted, 43

"ILEA Confidential," 27

I Like It Here: autobiographical aspects, 89; criticism of Great Tradition, 90–93; moral dilemma in, 90, 92; as travel book, 90–91; writing of, 18, 89
"In Memoriam W. R. A.," 46
"Investing in Futures," 37
Isherwood, Christopher, 8
"I Spy Strangers," 34, 35, 40
I Want It Now: characteristic hero, 104–5; as fairy tale, 105–6, 142; hypergamy in, 105; social milieu of, 104; writing of, 20

Jacobs, Eric: on Amis's dependence on women, 3; on Amis's female characters' resemblance to Elizabeth Jane Howard, 21–22; on Amis's lack of academic honors, 12; on Amis's life after moving out of parents' home, 3; on Amis's resemblance to Maurice Allington of *The Green Man,* 69; on Amis's typical day, 23; argument over editing Amis's letters, 148n. 19; as critic of *The James Bond Dossier,* 19, 73; as critic of *Take a Girl Like You,* 18; as critic of *You Can't Do Both,* 24, 136; biography as possible inspiration for *The Biographer's Moustache,* 136
Jake's Thing: autobiographical aspects, 115; connection to *Lucky Jim,* 115; charged as misogynist, 114–15; interpretation of "thing," 115–16; writing of, 22
James, Clive, 141
James, Henry: *Ambassadors, The,* 91; influence on Kipling, 30; *Turn of the Screw, The,* 69
James, M. R.: Amis's appreciation of, 68, 72; "Casting the Runes," 70; "Count Magnus," 38, 70; "Mezzotint, The," 38, 72; "Oh, Whistle, and I'll Come to You, My Lad," 33, 68; "Treasure of Abbot Thomas, The," 70
James Bond Dossier, The: Bond as Byron, 74; Bond as Everyman, 73–74, 150n. 17; defense of Bond, 75–76; Fleming effect, 74; iconoclastic aspect, 73; M's

INDEX

role, 75; villains, 74–75; women, 76; writing of, 19
Jennings, Elizabeth, 41
Johnson, Paul, as critic of Angry Young Men, 17
Jones, Mervyn, 28
Jones, Monica, 14
Joyce, James: as modernist, 140; "Painful Case, A," 33

Keats, John, 43, 44
Kilmarnock, Lady. *See* Bardwell, Hilary
King's English, The: influenced by Orwell and Fowler, 31; writing circumstances, 30
Kipling, Rudyard: "Beyond the Pale," 33; *Kim,* 80; as subject for Amis, 28–30; as subject for Orwell, 16; as subject for study, 140; as tragic poet, 42
Kornbluth, C. M.: as co-author with Frederik Pohl, 49; "Marching Morons, The," 50
Kuttner, Henry, "Vintage Season," 50

Lane, Homer, 134
"Larger Truth," 45
Larkin, Philip: on Amis at Cambridge, 11; on Amis and the Movement, 14; on Amis at Princeton, 10; on Amis's conservative stance, 17, 23; on Amis's departure from Cambridge, 12; "Aubade," 6; "Church Going," 60, 130; connection with *The Green Man,* 21; connections with *Lucky Jim,* 5, 14; connections with the Movement, 15; friendship with Amis, 5–6, 25; "I Remember, I Remember," 128; on *The Legacy,* 13; *Less Deceived, The,* 5; use of "bum" in tirades, 89–90
Latham, Philip, "The Xi Effect," 52
Lawrence, D. H.: as author in Great Tradition, 91; as bogus travel writer, 90; as liberating writer, 134, 136
Leavis, F. R.: *Great Tradition, The,* 90, 91–92, 140–41, 143; influence on the Movement, 15; as moral critic, 143; negative evaluation of Amis, 11, 152n. 5

Le Carré, John, 79
Legacy, The, postmodern aspects, 13
LeGuin, Ursula K., 52, 53
Lewis, C. S., as participant in "Unreal Estates," 50
Lodge, David, 140
Look around the Estate, A, 45
Lucky Jim: anger in, 83; connection to *I Like It Here,* 18; connections to Larkin, 5, 14; connections to the Movement, 15; as fairy tale, 86, 142; "filthy Mozart," 84; linguistic concerns, 85–86, 144; narrative method, 83–84; rebellion against culture, 84–85; wins Maugham prize, 18; writing and publication of, 13–14
Lycett, Andrew, on writing of *Colonel Sun,* 20

MacDonald, John D., Amis's favorable opinion of, 144
MacLean, Katherine, "Unhuman Sacrifice," 50
MacLeod, Norman: as critic of *I Like It Here,* 151n. 5; as critic of linguistic aspects of Amis's writing, 151n. 9
Magazine of Fantasy and Science Fiction, The, 51, 52
Manning, Norman, 8
Marlborough school, 4
"Mason's Life," 37
Maugham, W. Somerset: as critic of the Movement, 15; as definer of love, 125; "Door of Opportunity, The," 33; literary prize, 18
McCarthy, Mary, 10
McDermott, John, *Kingsley Amis: An English Moralist,* 141
Memoirs: aborted "orgy," 18–19, 25; lack of information about first marriage, 7; meaning of final poems, 24; self-telling frankness, 19; as unconventional autobiography, 25; writing of, 22–23
Millhauser, Steven, *Edwin Mullhouse,* 136
Montgomery, Bruce (Edmund Crispin): collaboration with Amis on oratorio, 13; creator of Gervase Fen, 63;

Montgomery, Bruce (*continued*)
  friendship with Amis, 25; friendship with Amis and Larkin at Oxford, 5; taken in by "Who or What Was It?," 37
Moore, Tom, 42
"Moral Fibre," 35–36
Morris, William: *News from Nowhere*, 57; as social thinker, 27, 85
Morrison, Blake: as critic of the Movement, 15, 45, 64; on Orwell's heroes, 15–16
Motion, Andrew, on Amis's and Larkin's group at Oxford, 5
Movement, The, 14–16, 41
"Mr. Barrett's Secret," 38–39
Mr. Barrett's Secret and Other Stories, 38–40
Muir, Edwin, "The Breaking," 42
Mummy Knows Best. See *Egyptologists, The*
Murdoch, Iris, 6
"My Enemy's Enemy," 34

Nabokov, Vladimir: Amis's disdain for, 23, 29, 143; "First Love," 33; *Real Life of Sebastian Knight, The*, 136
"New Approach Needed, A," 46
Newbolt, Henry, as favorite of Amis, 43, 44
New Maps of Hell: connections with *The Alteration*, 56; defines science fiction, 48; emphasis on dystopias, 48–50; origins in Gauss lectures, 10; as pioneering study, 47; publication of, 18; recommendations for genre, 50
New Statesman, 5, 28
New Wave, 51–53, 124
"1941/A," 39, 55
Niven, Larry, 53
"Nocturne," 46
"Notes on Wyatt," 45
"Nothing to Fear," 18, 45

"O Captain, My Captain!," 44
"Ode to Me," 46
"Ode to the East-North-East-by-East Wind," 45

"O'Grady Says," 46
Old Devils, The: autobiographical aspects, 121–22; as ensemble novel, 122; favorable reception of, 121; fear of death in, 45; narrative method, 122; old age as subject, 123; sexual conflicts in, 122–23; Welsh setting, 9; wins Booker Prize, 22, 121; writing of, 22
On Drink, 26
One Fat Englishman: autobiographical aspects, 98; characteristic hero, 97; as comic inferno, 101; connection to *I Like it Here*, 97; as morality play, 142; narrative method, 98; question about hero, 98–100; theological aspects, 99; writing of, 19
Orwell, George: anti-intellectualism, 16; birth year, 1; as defender of popular literature, 73; at Eton, 4; influence on Amis, 15–16, 148n. 13; as influence on *The King's English*, 31; influence on the Movement, 15–16, 44; on Kipling, 29; on morality, 143; *Nineteen Eighty-Four*, 55, 56, 58–62, 75; politics of, 145; "Politics and the English Language" 31; as realist author, 140
Osborne, John, *Look Back in Anger*, 16–17, 59
Owen, Wilfred, 15
Oxford Book of Light Verse, The, 42–43

Parker, Charlie, 124
Peach Key, 148n. 16
Peterhouse College, Cambridge, 11–12
"Pill for the Impressionable, A," 45
Piper, H. Beam, "He Walked around Horses," 30, 39, 52
Plath, Sylvia, 36
Pleasure of Poetry, The, 41
Pohl, Frederik: Amis's admiration for, 49; as co-author of *The Space Merchants*, 49; on decline of science fiction, 52; "Midas Plague, The," 50; "Tunnel under the World, The," 52
"Point of Logic," 45

INDEX

Pound, Ezra, 36
Powell, Anthony, Amis's admiration for, 25, 28
"Prelude, The," 5

"Reunion, A," 46
Rhode, John, 2, 65
Richardson, Samuel, *Clarissa*, 93
Riverside Villa Murders, The: autobiographical aspects, 64–65; connection to father's reading habits, 2, 65; as golden age mystery, 65–67; postmodern aspects, 66; writing of, 21
Roberts, Keith, *Pavane*, 54, 57–58
Rochester, Earl of, "A Satire against Mankind," 43
Rodden, John, *The Politics of Literary Reputation*, 140
"Romance," 45
Rossetti, Dante Gabriel, 7, 47, 50
Rosten, Leo, 25, 26
Roth, Philip, 36
Rudyard Kipling: on "Baa, Baa, Black Sheep," 29"; as essay, 29; on Kipling as short-story writer, 30; on Kipling's incipient modernism, 30; on Kipling's politics, 29–30; on *Stalky and Co.*, 29
Ruskin, John, 27
Russian Girl, The: bad art as subject, 132–33, 144; fairy tale aspects, 131–33, 142; sexual conflict in, 131–32; as traditional novel, 131; writing of, 23
Russian Hide-and-Seek: absence of belief as theme, 58, 60–61; connections to *Nineteen Eighty-Four*, 58–62; as future history, 58; Margaret Thatcher's comment about, 58, 148n. 18; writing of, 22

"Sacred Rhino of Uganda, The," 4
Safire, William, as grammarian, 32
Salwak, Dale, as critic of Amis's characters, 141
Sassoon, Siegfried, 15
Sayers, Dorothy, 65
Scott, J. D., "In the Movement," 14

Shakespeare, William: *As You Like It*, 116; *Romeo and Juliet*, 59, 61; sonnet 129, 87; sonnets, 43
Shaw, George Bernard, 136
Shaw, Irwin, "Act of Faith," 33
Shawcross, William, 28
Sheckley, Robert: as humorous author, 50; "Pilgrimage to Earth," 50, 52
Shelley, Percy, Amis's disdain for, 43, 45, 55
"Shitty," 46
Simak, Clifford D., as author of pastoral science fiction, 57
Simon, John, as grammarian, 32
Snowdon, Lord, 25
Socialism and the Intellectuals, 16, 27
"Something Nasty in the Bookshop," 45
"Something Strange": connection to Aldiss's "Outside," 32; connection to "New Wave," 37
"South," 46
Spectator, The, 14, 28
Spectrum anthologies, 50–51
Spillane, Mickey, 62
Stanley and the Women: autobiographical aspects, 121; critical reception of, 117–18; madness as subject, 119; narrative method, 118; sexual conflict in, 118–21; writing of, 22
St. John's College, Oxford, 5–8
Stoker, Bram, *Dracula*, 38
Sturgeon, Theodore, "Killdozer," 50
Suvin, Darko, 48
Swift, Jonathan, *Gulliver's Travels*, 48, 149n. 4
Symons, Julian, as critic of detective story, 62–63
Szamuely, Tibor, friendship with Amis, 17, 25, 28

Take a Girl Like You: characteristic hero, 93–96; as departure for Amis, 92–93, 97; fear of death in, 45, 93, 95, 144; moral dilemma in, 95–96, 144; narrative method, 93; theological aspects, 96; writing of, 18

Taylor, D. J., as critic of Amis's influence, 140, 141
Taylor, Elizabeth: Amis's admiration of, 25, 89; "Summer Schools," 33
Tenn, William, "Null-P," 50
Tennyson, Alfred, as poet of loss, 42
That Uncertain Feeling: autobiographical aspects, 86–87; characteristic opening, 86; connection with "Moral Fibre," 35; hero compared to Jim Dixon, 87; hypergamy as subject, 87–88; infidelity as subject, 89; love and work as subjects, 87–89; moral dilemma in, 87–89; narrative method, 86; original title, 141; writing of, 18
"Their Oxford," 46
Theroux, Paul, as critic of *Rudyard Kipling*, 29
"They Only Move," 45
Thomas, Donald, as biographer of Robert Browning, 39
Thomas, Dylan: derided by Amis, 41, 89, 122, 124; publication by Fortune Press, 12
Thomas, Edward, 41, 42
Thomas, R. S., 42
"To a Baby Born without Limbs," 81, 96
"To Be a Pilgrim" (hymn), 61
"Toil and Trouble," 39–40
"Too Much Trouble," 37
"To See the Sun," connections to *Dracula*, M. R. James, 38
Treece, Henry, *The Green Man*, 150n. 15
Twain, Mark, 25, 28, 46
"Twitch on the Thread, A," 40
"2003 Claret, The," 37

University College of Swansea, Wales, 9–10
Upward, Edward, 1

Vanderbilt University, 12
Van Vogt, A. E.: as *Astounding* author, 49, 50; "Resurrection," 51

Wain, John: connections to the Movement, 15; friendship with Amis at Oxford, 7; pushing of Amis's work, 14
Wallace, F. L., "Student Body," 52
Waugh, Evelyn: Amis's attitudes towards, 28, 30; as author of war fiction, 34; birth year of, 1; *Brideshead Revisited*, 40; as Catholic novelist, 100–101
We Are All Guilty: connection to *Russian Hide-and-Seek*, 130; origins of, 129; personal responsibility as subject, 129–31; writing of, 22
Wesker, Arnold, 25
West, Richard, 28
What Became of Jane Austen? And Other Questions, autobiographical sections, 23, 148n. 1
Whitman, Walt, 43–44
Who Else Is Rank: connections with short stories, 33; writing of, 13
"Who or What Was It?," connection to *The Green Man*, 37–38
"Why Lucky Jim Turned Right," 17, 27
Williams, Raymond, 50
Wilson, Angus: as author of study of Kipling, 29, 30; "Fresh-Air Fiend," 33
Wodehouse, P. G., "Jeeves and the Song of Songs," 33
Woolf, Virginia, 140
Wyndham, John, *No Blade of Grass*, 48

Xenophon, *Anabasis*, 134

Yeats, W. B., "Easter 1916," 44
Yevtushenko, Yevgeny, Amis's attitude towards, 25, 148n. 1
You Can't Do Both: autobiographical aspects, 18, 133–34; characteristic hero, 134–36; connections to *The King's English*, 151–52n. 25; connections to other Amis novels, 136, 144; fear of death in, 46, 136, 144; narrative method, 135; religious aspects, 134–35; writing of, 23

Zoline, Pamela, "Heat-Death of the Universe," 53

The Author

William Laskowski is chair of the English and Communication Arts Department at Jamestown College. He has written about science fiction (particularly the authors Larry Niven and Jack Vance), Georgian poetry, George Orwell, Tom Wolfe, and Richard Wagner. He is the author of *Rupert Brooke* (TEAS 504).

The Editor

Kinley E. Roby is professor emeritus of English at Northeastern University. He is the twentieth-century field editor of Twayne's English Authors Series, series editor of Twayne's Critical History of British Drama, and general editor of Twayne's Women and Literature Series. He has written books on Arnold Bennett, Edward VII, and Joyce Cary and edited a collection of essays on T. S. Eliot. He makes his home in Naples, Florida.